ONE MORE MOON

Goodbye Mussolini! One Woman's Story of Fate and Survival

Ralph Webster

Copyright © 2017 by Ralph Webster
All rights reserved. This book or any portion thereof may not be
reproduced or used in any manner whatsoever without the express written
permission of the publisher
except for the use of brief quotations in a book review.
Printed in the United States of America
First Printing, 2017
ISBN: 1979461651
ISBN 13: 9781979461658
Library of Congress Control Number: 2017917238
CreateSpace Independent Publishing Platform
North Charleston, South Carolina

for Ginger

Some things in life cannot be accomplished without the love and unrelenting support from another. This was one of those times.

RGW, 2017

CHAPTER ONE

*'TIS the last rose of summer
Left blooming alone;
All her lovely companions
Are faded and gone;*

– Thomas Moore, 1805

Midmorning on February 21, 1935, two gas fitters connecting a gas line to a new bungalow at the Springfield Estate off Corbets Tey Road in Upminster, England, a suburban East London village, spotted an unusual sight for that day and year. A small airplane was flying over their heads. This was noteworthy because airplanes seldom flew over this specific location, and it was especially unusual to the two men as they typically were occupied with their work underground and happened to be taking a short break when the event occurred. Pertinent or not, this was the explanation given as to why both men happened to look up into the sky at the same exact moment on that particular day.

Police reports would suggest that the aircraft, later identified as a six-seat de Havilland DH84 Dragon airliner, was flying at an altitude of approximately three thousand feet and a speed of about eighty-five miles per hour. During the inquiry that followed, neither of these facts was deemed relevant or significant to the event that was to occur only moments later. As the airplane passed through the dark clouds overhead, the two workmen reported seeing something quite out of the ordinary. According to the men's statements taken early that afternoon: "suddenly, what looked like two packages fell away from the plane" and fluttered to the ground "like sheets of paper."

They reported hearing a noise, best described as a curious thud. As this sound appeared to have taken place only a short distance from where they were standing, the two gas fitters ran quickly to the nearby cabbage field to search for what had fallen. Upon investigation, they were astonished to find the broken bodies of two well-dressed young women lying face down on the ground. According to one of the men, "their hands were clasped, and one had a tight grip on the other's coat."

You can well imagine that an incident such as this would be reported across the globe and followed intensely by thousands and, perhaps, millions of readers. And it was, as this was not an ordinary story. Within days, newspapers throughout the world carried the startling and grim details on their front pages. An investigation into these deaths began immediately.

The women were identified as sisters, Americans, in their early twenties, well traveled, and reportedly "familiar with the civilities of European social life." One was characterized as more of a leader; the other as more apt to follow. They were reportedly the daughters of a high-ranking and well-regarded American government foreign service official whose name was withheld out of respect for the family's privacy.

As you might conclude, there were many questions. And early on, there was much speculation as to whether this was a double suicide, a tragedy of love or youthful disillusionment, perhaps even a homicide resulting from an argument, or simply a malfunction of the external door from the main cabin. Several newspapers suggested that the women may have been despondent over illness; one of the women had been known to suffer from severe bouts of asthma. Even as the bodies lay in the Hornchurch police mortuary, some reports even hypothesized that this terrible event was in some way tied to a shipment of gold bullion that had been reportedly lost while being transported by the very same airline the preceding week. This theory was quickly dispelled when it became known that three members of the Sabini gang were responsible for that theft.

Every story has a beginning, and this seems to be as good a place to begin as any other. Now the question for you to consider is: *What could this tragic event have to do with a guesthouse, the Pensione Alexandra, located fourteen hundred miles away in Naples, Italy?*

CHAPTER TWO

Me? Own a pensione? I was convinced my daughter, Mela, was crazy in the head when she came home that otherwise unremarkable late-October day in 1934 and announced the news that Bertie Allen, the odd Englishwoman who owned the Pensione Alexandra overlooking the Bay of Naples at Caracciolo 13, was thinking of selling. I had no idea why Mela was so excited. For heaven's sake, why should Paul and I be interested in hearing about a pensione that was for sale?

But that was how Mela was, a girl of seventeen years, forever dreaming, with a mind that could never sit still. Mela was very smart when it came to so many things, but she was constantly puzzled by the oddest assortment of distractions. She spent far too many of her waking hours each day wondering about what might be. Some days, that head of hers was completely in the clouds. What did she know of life? What did she know of fate? What did she know of disappointment? I couldn't help but smile when Paul told me Mela reminded him of how naïve I had been about these things when I'd first stepped off the train in Naples at the age of twenty-one in those months before we married.

I suppose that operating a small guesthouse like the Pensione Alexandra would not be as ridiculous as trying to manage a huge hotel like the Palazzio, with the bellmen, waiters, chambermaids, and cooks always holding out their hands and asking for tips. No one cared that the Palazzio was careful to warn guests about this practice and that the help was not supposed to act that way. Gratuities for these kinds of services were included as a service charge on the hotel bill specifically to prevent this bothersome behavior.

Most of us understood. These were difficult times in Naples. People needed money. What was the harm in asking? Unsuspecting tourists were fair game. They couldn't tell one coin from another and always fell prey to the sad looks of children. Look at all the *lazzaroni* on the streets, always begging for money. It seemed everyone was trying to make ends meet, even the authorities. The authorities? Ha! They just turned a blind eye. And what about the inspectors from the city hall? They had their hands out asking for money too. Most Neapolitans were simply trying to put food on their tables and keep roofs over their heads. Naples was a city of survivors, where people, from the youngest of age, learned how to get by from one day to the next using their cunning and wit.

A pensione? Crazy in the head! Paul and I did not have the money. We had no experience. Who would stay there? Who would cook? Who would mop? Who would make the beds? Who would launder the sheets? What about Mussolini's Fascists and all their silly regulations? What did we know about operating a pensione?

Now I can only laugh and smile when I think about that time. I remember how I caught Mela's dream. It was an idea that refused to leave, an irritating mosquito bite I continued to scratch. And day after day, that little bite began to itch more and more until, just like Mela, I started to imagine what might be. That was when that crazy little bite grew so large that it did not matter how much I scratched. It became my dream too.

And today? Today, I sit quietly for hours and hours and ponder those moments. I relive those memories. I picture the Pensione Alexandra in the early evening with its beautiful sunsets. I dream of the magnificent view of the Bay of Naples and feel the caress of the gentle breeze on those nights we sat on the balcony after everything in the kitchen was put up and our work was done for the day. I imagine the moon when everyone slept, and how I always knew that I could speak and it would listen. I remember the people of Naples, how they always overflowed with both the joy and the misery of life, and how crazy and alive Naples always felt, like a heart that never stops pounding. How could I forget that old man Vesuvius, his pipe spewing smoke and his mouth spouting fiery red lava, watched over us at night?

The Pensione Alexandra never made us wealthy, but it did enrich our lives. It changed us and made us become so different from the way we were. It brought the world to our windows. I was given a perch to observe the people of Europe struggle and suffer through unimagined and horrible times. I watched impassioned joy and tearful loss. When I think of those moments and the many people who passed through our doors, the memories make me smile and laugh and cry and catch my breath all at once. They bring me delight. They make me sad. They remind me of happiness, uncertainty, anguish, fear, desperation, and longing. They make me grateful for the life I have lived. These memories will never fade. They will always fill my heart.

Me? A pensione? Crazy in the head! That's what I told Mela that otherwise unremarkable October day when she came home and told us that Bertie Allen was selling the Pensione Alexandra. What on earth did we know about running a pensione?

[handwritten: Kind of redundant]

CHAPTER THREE

Meshugenah! I know that is what Mother would have said had she still been alive. I can imagine the concern in the sound of her voice. I can hear her very words: "Elsa, why on earth would you buy a pensione? You are much too old to carry on like that. You are a fifty-one-year-old woman with an aching back and bad feet. Your husband is lazy. He sits all day long waiting to win the lotto and smokes too many cigars. He is an old man. Your children are fully grown. You will soon be a grandmother. What do you know about managing a pensione? What do you know about cooking and cleaning or mopping a floor? It is time for your children to make their own lives. You know Mela will meet a nice young man, marry, and have babies to care for. You will be left all alone. What are you thinking? You are *meshugenah!*"

Father's eyes would have twinkled, and in his gentle, calm manner, he would have said, "Elsa, ever since you were a young girl, you have always been a little bullheaded and much too stubborn for your own good. If I gave you my advice, maybe you would listen, maybe you would not. It is your mother's fault. She spoiled you when you were a child."

So, perhaps they were right. Perhaps, just like Mela, I was a little crazy in the head. Mother and Father were no longer there to help guide me and give me advice, but I could still hear their voices telling me to be cautious, to be careful, to go slowly, to take one step at a time, just like when I was a child growing up in Germany.

Life was different now. I was older. This wasn't Koenigsberg. This was Naples. I was married and had raised four fully grown children of my own. With the growing madness sweeping Germany and our little Fascist egomaniac with his bold ideas for Italy, we were living in a time when it seemed that the whole world was destined to become a little crazy in the head. None of us needed to be reminded.

The Pensione Alexandra had been a guest house in Naples for more than forty years. Bertie Allen had always been the innkeeper. It had been her dream when she'd moved from a central London neighborhood to Naples as an attractive and entrepreneurial thirty-five-year-old widow. Her much older husband had succumbed to one illness or another. When he had died, she had been left with a meager savings, far less than she had expected and far too little to continue the lifestyle she'd anticipated in London.

On a rainy-day whim, she'd closed her London home, kept only her prized possessions, and moved to Southern Italy, to sunny and carefree Napoli, to venture out on her own with the hope that she would not outlive her money. That was when she'd opened the Pensione Alexandra. I think most of us would agree: when Bertie Allen embarked on her Italian adventure, she might have been a little crazy in the head too.

The Pensione Alexandra was named after Queen Alexandra of Denmark, wife of King-Emperor Edward VII, Queen of the United Kingdom of Great Britain and Ireland and Empress of India. At first, the pensione had possessed a different name, one that has been long forgotten. Bertie renamed it the Pensione Alexandra in 1902 after the king and queen's coronation. To be perfectly honest, when Paul and I first became the owners of the pensione, I found it hard to imagine any reason why Bertie Allen had chosen such a respectable name, other than that she was an Englishwoman giving tribute to her queen.

I must quickly dispel you of any wrong impressions. It is true that, in its day, the pensione had developed quite an international following, particularly since English was its resident language, an appealing attribute and somewhat unusual in Naples at that time. The Pensione Alexandra was the largest of four pensiones overlooking the Bay of Naples on Via Caracciolo and the only one the 1930 *Baedeker Guide* saw fit to describe as "English and good." Many fine guests from throughout the world had spent their nights at the Pensione Alexandra. Some had even lived there. And frequently, multiple languages had filled its parlor and breakfast room, at times too loud and, upon occasion, in disharmony.

Unfortunately, despite the pensione's past success, the years had not been kind. They had extracted their toll. The beds were in varying stages of disrepair, and the appearance of the public areas had suffered from overuse. Even the furniture had become a little tired and worn around the edges. I suppose what I am trying to diplomatically say is that, even then and certainly now, being named for a queen did not mean that the Pensione Alexandra was fit for a queen.

When the Pensione Alexandra first opened, Bertie Allen made quite a name for herself in Naples. She developed a reputation as a rather odd bird, particularly in the more cultivated, more polite northern European circles of Neapolitan society. Her behavior certainly attracted attention. She was a woman about town. I am sure she faced an uphill battle and ridiculous obstacles. Can you imagine? An Englishwoman operating a guesthouse in the machismo world of Naples in 1894.

Moreover, I understand that, in her attempt to generate additional income, there were many evenings when Bertie opened a second set of doors and offered her services as somewhat of a self-acclaimed clairvoyant. Thus, not only was the pensione a guesthouse for weary visitors, it served as a gathering place for seances and other mysterious forms of communication with the world that existed beyond the reaches of man's natural vision.

The specifics will forever remain unknown. Perhaps these activities had something to do with the escapades of her dear departed husband, a well-known eccentric who shared a penchant for stuffed animals, particularly large, feathery birds of all varieties, as these were the prized possessions that accompanied Bertie Allen when she moved from London to Naples. The result was that the Pensione Alexandra housed an extremely odd collection of furnishings and taxidermical delights, furnishings that made it highly unlikely that Queen Alexandra, or any other queen for that matter, would ever see fit to visit, let alone spend a single night there.

CHAPTER FOUR

There is an expression I learned when we moved to America, *skating on thin ice*, which might best characterize our family's financial situation on that day Mela came home and told us about her dream. When I learned that Bertie Allen wanted to sell the Pensione Alexandra, it was our pressing money problems that actually caused my ears to perk up and my mind to start considering this farfetched idea. I can't imagine there was any other possible reason.

The issues with money were a relatively recent phenomenon. Paul and I had been fortunate. For well more than a decade, our family had enjoyed a comfortable lifestyle, certainly when measured by the standard of living in Naples. Over the years, like nearly everyone else, we had experienced our share of upturns and downturns when it came to finances. Italy's economy remained somewhat of an unexplainable mystery, always unpredictable and chaotic. But we'd had more than our share of good luck. For us, the downturns had usually been short in duration and always followed by periods of moderate prosperity.

However, this time was different, and our fortunes had taken an unforeseen turn. For several years, they had been descending deeper and deeper in a seemingly never-ending downward spiral. On that particular day in October of 1934, I could see little light at the end of a very dark tunnel. Paul continued playing the lotto each week, picking his numbers based on one silly superstition or another and praying each Saturday evening for lightning to strike. But winning the grand prize in the lotto seemed a rather unlikely solution. The most he had ever won was hardly enough to take the family out for a Sunday afternoon dinner at one of the eating houses in Posillipo.

It would be misleading for me to say that we were broke. We certainly were not penniless, but it would be correct to say that more pennies were going out than coming in, and we were heading in a direction that could not continue for any extended period of time. Some days, we robbed Peter to pay Paul. Unless something changed, a crisis was certain to be not far off in our future. I didn't need Bertie Allen and her seances to make that prediction. From where I was standing, there could not have been a better time for Mela to dream this dream. The Pensione Alexandra offered an opportunity that deserved our attention. If we were successful, it could become a much-needed answer to our prayers.

Forty years earlier, in 1894, at the invitation of his uncle and with the encouragement of his mother, twenty-one-year-old Paul had moved from Germany to Naples. He was to be groomed to someday take over his uncle's export business. Aunt Betty and Uncle Arthur had no children of their own and needed someone to be trained in the business. Aunt Betty, in particular, was worried that if something happened to her twenty-year-older husband, Uncle Arthur, she would be incapable of providing for herself. Paul's mother, Uncle Arthur's widowed sister living in Stuttgart, provided a timely answer to this perplexing problem. She had three sons – one studying medicine, one dabbling in antiques – leaving the third son, Paul, who was more than a little uncertain about his life and in need of a future.

Paul's brothers would move to America to pursue their careers, but Paul had shown little interest. He had no aptitude for the language and not much enthusiasm for the adventure. Paul's mother's plan was to join her two sons in America. However, she refused to move until an answer could be found to the pressing question of what to do with Paul. The opportunity for her uncertain son Paul to move to Naples, where he could become an apprentice to Uncle Arthur, became the ideal solution for all parties involved.

Paul clearly had a head for the business and a particular flair for salesmanship, and with time, he showed great promise. His responsibilities grew. We married and had four children. He was capable and conscientious, perhaps, at times, a bit lacking in self-confidence, but his hard work paid off. Twenty years after arriving in Naples, following the death of his uncle, Paul took over the operation of the export business just as planned. He gained the means to support his aging Aunt Betty and to provide for our growing young family.

Flourishing and successful, in its better days, Paul's business was the largest *tartarari* wholesale house in Naples, exporting tartar deposits collected from wine barrels, a key ingredient in the making of cream of tartar baking powder. He could proudly report that, under his direction, the business had grown to include a number of large customers, several in America.

War came in 1915 when Italy joined Britain, France, and Russia in the fight against Germany and Austria-Hungary. Paul's family responsibilities and age kept him from the army, but World War I extracted a terrible toll from Italy. While Naples and Southern Italy escaped much of the bloodshed, the cost in life and treasure for the nation of Italy was devastating. Everyone was affected in one way or another.

When the war ended, Italy, like much of Europe, suffered high unemployment and hyperinflation. This was a difficult time, yet the *tartarari* business survived, and our family continued to enjoy a certain amount of prosperity throughout the next decade. We were never wealthy, far from it, but we were well positioned in the middle class. We could afford to provide for our children and live a comfortable life.

Our luck ran out when the Great Depression expanded beyond America's shores. It was not to be avoided, and we felt it all the way across the Atlantic in Italy. That was in the early 1930s. The Great Depression marked the moment when our financial situation began to deteriorate. Decreased demand from America meant Paul's warehouses in Italy overflowed with tartar. It could only be sold at a greatly reduced market price, much lower than what Paul had paid his suppliers when he'd first purchased the tartar. The difficulty was that Paul was dealing with borrowed money. Whenever the tartar in the warehouses was sold, Paul received less than what he owed the banks. The bankers did not care. That was Paul's problem. They expected to be repaid.

Matters became much worse when Paul's business encountered a devastating fraud committed by a longtime trusted supplier. Shipments were lost. Paperwork disappeared. Bank transfers failed to take place. The result was a lengthy procession of lawsuits and legal proceedings. The fact that this fraud was perpetrated by someone Paul had done business with for so many years and considered a friend made it all the more difficult to accept or understand. Clearly, this was an indication of how desperate the times were.

Fortunately, a small inheritance upon Aunt Betty's passing helped a little, but unfortunately, it was not enough. The banks kept asking for their money, and the debts continued to mount. We were forced to face reality and tighten our belts.

First, we gave up our extravagances, like the membership dues for the German club. Then we could no longer afford to keep our maid, Elise, who had been part of our family for eighteen years. When the children had been young, we had hired her to be their governess. When they'd grown older, I'd felt sorry for her and kept her on.

Instead of sending her back to Switzerland, I asked her to become our maid. I honestly have to say that letting her go was a bit of a blessing. She had been with us too long, and she wasn't the best maid. But I never had the heart to send her away until we had no choice. We cut back on many household expenses: the seamstress who did the mending, the old woman who washed and ironed the clothes, even crazy Consolato, who drank too much wine and who had no teeth. He came each week to beat our rugs and wash the windows.

I suppose everything is relative. We knew these were luxuries. If we had not had them, they might not have been missed. But we had become accustomed, and the adjustment was difficult. It really wasn't that we couldn't do these things for ourselves. We certainly were able. What made it hard was that our children had grown up with these wonderful people. They were like family. The children thought of them as their friends, companions, and playmates. Even as difficult as Elise had become, she was my friend too.

Finally, there came a time when we could no longer afford private school for the twins. In Naples, private school was a necessity. Paul and I never considered a good education for the children to be a luxury, and the public schools were not very good. But we did not have enough money. By then, the two older boys were already grown and had left home, but the twins, Mela and Arthur, were not even fifteen years of age. They were both promising students, but they wanted to contribute. The two decided to quit school so they could go to work and help with the family finances.

One More Moon

I know there were countless others in Naples whose situations were far worse. We knew we had been fortunate and rarely felt sorry for ourselves, although Mela may have felt differently at times. Our relatives in America generously sent their hand-me-down clothes to their poor relations in Italy. As a teenage girl, Mela found herself the recipient of clothes that did little to improve her appearance, despite her frequent efforts to rip out seams and sew alterations. No matter what, we always had enough to eat. As a family, we remained close and caring. However, this change in circumstances should not be understated. There had been some rather depressing moments.

When times were more affluent, our family developed an affinity for tea, considered by many to be somewhat of a local luxury. A first cousin living in London was married to a man who imported tea from China. Tea was very expensive in Naples. Like salt and tobacco, a special tax was imposed, making it overpriced, in limited supply, and an extravagance most could not afford for everyday use. During our better days, we would order tea from our London cousins. It was an indulgence we were able to enjoy.

As our finances became less and less secure, Mela recognized that many of our friends liked tea too. She decided to order a supply from London to sell for a small profit, another way to contribute to the household finances. Mela was out and about delivering tea the day she learned Bertie Allen was interested in selling the Pensione

Alexandra. When Mela rode the trolley down the Via Roma to bring tea to my good friend Lonnie Fabricatore, Lonnie told her this news.

Like much of life, often there are things that are not always exactly as they seem. When we decided to purchase the Pensione Alexandra, I assumed Bertie Allen wanted to sell because she was getting old, was ready to retire, and wanted to return to England. Sometimes, only experience teaches us the questions to ask before one acts. It was only later, months after we took over its operation, that I learned Bertie Allen had never disclosed her real reason for selling. She had been convinced that Mussolini would invade Ethiopia and the League of Nations would impose sanctions against Italy, which would hurt tourism and destroy her business.

Bertie Allen was right about Il Duce's Ethiopia adventure. What a bungled mess that became. Mussolini and his followers were convinced they could rebuild the Roman Empire. At least Mussolini thumbed his nose at the League of Nations, which was quickly becoming a rather toothless tiger, and the sanctions had little effect. If the sanctions had been effective, I am not sure what we would have done. Of course, we could not imagine then that, within a few short years, a much larger and perilous storm cloud would appear on Italy's horizon. At least there would be some sunny days before that cloud arrived at our doorstep.

CHAPTER FIVE

Money and risks aside, agreeing to buy the Pensione Alexandra was not an easy decision for Paul and me to make. We had to compromise, and I must tell you, I was raised to become the supportive wife of a merchant, not the proprietress of a pensione. At my age, there were expectations and duties to fulfill. Operating a guest house was not one of them.

It hasn't mattered where I have lived; there has always been a way of life and a way one is expected to act. Naples was no exception. In Italy, at the time we acquired the pensione, the social class structure was very strong. Once pigeonholed, whether wealthy or poor, noble or common, young or old, man or woman, there were certain norms to be followed. The rules may have been unwritten, but we all knew what they were. We kept to our own, knew where we belonged, stayed within our circle, and conducted our lives well within the lines. What I am trying to say is that a woman in my position was not supposed to have to concern herself with the rather ordinary and mundane task of managing a pensione, a role Mother would have found to be beneath my station.

I remain convinced that children have a better sense of these matters than adults, particularly better than we did at those times. Adults can make life messy and complicated. Children don't care to understand or observe the little differences. They just want to have fun and play with other kids. But even back then, when our children went to the park, we insisted that certain rules of society be followed. Our governess was under strict instructions to keep them apart from many other children and to be certain they played with only those within our social circle. Can you imagine? Before we owned the pensione, the concierge in the apartment building addressed Paul as *l'Eccellenza* and referred to the children as *i signorini*, the little lords. This may all sound ridiculous today, but that was the tradition in Naples, almost caste-like. We all knew our place in society and the roles we were to perform. One thing life has taught me is, whatever the issue, somehow children know how to simplify what adults know how to complicate.

It would have been as unthinkable for one of my children to work as a chambermaid in someone's home or a manual laborer in a factory as it would have been for me to have a career, consider any type of employment, or, for that matter, concern myself with money. Me? Earn a living? My time was to be spent on more appropriate activities. Someone in my position was expected to live a life of leisure and responsibility, and not to have to deal with the chores of daily life. Others more suited to those tasks could handle them.

I tell you all of this so you will understand how significantly our lives changed when we began operating the Pensione Alexandra. And as I say these words, I realize how much they make me sound like a prima donna, even a snob. But I don't believe I was. Snob or not, I was a realist. I knew how I was expected to act, but more importantly, I knew what I needed to do.

Of course, the world has changed a great deal from the way it was back then. The role of women was different. Respect for women was different, and in Italy, when it came to women, everything was different. In Naples, it was a man's world. There was no doubt about that. I suppose the role for women was not dissimilar to many places. We all had our roles, and nearly all the rules were made by men. Then, while nothing was cast in stone, Paul was the family breadwinner, and when it came to family decisions, there was no question that his word was final. It had always been that way. We had never known differently. We all deferred to Paul.

What made Italy particularly unique during this time was our dictator, Benito Mussolini, Il Duce. Life under Mussolini and the Fascists meant that people had less control of their personal lives and the government controlled as much as they could. In 1934, when we acquired the pensione, I lived in that Fascist world. This was a society where boys were expected to grow into soldiers and fight for Italy's glory and girls were encouraged to increase the production of babies. This was a society where bachelors paid extra taxes for not being married and where girls were rewarded for having the most babies. Mussolini had an empire to build. Empires required armies of men to conquer additional lands. Additional lands were needed to support a population expected to grow because the women were pregnant and new babies were about to be born. That was Mussolini's plan.

Fortunately, by then, I was much beyond my baby-producing years and thus excluded from having to concern myself with the daily rigor of Mussolini's plan for women. If I had a concern, it was what this might mean for Mela. But that really isn't what this story is about, and Mela was not all that interested. I just want to give you a broader sense of the role women were expected to play when I was about to become the proprietress of the Pensione Alexandra. The expectations for women were well defined. Women were expected to maintain the household, raise the children, and support the men. I know there are those who question whether it was Mussolini who actually made the trains run on time in Italy but, there should be no doubt that his well-functioning empire relied upon everyone making their contribution and doing their part.

That is how our life was the day when Mela arrived home with her dream of owning the Pensione Alexandra. Paul's first reaction was to show little interest and express even less enthusiasm. He had other things on his mind. Poor Paul. I felt so bad for him. He was always busy with the stagnating and deteriorating tartar business. Most of his time was spent attending legal proceedings. His hands were tied, and he had become terribly depressed. The pressure of our precarious financial situation was an enormous worry. Almost overnight, we watched Paul's personality change from optimistic to pessimistic. He seemed to have aged. He lost weight. His self-esteem and self-confidence suddenly disappeared. Paul and I were managing as best we could. Our marriage remained strong, but I would be less than honest if I did not say that this was a stressful and difficult time.

Paul and I both were keenly aware that something had to be done to turn things around, but keep in mind, he had his role, and I had mine. It was acceptable for Mela and me to make small contributions to our finances. Mela could babysit, do some tutoring, and sell a little tea. Perhaps she could find work as a clerk in a store. With the boys' rooms vacant, we could take in an occasional border, but there was little more that I could do to contribute without overstepping my place. The difficulty was we all realized that those few minor money-raising enterprises Mela or I might attempt would not be enough to solve our financial problems. Unless Paul successfully picked all the numbers in the lotto, a better solution would be required. Changing who did what would require one of us having to give what the other would take. Acquiring the Pensione Alexandra was not my decision to make. It was an endeavor I could pursue only with Paul's blessing.

With Mela's and my encouragement, Paul had little choice other than to reluctantly approve of the idea of considering the pensione. It was tough for him to accept the fact that he might share his role as the breadwinner in the family. And he made it clear that, if we were to make this purchase, it would become my responsibility. It would be up to me to figure out how to make it work.

He would give his support when he could, but apart from that, I would be left on my own. The best he could do was to become my reluctant partner.

With all that in mind, I took a deep breath and hesitated for a moment to reconsider what this might mean. Then the opportunity to solve a big problem prevailed, and I jumped in with both feet. The moment I landed, I received an immediate education. Within days, I learned that dreaming of owning a pensione was not the same as actually buying a pensione. Later, I would learn that buying a pensione is not the same as operating a pensione. Often, there are times when the best way to learn is through experience. In my case, it was by the seat of my pants. I was determined to succeed. Once I jumped in, I found myself far too deep to be able to jump out.

CHAPTER SIX

After many face-to-face meetings and a little haggling with Bertie Allen, the purchase price and terms of purchase were agreed upon, on the condition that I would find a way to raise the necessary money to complete the sale. We had a prolonged negotiation, but I came away convinced that the Pensione Alexandra would, with time, enable our family to fully repay our debts and regain our financial footing. Then I overcame my naturally shy tendencies and wrote letters to friends and relatives in America, asking for their help.

My oldest brother, a Boston banker; Paul's brother, an ear, nose, and throat specialist living in New York; and my sister in Chicago, whose husband had a successful career as an engineer were so swayed by my plea for help from the other side of the Atlantic that they wired the necessary funds within days.

I know this was an imposition, perhaps an act of charity. Believe me, I could not have been more grateful for their generosity. There was not a single moment of hesitation. They never asked when they would be repaid. I am sure they doubted whether they would see their money again. Today, I imagine they thought I was crazy in the head. I know that not a single one of them could picture me as the owner of the Pensione Alexandra.

Rather than talk about the price, I should tell you what we bought when the negotiations to purchase the Pensione Alexandra were completed. As with most entrepreneurial endeavors, there were any number of surprises. The first was to learn that the purchase did not actually include the building at Caracciolo 13. No, we were to purchase the lease for two of the six floors in the building at that address, the particulars to be renegotiated with the landlord, Signor Spinelli, a very thin and nervous man with a wispy, dark mustache waxed to curl up on either end. Clearly, buying the lease instead of the building significantly reduced the Pensione Alexandra's purchase price, certainly a point in our favor. Unfortunately, there was a different issue. I found myself having to deal with Signor Spinelli.

Signor Spinelli was such an odd character, almost classic in the Neapolitan sense, and a person who, to this day, remains impossible to forget. And even though I poke fun at him as I tell you this story, the truth is, the longer we knew him, the better we cared for him, and with time, he became a member of our extended family. He was one of those people whose friendship never wavered and who stood with us when times were tough. But when I first met him, I did not know what to think.

Signor Spinelli wore a misshapen hairpiece that created the strange sensation that it was moving about his head. The hairpiece reminded me of our old cat before, during, and after she died. He always held a sweet-smelling cigarette between his yellow-stained fingers. And in conversation, he spoke rapidly, with a whisper-like voice that might best be described as spooky.

His mannerisms were dramatic, and his words were often punctuated with much annoying hand movement. He had a very distracting habit of winking, first with his left eye, followed in quick succession by the right, like a nervous tic except that it wasn't. Fiftyish and a bachelor, he acted as though he considered himself quite the ladies' man. I will always remember the smell of his cologne – an excessive amount, the scent lingering for days. We could always sense when he was standing nearby or where he had been. He usually sported a bright red handkerchief in the pocket of his suit coat, which was always pulled carefully about his shoulders. If I were to draw you a picture, it would be of someone who worked hard at crafting the image of a man about town.

I believe my age and seniority helped our relationship. As I was a few years older, he remained very polite and was always deferential in our business dealings. As for me, I found it difficult to refrain from reaction whenever I met with him. I have never known such a strange person before or since.

It was always *mia cara signora* this and *mia cara signora* that. In fact, because of his many invitations to sit and discuss our lease over coffee, it became quite apparent, particularly when he tapped his hand on my knee or held my arm to emphasize one point or another, that he'd taken a liking to me and enjoyed my company. I chose not to reciprocate. The thought of his well-manicured fingernails – I am sure he wore polish – still makes me shudder, and not in a positive way.

I suppose, for some, he could be very charming. He often spoke of his exploits and, at times, boasted about his conquests. Fortunately, I learned that I had not forgotten my ability to charm as well. Clearly, he was not experienced at negotiating a business transaction with a woman, at least not eye to eye. And I am certain that if he were asked, eye to eye might not have been the negotiating position he would have preferred. To this day, I remain absolutely convinced that, as a result of his constant desire to impress me and to teach me the finer points of conducting business, we were able to conclude the *negoziati w*ith a lease very favorable to my interests.

The most significant concession was that Signor Spinelli would exchange the two half-floors, which had been used by the pensione for the previous forty years, with one entire floor. Now, instead of the pensione being located half on the second floor and half on the third, the Pensione Alexandra would occupy the entire third floor, creating a much more agreeable floorplan and better surroundings for our guests. Accomplishing this would necessitate knocking through the wall along the middle of the third floor and building a number of walls to create new sleeping rooms, a reasonable and practical solution to a much-overlooked problem and with a cost that Signor Spinelli graciously suggested we would mutually share, with the understanding that his contractors would perform the work.

Removing the wall from the middle of the third floor resulted in an unanticipated bonus when it was discovered that the old kitchen had become invaded by cockroaches, a situation that, whether or not previously known, had never been disclosed. Our agreement stipulated that, in the case of this or a similar unforeseen event, Signor Spinelli would furnish us, at his own expense, with a new kitchen, which was to be conveniently located adjacent to the breakfast room. Although a little smaller than the old kitchen, it was to be freshly painted and clean. Most importantly, the lease contained a clause assuring that the kitchen would be inspected every three months and would remain cockroach free provided that we kept it fully cleaned and scrubbed.

Another item of prolonged negotiation concerned the lift. I no longer remember the particulars, but there was an issue with the elevator, a problem that Bertie Allen had failed to successfully address and that she had avoided for forty years. Signor Spinelli speculated that the problem had something to do with Bertie's communication with the afterlife. For reasons that never became completely clear, the elevator, when filled with guests, was only to be operated in one direction. It would take guests from the ground-floor entrance up to the third-floor reception area, but for their return, guests were required to walk down the three flights of stairs. I imagine this had something to do with the weight that the elevator could carry on the descent, but I was never advised as to the exact reasons. Again, with Signor Spinelli's assistance, this important issue was resolved to our mutual satisfaction. The necessary repairs were made, and the elevator was able to carry passengers in both directions, a major improvement to the pensione's future operation.

So, one might ask, *what did we purchase when we bought Pensione Alexandra?* Once all negotiations were completed, we purchased the terms of a renegotiated lease and the forty-year-old contents and furnishings of a pensione that could accommodate thirty-two guests. We bought dining tables and chairs, dishes and cutlery for sixteen, serving dishes, and coffee urns. This allowed us to serve meals in two seatings, a major undertaking considering that meals could possibly be served three times a day and dishes required handwashing between servings. We acquired old armchairs and couches, lamps, rugs, side tables, beds, mattresses, armoires, linens, pillows, pots and pans, ashtrays, a sign, some advertising placards, the name and reputation of the Pensione Alexandra, and many stuffed animals, particularly feathery birds that had suffered greatly and taken on the odor that grows naturally with advancing age – an odor that, I was certain, would not be improved even if the birds spent several days in the company of Signor Spinelli and his cologne.

Only days before Christmas of 1934, we took possession and moved in. It was clearly not the height of the Naples tourist season, but we didn't care. We continued to keep our apartment at Corso Vittorio Emanuele 24, which, by foot, was only fifteen minutes away. But my plan was that we would spend most of our time at the pensione, often sleeping there. I was so excited. I felt as if we would be staying at a seaside villa overlooking the

Mediterranean Sea. I had to pinch myself. I was afraid that lightning might strike.

I still have very vivid recollections of that first night. I insisted we sleep there. Paul, Mela, and I huddled together in those strange surroundings with strange furniture and the oddest assortment of furnishings. Late that night, I dreamed that Bertie Allen's old guests had returned for a seance. Dressed up as birds, they were peering at us, the three trespassers, through dark, beady, unforgiving eyes. When confronted, they told me we could not leave because Bertie had fixed the elevator so it would not go down and that she had locked all the windows. Needless to say, it was a very strange dream. I fail to recall how it ended.

The next morning, we organized ourselves and went from room to room to hunt for any mysterious treasures that might have been left behind. We couldn't contain our laughter when Mela opened one chest of drawers and discovered an old Ouija board. She convinced us that this was the very board Bertie Allen had used to converse with her dearly departed husband and other friends. Later, when the renovations were complete, we hung it on the wall in the breakfast room, and it became the topic of many wonderful conversations with guests.

What did it matter? We owned a pensione, and I was the *madre della casa*. I remember thinking that one of Bertie Allen's mummified birds might be a pigeon who would do his business on my crazy head. In Naples, that December of 1934, a pigeon doing his business would be the sign we were hoping for, the sign of *buona fortuna*!

CHAPTER SEVEN

As I sit here and tell you this story, I find it hard to believe that those events took place so long ago. So many years have passed that, some days, I don't understand how all of this happened or whether these memories are actually real. Perhaps they are a dream. So much makes little sense. One moment, we were buying the Pensione Alexandra hoping to repay our debts and solve our financial difficulties. The next moment, I was negotiating the lease with Signor Spinelli, whose hairpiece reminded me of the family cat. Now it is nearly fifty years later, and I find myself living in Portland, Oregon, a place I had never heard of and never imagined existed. How can I be almost a century old? It seems as if it were only yesterday that I first stepped off the train in Naples, married Paul, and cared for my four bambinos.

I suppose how I arrived here matters to only a few by now. Life moves on. We all hope the world becomes a better place for each succeeding generation. I remember when the airplane first flew and when I saw men walk on the moon, which, when you think about it, is really quite amazing. But despite our scientific advances, no law has been passed to prevent old men from sending the young to fight their wars and die, which is something I will never be able to understand.

The simple fact is that I am here and it is now. Paul seems a distant memory, and my children have grown old, with children and grandchildren of their own. I am fortunate that many live nearby, that they allow me to live here and are able to keep me under their watchful eyes.

Now, for a reason I cannot fathom, I survive as the last one standing of my family's entire generation. My life has been quite fulfilling. There are few my age who can state that every one of their descendants is still living. They tell me I am an endangered species. I have no idea who decided this, or why I was the one chosen to finish this chapter of life, but here I am, the innkeeper, left with the last key to unlock the stories that will soon be long forgotten. Perhaps whoever selected me thought that the years I spent as the proprietress of the Pensione Alexandra prepared me to take on this final role as the family storyteller. I truly have become the keeper of the secrets.

I can honestly say that becoming this old is a cursed blessing. Obviously, there is little I can do to change the situation I find myself in. I only hope that, when my endangered days are over, they do not see fit to preserve me for display. Ashes to ashes would be my request. I think

I would rather stay aflutter in the wind. What is it the grandchildren say to me? *I have to roll with it.* That seems to be a good expression. I tell them, *I will roll with it* until such time as I am unable to roll over. Then they should toss me aside. The next generations have their lives to live, and my only advice is: the sooner they begin the better. It is all right to be a little selfish. From my perspective, the good years should be enjoyed. Life passes in the blink of an eye.

Reaching ninety-eight years gives me hope and a sense of anticipation. I feel that, if I have made it this far, I should try for one hundred. It is a nice, round number and seems to be a reasonable goal as long as my mind remains clear. I look forward to each new day, and I like the thought that each new day brings me one step closer. My children, grandchildren, and great-grandchildren are all rooting for me. And I could not be more fortunate. I continue to have the joy of rooting for all of them. We are able to learn of one another's adventures. I am the first to admit that now mine are a little less adventuresome than theirs. Sharing these adventures is a gift that only generations can give to one another.

I am truly loved, but I admit to having days when I feel more cherished than loved. I have come to understand the difference. Cherish is something one does with a prized antique sitting in a favored place on a mantel or to a silver bowl brought out and polished to look good when the guests arrive. Cherish lacks the emotion of love. Love has more depth and dimension. I am certain you can cherish someone you love. I am not sure if you must love someone you cherish. By my measure, cherish is not love.

Please don't misunderstand. My family is not the reason for expressing this thought. I know they love me. Actually, I am talking about those days when the staff cleans my room. That is when I feel cherished and when I join the others for our frequent playdates in the hallway. Sometimes, these playdates last for hours. Often, I wish that we would be given rugs for our naps like they did when we were children. Picture these hallway playdates as something like school recess at a playground that has no slides or swings. I ask you, what child wants to go to a playground without swings or slides? Those kinds of playgrounds were not interesting when I was a young child in Germany, and they do not hold my attention now. Now my playground only offers small park benches built to hold one person. I suppose the only positive thing about these benches is that they do have wheels. Instead of running and playing, most of my playmates sleep, and too many of them snore. Those are the moments when I feel a little more cherished and a little less loved, when I feel that I am an antique put out for display. Like I said, there is a difference between cherish and love.

I know some of my playmates enjoy this form of recreation. They like the social aspect of our hallway playdates. That's ok, to each their own. For me, the hallway is more like a gym for the ancient. Sometimes, I think I should invite my great-grandchildren to visit on Halloween. The hallway could be decorated to look like a haunted house, and my playmates and I could sit in our chairs pretending to be dead, which, with practice, should not be very hard to do. We would startle the children when we moved. It would be great fun but probably against the rules. I am sure those in charge wouldn't allow it. As I said earlier, everywhere I have lived, there has been a certain way of life and rules to be followed. Even at my age, this remains true.

Please excuse my behavior. Don't get me wrong. I am not sad. A little cynical? Yes. But I am certainly not depressed. That is not me. Quite the opposite. I feel complete. I am lucky to have lived the life that I have lived and am not ready to roll over. What's the other thing the great-grandchildren tell me to say? *Let the good times roll.*

Now, before I lose your attention, I have one or two more things to say. It is no surprise that, when you reach my age, many parts of one's anatomy don't work as they once did. In other words, rolling in any direction has become difficult. I have no idea how many functioning body parts I have left, but it does seem that, one after another, they tend to fail. In my endangered position as the last remaining member of my family's generation, one of my responsibilities is to explain these *other* important facts of life. This is what happens. It should be expected.

I imagine that the first facts of life you learned as a teenager were far more interesting and, I hope, kept you more entertained. In any case, now there are days when it seems that more parts fail than continue to work, simply a function of age. There is little I can do to prevent this from happening. My eyesight is poor, and my hearing is worse. Believe me, now that I have lost two of my five senses – and those two in particular – there are times when, even in a room filled with people, I can feel all alone. To be perfectly honest, often, there are days I find myself wishing a certain third sense would fail. That would be the sense of smell. I am prompted to say this particularly on those playground days, when I am surrounded by my playmates, who are close in age to my own. When I sit on the park bench with wheels, I yearn for the lingering smell of Signor Spinelli's cologne. Being old does not mean I have lost my sense of humor.

Although one by one, my senses are fading, my family tells me that my mind remains amazingly clear. Amazing is a curious word. Often, it seems that nearly everyone who lives here has reached the age of amazing. We are reminded of that every day. I would prefer that my family would say my mind is *most* amazing, which is what I tend to think. Even to this day, I am able to remember the details of memories with the most amazing clarity. I take great pleasure in reliving those moments. With regard to the necessities of everyday life, the wonderful staff here at this facility makes it a point to remember. They take good care of me and always remind me of what I forget.

There is one additional thing to mention. It is a conclusion that I am sure you will draw. And I suspect it is a conclusion you may have already drawn. I readily admit to being at a stage in life where others will hear me talk far more than they see me listen. Throughout my life, I have always enjoyed observing the human race and offering my commentary, whether asked for it or not. My children tell me this trait continues. Sometimes they say I talk too much. Often they remind me that I fail to stop. Personally, I consider myself colorful, descriptive, detailed, and even prescient, particularly when I repeat stories from the past when, based upon my firsthand knowledge, I am able to foretell what happens next with a high degree of certainty.

Only now, my failing eyesight and loss of hearing cause far more commentary and far less observation. You are right to conclude that is another way of saying I speak far more than I listen, which brings up this final issue. Now there are days when I am not entirely certain as to whether there is an audience to hear me or, for that matter, who they might be. This seems to matter less and less. To me, it is only a minor annoyance. I just continue to talk. And like the grandchildren encourage me to do, *I keep on rolling.*

CHAPTER EIGHT

Today is not particularly different than any other day. I suppose that is a function of my age. Some say that if you live long enough, most things seem the same. Perhaps this is because the little differences don't appear as important as they once did. For me, only the mornings and the sunrise remind me of the days as they pass. But counting the days this way has little to do with my age. It is mostly due to the "lights out" rule they have here. I keep telling them that they need to change it. Old people do not need to be told when they should go to bed. I am considering organizing a sit-in in the hallway. It wouldn't be very hard to do. I would have plenty of patient volunteers.

When we lived in Naples, Paul and I loved to stay up late and wait for the moon. Then there were more perfect nights than not. The pensione would be draped in light as the moon made its way over the Bay of Naples, and the stars would fill the sky. Sometimes, we made a game out of counting the shooting stars, especially on those warm August nights when the tourists thought the temperatures were too extreme to visit Naples.

With the wind gently blowing across the water, the nighttime air would be fresh and clear, a welcome relief from the daytime. I loved our evenings on the balcony, often only the two of us, when it was peaceful and we had time to catch up on the day's events. Other evenings we would sit for hours in quiet conversation with guests. It's funny now that, because I am told when to go to bed and turn off the lights, I cannot remember the last time I saw the moon or, for that matter, the stars. It is as if I have lost the moon. Sad, no. Different, yes.

Now, most mornings, I awake at daybreak. I like to roll over in my bed and spend a few moments staring out the window. What I see is all so curious. My old Naples friend, Vesuvius, has been exchanged for the profile of Mt. Hood. And the blue of the Bay of Naples and the Mediterranean Sea have been replaced by a parking lot and a school playground. At least the school playground has slides and swings. That makes me feel a bit better.

In Naples, the early mornings were always such a busy time of day. The entire world would come alive at daybreak. I have always thought that the people in Naples live a more carefree life than anywhere else in Italy and, perhaps, even the world. Even when Mussolini took control and the Fascists told us what to do, Naples still had its own sense of order and balance. Until Mussolini betrayed us, I thought life in Naples was protected by the sun and the moon and Mount Vesuvius and the Mediterranean Sea.

Within those borders, nearly everyone seemed cheerful and engaged, happy to be on this earth.

I know now that many were not as carefree and happy as I thought them to be. For most, it was a difficult life, and there are many who would not describe life under Mussolini's dictatorship as freedom. Yet in some ways, that was what it appeared to be, and for many years, Il Duce seemed our protector, sheltering us from our troubles, almost a father figure. There was a "come what may" attitude of survival that nearly everyone seemed to share. It was almost childlike. You could feel it.

Many days, life on the streets was a celebration that never ended. From morning till night, the streets resounded with shouting and singing and the rattle of the vendor's carts and the voices of children. Of course, over the years, much changed. Progress is like that. I still remember when they banned the shepherding of goats through the streets. Out with the old and in with the new, I suppose. But the Napoli I remember has never changed. These memories are meant to be.

I loved looking out our windows and watching Naples come alive each day. The street merchants would be out as soon as the sun came up. Pushing their wooden carts through the little streets, they would sing their songs to sell their wares: fruits, vegetables, eggs, breads, fresh flowers. Everything we would need they would have. It was a continuing parade. All the vendors would pass by our windows: the knife sharpeners, the letter writers, the men with their sewing machines, the barbers, the men with the ice. The old, lumbering cow would walk behind the man who sold the cow milk. Every morning was like a big, open-air festival filled with people and everything imaginable. All the windows would open, and everyone's heads would pop out. The laundry would be hung on lines connected by pulleys. All the gossip would be heard. Every question would be answered. Voices would fill the air from every direction.

I always felt a little sorry for the man with the cow, because most of us bought our milk from the man with the goats. It was less expensive. Boys and men would herd their goats through the streets. They would always follow the same routes. The women would give their milk bottles to the goat man, and the nearest goat would fill the bottle. It was the same day after day. It had been that way for centuries.

Elise, our maid, would send the basket with the money down from the window by rope to retrieve whatever we needed, even the milk. And if one of the street vendors didn't have something one wanted, they knew someone who did. The price of everything was known because negotiations would take place between each window and the street. Everyone would listen. We didn't have telephones; we had windows. That was our party line. It was a system that worked.

America is not Italy. Portland is not Naples. Such a contrast. Here, I am always amazed by how peaceful it is so early in the morning, exactly the opposite of our life in Naples. There is no movement, only the quiet to wake me. Just as amazing is my surprise that I have been granted the gift of another new day. In that single moment of recognition, my eyes blink, and I put my hands on my chest to be certain that my heart still beats.

As the sunlight slowly crosses the window, as if on a schedule, my old friend the pigeon will perch on the sill. With my failing eyes, all I can make out are the broad outlines of his silhouette. He appears to peer silently, intense and unmoving, reminding me of the good luck the pigeon brought us when we owned the Pensione Alexandra. Some mornings, I wonder how long he has been sitting there contemplating our connected memories. What does this pigeon think at the sight of this old woman as we stare at one another? I imagine our eyes lock and refuse to blink. We share our confusion, even our secrets. Then I smile knowingly and nod politely, just as I would wish good morning to an old and dear friend.

Some mornings, it is as if I can feel the sound when the pigeon scratches the window sill with his tiny feet. Something I can't explain makes me turn my head, and I try to listen. Isn't it odd to have the sensation that I can see and feel a sound even when my eyesight fails and I can no longer hear?

My hearing has been poor for more years than I can remember. Now it fails completely. When Paul was alive, he would tell me that my ears didn't work. What a strange thing to say. Of course, he was still learning the English language then, and expressions were confusing for my dear Paul. Paul found it difficult to adapt to change. Our lives travelled quite a distance. So many languages. So many customs. So much to learn. So many expressions. Difficulties and uncertainties. Never enough time. But here I am, greeted by another new day.

Paul was right. My hearing became more and more dreadful. He would get so frustrated trying to talk to me. I couldn't hear a thing, not a sound. My ears did not work. I don't remember when my hearing stopped completely, but it stopped, probably a gift from my father, a sign of advancing age. By then, Paul and I had been with one another so long that it hardly mattered. We had learned to communicate in our own silent way. I always felt I could see his sound even when I couldn't hear it. Paul and I, together we grew old, he looking more like his father, me acting more like my mother, differences that became harder and harder to distinguish. Finally, I could not see or hear him at all. He was no more. It was as if he simply disappeared.

How bittersweet it is that thirty years have passed since Paul held me in his arms. We laughed and cried through much of life together, when the children were born, when our parents died, the years we were all alone together after everyone left.

Losing my sense of hearing was so frustrating, but Paul made me feel so much better. Since I couldn't hear the music when we danced, he would tap his fingers softly on my back so I could stay in step. I still miss his caress, his smile, his face, and the silent words he said, words that I could not hear. I still miss the touch of his sound. I miss his gentleness and the quiet way he would listen. I miss how he would laugh. We were so close. It seemed as if my world effortlessly continued when I left the arms of my parents and moved into Paul's arms. I just lightly danced from one stepping stone to the next.

It is all so curious, the things one remembers in the morning, when it is quiet and there is time to think and to listen to oneself talk. Father used to tell me I had busy hands. I suppose that is true. My hands have always stayed busy, holding a book, drawing and painting, playing solitaire, making birthday cards, knitting, crocheting, making puppets and stuffed animals for the children, writing letters, keeping journals. What a strange person I must be. I rarely move, but I am never idle. Paul said my ears do not work, and Father said I had busy hands. I wonder if that is how I will be remembered.

So, in the early morning, it is the light through the window that wakes me. Even on the dimmest of days, it is a pleasant surprise during these early hours. I still find my own peaceful moments. Gray and misty or crystal clear, there are days I wonder if Portland will ever make up its mind. No, Portland is not Naples.

When we lived in Naples, the sky seemed endless. It reached to the end of the world. The sun shimmered across the Mediterranean. I remember each day as sparkling, a wonderful prism filled with color and reflection. Mount Vesuvius felt so close, always within our grasp, always keeping watch, a shoulder to the sea.

At my age, little of this matters. Like I said, my request is simple. It would be to see the moon one more time. Perhaps that will happen if they change the rules. Everything is quieter and easier now. I laugh, and I cry. The little differences between these two bookends are not so important. I am grateful for each new day. I am amazed by each new morning.

CHAPTER NINE

Things do have a way of working out. Two sides seem to always find a middle. Taking possession of the Pensione Alexandra in the heart of winter became a blessing in disguise. We needed time for the repairs and construction. Of course, I was too busy to know and too worried about money to find this comforting. All I knew was that there was much work to do before we could be ready for guests. I was anxious to roll up my sleeves and get to work. My days of living the leisurely life were over. Now I had a pensione to operate.

Dust was everywhere, on the floors, on the stuffed birds, in my hair, everywhere. As soon as we cleaned the dust from one spot, it would mysteriously move to another of its own free will. Signor Spinelli and his crew of workmen created new mountains of dust each day as they took out the third-floor wall with their sledgehammers, built the new kitchen, and rearranged walls for the new sleeping rooms. More than once, every inch of the third floor had to be scrubbed and cleaned. Every window pane had to be washed. Carpets needed to be cleaned. Floors had to be waxed. The chandeliers had to be dusted. Furniture had to be repaired and replaced. This was my pensione. I wanted it spotless. I wanted it sparkling. I wanted it perfect.

It helped that winter in Naples is the low point for tourists. Even with the Mediterranean climate and mild weather, guidebooks encouraged travelers to avoid Naples until April. For us, this loomed as a potential serious problem. We needed paying guests sooner rather than later, but first, we had little choice. We would take the time necessary to put our new house into order.

Renovations began the day after Christmas, when the three workmen arrived to survey their project and begin their work. I remember watching them arrive from the window. It was a typical Naples scene, one I had seen many times before. They walked merrily down the street, in unison, one behind the next, three men, all wearing white pants with matching caps on their heads, holding the long ladder in one hand and their lunch buckets in the other.

I was surprised to learn, as I thought that I would be in charge, that the crew would work under the direct personal supervision of Signor Spinelli, who informed me he was pleased to continue his everyday visits and offer this service at no charge. This would be his gift. He immediately became a distraction for everyone. It was only a matter of days before I began thinking of him as a very small annoying fly wearing a wig, waving its arms simultaneously in all directions. He would shout confusing instructions in a loud version of his spooky voice, and he refused to leave. Mela teased and told me I was his muse.

Most of us are familiar with how much a nuisance a fly can be in wintertime. So, with Mela's strong encouragement, I finally was able to make it clear to Signor Spinelli that his solicitations would not be returned. We would all be better off and make more progress without his daily visits. He understood when I told him that if he expected me to financially fulfill the terms of our lease agreement, he'd better stay out of everyone's way. It took me two days to gather my nerves for that conversation, but it was necessary, and it worked. I remember being so relieved and so proud. It was my first executive decision as the proprietress of the Pensione Alexandra.

The construction was not all that required attention. Arrangements with the various services and suppliers were needed for when we opened. Our guests would expect breakfast each morning. Some would want midday and evening meals; others would ask for picnic lunches. Deliveries needed to be scheduled.

We would need ice, a steady supply of breads, milk, eggs, fresh fruits, vegetables, meat, fish, and various staples like tea and coffee. I had to find a washerwoman so linens could be laundered. We had to be prepared because guests could arrive and depart on any day. We had been warned of fleas and bedbugs and what that could mean for our reputation. No chance could be taken. Fortunately, we could continue much of what had been arranged previously by Bertie Allen, but even so, this was

Naples. I wanted to make it clear to one and all that the new owner was tough and not to be taken advantage of. In Naples, we were all too familiar with clerks who might shortchange the customer when no one was watching or the butcher who might put his thumb on the scale to charge just a little more.

There were days I felt as if I were walking in circles. I had the feeling that I was the only one in a hurry. Everyone else seemed to be working at their own comfortable pace without a care in the world. Both Paul and Mela avoided me. Our funds were limited, and everything was a mess. We needed guests in order to make money. Money was needed for supplies, which were needed to open the doors. We needed the doors to be open in order to receive guests. And we needed all the help we could find, except we had little money to pay for it. I felt completely ill prepared for my new station in life, and I loved every moment.

Now I can only laugh when I think about those first days. Back then, I am sure I cried and kept my reluctant partner, Paul, awake each night. I remember the day when I hired Consolato, the old man with no teeth, who drank too much wine and who used to clean our carpets and wash our windows and do other odd jobs. I employed Consolato to paint the rooms and hang the wallpaper in the breakfast room. Consolato was like family. We had known him for years. When they were young, the children adored him. He would always put the chairs in a line, and they would pretend they were riding in a train. I knew he would listen to me. I was used to his strange habits, how he always arrived with the same two refilled wine bottles: one white for midday and one red for late afternoon.

I also knew that Consolato would work for whatever wage we could afford to pay. What did I know? I was so inexperienced. I forgot to ask if he had ever hung wallpaper or painted a room. What a mess he made. And the wallpaper? He hung it in the breakfast room with the pattern upside down. I am sure the look on my face was priceless when he proudly unveiled his work. At first, I was concerned, but the very next day, the wallpaper fell from the walls as if it had a mind of its own and knew something was wrong. Then I helped Consolato mix new paste and together, we put it back up the right way. Like I said, things have a way of working out.

Every day, the voice of my mother filled the back of my head. *Meshugenah! What was I thinking?* She was right about my children. They were fully grown and living their own lives. Mela was home but had little time to help. Paul was of little use. With time, we would hire help – a cook, a chambermaid, and a laundress. For now, I would be all three. I would also be the advertising director, the receptionist, the bookkeeper, the busboy, and the dishwasher.

Now that Signor Spinelli had stopped making his daily visits and shouting his instructions, it was amazing to see the progress the workmen made. When the children were little, I enjoyed helping them with craft projects and painting little drawings. Now I learned how to use a big paintbrush to paint the walls. The workmen just laughed, but someone had to clean up after Consolato. I am sure that I was a ridiculous sight. At the movies, I had watched newsreels from America and had seen Katherine

Hepburn and Marlene Dietrich wear trousers, so I made myself a pair, one of the few times in my life that I have worn pants. No one had ever seen someone like me, the lady of the house, do work like I did those days. Paul did not know what to think. I quickly learned that you do what you have to do. Bertie Allen became my hero. The Pensione Alexandra was rapidly changing my life.

Day by day, the improvements took shape, and with a little elbow grease, the pensione began to take on an air of respectability. Those four weeks were a flurry of activity and seemed much longer than they really were. We didn't have a moment to spare as the third-floor wall was removed, the cockroaches exterminated, the new kitchen and plumbing installed, the elevator repaired, everything moved from the second floor to the third, and all rooms thoroughly cleaned and painted. Fortunately, the mishaps were minor. Mela would probably disagree, since a very heavy marble table fell on her foot, requiring a cast to be worn for a number of weeks. Before the end of January, most of the work was completed. Suddenly, we were ready to be open for guests.

The night before we opened, we hardly slept. There were still some bedrooms that were not finished, but I wanted to make certain that what was complete was perfect. We certainly had no reason to believe that we would be filled to capacity anytime soon, as the tourist season was still a few months off. At least we had most of the rooms ready. I hoped that would help pay the bills.

A very proud Signor Spinelli joined us that evening. We celebrated with a bottle of Champagne, and I helped Paul hang the newly painted sign outside the front entrance. With little sleep, I was up before daybreak the first morning, yelling at Mela and Paul, "We have to be ready for guests. They could arrive at any time."

By sunrise, I was out the door and on my way to the seaport, where the ships docked. I wanted to be first in line to meet the passenger ship from Genoa and the boat from Palermo. I still remember standing there with my little sign that said "rooms available." You never knew who might need a room. I asked Mela to do the same at the train station before she went to her job. She could meet the first train from Rome.

We were unsuccessful that first morning, and the next morning too. We knew it would be slow. It was still the last days of January. But late on that second day, I was astonished when a middle-aged man appeared at our door to inquire about a room. He asked to see the rooms. As I watched him inspect them and try the mattresses, I became convinced he was a city inspector or someone from the tourist police. I remember saying to myself, "I know what he is up to."

But as it turned out, he wasn't an inspector at all. He really was to become our first paying guest. The next morning, I am certain I served him the biggest breakfast of his life. I couldn't contain my excitement. I took the money he paid and pinned it up on the wall. The refurbished Pensione Alexandra was open for business, and the new owner was ready to receive the next guest.

CHAPTER TEN

One guest was not enough to pay the bills, and neither were the few guests that followed. Those first days we were open were difficult, slow, and more than a little disappointing. After four weeks of constant motion and expectation, reality started to sink in.

I remember sitting alone in the reception room, playing solitaire, waiting for something to happen. Even playing solitaire was difficult. I had tried knitting but found myself worrying that the milk would spoil or the ice would melt. Now I can still feel the anxiety and anticipation. One moment, I wanted to jump up, and the next moment, I wanted to fall down. The last few rooms were almost done. Consolato was nearly finished painting. The family continued to avoid me. I was upset with everything and everyone. I was so anxious for the pensione to become a success, yet there was little I could do that would make a difference. Perhaps it is a quirk in my personality, but even now, I find it difficult to be an optimist on those days when it rains.

There was always much to learn, and I was still learning. One of the first lessons was that it hardly mattered whether we were open for guests, whether I met the ships arriving at the port or the trains arriving at Centrale holding my little sign that said "rooms available," or that our sign on the street was freshly painted. If tourists were not arriving in Naples, there was little likelihood that the Pensione Alexandra would have guests. And if, somehow, tourists had previously arrived in Naples, chances were that they had already found a place to stay and were satisfied. All we could do was hope someone would walk through our doors. While I was waiting, I tried to keep my hands busy playing cards. From time to time, I stood behind Consolato with a paintbrush. I admit to having moments when I considered asking to share his wine.

Paint buckets, a ladder, and a drop cloth were still in one room when the miracle I was hoping for came from the least expected source. It may have been that the Pensione Alexandra was not fit for a queen, but suddenly, it appeared that the Pensione Alexandra was fit to house a number of her favored subjects, a squadron of airmen from Her Majesty's Royal Air Force.

I will never forget the moment. It was the last Saturday in January. Paul, Mela, and I were having our coffee late that morning. There was not a single guest staying in the pensione. All the rooms were empty, and no one was expected. When the telephone rang, Mela picked it up and quickly handed it to me. She was too nervous to talk.

It was the British Consulate calling with an emergency request.

Could the Pensione Alexandra accommodate thirty RAF flyers for several nights?

I do remember asking the caller to repeat his question. I wasn't sure if I had heard correctly. I have a clipping from an English newspaper that someone sent me years later. It explains what happened better than I can.

On January 15, 1935, Squadron 210 of the British Royal Air Force left the Seaplane and Flying Boat station located at Pembroke Dock, Pembrokeshire, Wales, on an 8,000-mile journey. The crew of thirty plus RAF flyers has been ordered to ferry four Singapore Mark III flying boat bi-planes in a formation flight to the big British base in Singapore to re-equip RAF Squadron 205. The Singapore Mark III is a new aircraft in the RAF's inventory, having been delivered only months ago for operational training and trials. She is fitted with four Rolls Royce Kestrel engines and has a top speed of 145 miles an hour.

The assignment promised to be lengthy but leisurely, with stops at various British bases along the way. However, en route, their journey has been delayed on the island of Nisida, near Naples, Italy, as a result of engine failure. Maintenance is required, and replacement parts have been ordered for the engines on two of the flying boats. Squadron 210 will continue its journey after all repairs have been made. The delay is not expected to exceed five to six days.

Mein Gott! I looked to the sky and said thank you. Even though I wasn't Catholic, my right hand immediately touched my forehead, the middle of my chest, my left shoulder, and then my right, as I made the sign of the cross. The pigeon had done his business. We'd caught our lucky break. We could not believe our good fortune. Just like that, when it was least expected, our pensione would be completely filled. Even if this was only for a few nights, it was a start. We looked at one another in amazement. I remember my relief.

It was only a matter of moments, as much time as it would take to count to ten, before my amazement turned to anxiety. There were so many questions and not nearly enough answers. How many eggs would thirty young British flyers eat for breakfast? How much bread did we need? Did we have enough coffee? What about lunch? Suddenly, the newly constructed kitchen, courtesy of Signor Spinelli, seemed much too small. Where would we put everything? How could we prepare all the food that would have to be served? Did we have enough serving dishes? Were the beds all ready? What about ice? We had never been filled to capacity before. Truthfully, we had no idea what our capacity really might be. And our visitors? They were to be approximately thirty healthy young men, certainly with large appetites. The reputation of the Pensione Alexandra would be at stake. And this was not one of my children calling with a practical joke. This was really about to happen.

CHAPTER ELEVEN

Paul was familiar with the island of Nisida. It was only a tiny bit north of Naples, near the Posillipo quarter, where we sometimes went for our Sunday afternoon meal. There was an old fort that had been turned into a prison, and on the quay, there was only an old building where they used to quarantine people with cholera during the epidemic. There was space to keep the flying boats by the fort, but there were no quarters to house the men.

Did we know when the men would arrive? If they were traveling by motor coach, it was possible that they could be at our door within an hour or two. We needed to be ready. The British Royal Air Force would be staying at the Pensione Alexandra.

I am convinced that if my old friend the pigeon had been watching, we would have made it roll its head and laugh. We must have been an incredible sight. Mela, Paul, and I were just sitting there in our chairs in the breakfast room with our mouths gaping wide open. We were unable to speak. At the very least, we were in shock. So far, Paul had been impressed with what had been done with the pensione, but that did not mean he was enthusiastic. He remained my reluctant partner, clearly not convinced that it might become a success. Now, in that single moment, everything was about to change.

As soon as I took a deep breath or two and collected my wits, I was out the door. My aching feet have never run so fast or so far. Forget the rules of society, my concerns for respect and dignity, or the fact that I was a fifty-one-year-old woman, soon to be a grandmother, who had long ago forgotten how to run and had an aching back. All those concerns ran out the door with me. Just remembering that day makes me dizzy.

I had to go meet with Don Mario, the butcher. He sold the best cuts of meats. I had to find Donna Peppina, who could provide fresh vegetables and fruits. I had to stop by the nearby fish market. I needed to find the man with the cows to make sure we would have enough fresh milk. We couldn't serve the men goat's milk. I had to find Vincenzella's father. Finding him was always a problem. By this time of day, he was sure to be sitting somewhere on a doorstep with friends, enjoying his wine and debating the world's problems. The question was which doorstep, but he was critically important. He was responsible for bringing the baked bread from the bakery in the morning. He needed to be on time, and he needed to bring enough bread. And it absolutely needed to be fresh.

Nobody had telephones. Produce and meats were sold from carts and small stands, not stores with cash registers and telephones. This was Naples. All arrangements and negotiations were to be face to face and eye to eye. We had to raise our arms, hands, and voices and agree on prices in the Neapolitan way. It was the way business was conducted. I insisted that everything had to be perfect. Everyone must promise to provide the best. And to everyone I met on the streets, I proudly announced the exciting news. The British were coming. The Pensione Alexandra might not have been fit for a queen, but we were certainly fit for the flyers from Her Majesty's Royal Air Force.

I know I'm repeating myself, but sooner or later, most things work out. Everything and everyone has to give a little to make things work somewhere in the middle. Perhaps it was never perfect, but few things ever are. I remember telling myself that Mother was right. A pensione? What was I thinking? I am too old, my back aches, and my feet hurt. All the while, Paul sat watching and smoking his cigar. He was speechless. He didn't say one word.

I still see the expression on Mela's face. Just imagine how she must have felt. For her, this was heaven. And once again, she had her head in the clouds. Here she was, an unattached girl anxious to discover the mysteries of life. She would soon be surrounded by thirty British RAF airmen. What a new experience this promised to be. We needed to keep our eyes on her. Paul would have to pay attention. I am sure she was already wondering how quickly she could remove the cast from her foot.

CHAPTER TWELVE

I know I prattle on and on. You certainly have every right to be impatient for me to tell the story, which I will in short course. I just ask you to indulge this old woman for a few more moments. There are a few things I need to say that will give this story much-needed perspective.

At my age, I have learned that every life, whether or not recognized, needs a center on which all else balances and rests. Whether one is at the beginning, middle, or near the end of life, this center provides a large-enough base so that everything you have ever done or ever will can sit securely atop it.

Some people spend their entire lives searching for that part of life that makes everything else seem complete and fulfilled. Some find it in their religion. Some find it in their family. Others find it in their passions and talents. I have had more than enough time to consider this question. There is no doubt that my husband, my children, and the generations they have created will forever be the most important, most meaningful parts of my life. But the time that made me grow in hundreds of different ways, that opened up my mind and my heart, gave me self-confidence, made me see that there was another dimension to my life as a woman, that didn't revolve entirely around children and a husband was the period when we owned Pensione Alexandra. I can sit everything else securely atop that time. Those years were to change and challenge the rest of my life and make me consider all that I had done before. I can think of no better way to say it.

Visiting with guests at the pensione, I had conversations I never imagined were possible, heard opinions that seemed revolutionary, learned about places, events, and people that were completely beyond my horizon. I made friendships that lasted a lifetime. I witnessed joy, love, sadness, passion, fear, tragedy, and struggle. I discovered emotions I never knew, emotions that I never imagined existed. I learned that I wasn't alone in my feelings and that others shared my confusions. I began to understand that, sometimes, our differences are not as great as they may first seem. I realized that contradiction is fuel for debate and often leads to a better answer, and I learned that being the loudest does not mean someone is right.

I was able to begin to know myself, to find out who I was, and to rule out who I was not. I learned that life, however rewarding, remains a difficult and challenging lesson, that there are things that do not turn out as they should, and that, frequently, there is nothing one can do to change what will happen. I learned that fate and luck are often two sides of the same coin, just like heads and tails, and that, at times, the course of one's life can be explained simply as a matter of which side lands face up.

For me, the time that we owned the Pensione Alexandra was when I learned how to stand confidently on my own two feet, something that, until then, others had always done for me, something I had never been taught to do, a choice I never was given to make. The lessons we were taught, when growing up in Germany's East Prussia were that wives, daughters, and sisters spent their time at home, where they would oversee the domestic duties and raise the children. I grew up in the Victorian era, and that was to be my place in life. I was to follow, to follow gracefully, and, above all else, to refrain from attempting to lead. I was to stand by my husband's side, to be a loving parent and a supportive wife. If I performed these roles well, my life would be fulfilled.

Learning to become independent was a lesson never imagined and certainly a goal never stressed. I was trained to always remain under the protective shield of parents or my husband. I never dreamed of anything that went beyond that shield. Even dreams need prompting, and I was never prompted. Today, there is much talk about glass ceilings. I grew up in a time when the glass ceiling was held up by four glass walls.

You may think me naïve. Perhaps I was. Many are thrust into circumstances that require learning these lessons early in life. For me, it was only after I fulfilled my roles as a daughter, a wife, and a mother, and after raising four children who no longer needed my help. I do not belittle my role. Yet now I know I was so busy supporting others that I missed my chance to do things for myself. I failed to learn that I was important, intelligent, and capable, and to become genuinely comfortable with me.

I suppose each generation distinguishes itself from the past in one way or another, that we each, in our own way, conclude that the world is more evolved, more modern, and certainly different from the one our parents knew. I am sure I was older than most when I discovered that my life might be different from my mother's, that I was not repeating what had always been done. The pensione did for that for me. The pensione distinguished me from my past.

I was fifty-one years old when I discovered my need for something more and when I developed the self-confidence to do more. What I did changed little for any world but my own. Yet that was when I moved from second fiddle to first violin, and that was when I knew for certain that I was not crazy in the head. My center was the Pensione Alexandra. That was when I became part of the world.

CHAPTER THIRTEEN

I never learned exactly why the British RAF chose the Pensione Alexandra for their stay, but I remain forever grateful. If I were to hazard a guess, they chose us because the Pensione Alexandra was one of the few guest houses in Naples advertising that English was spoken. Perhaps it was because we had the necessary rooms available. No one ever said, and I never asked. I suppose this decision might have been one of Bertie Allen's last gifts from her queen. All I know is that I was happy no one had advised the queen that the pensione's ownership had changed and that the new owners were not British. I am not at all certain we would have been selected if it had been known that the Pensione Alexandra was being operated by a German family living in Naples.

In any event, what a change this one event made to our lives. Can you imagine? Suddenly, the English language was all we heard and spoke. We went from empty to crowded in a single instant. Mela was thrilled to be able to practice her English and found herself in the company of many willing tutors. My language skills were a little rusty but good enough to be understood and to generally understand what was being said. Perhaps there were moments of confusion, but I was able to carry on a conversation. Paul found this a convenient time to purchase a box of better cigars and a few more lotto tickets. And once again, we learned what we needed to do by the seat of our pants.

When the men arrived, we had been told that they would stay for only a few days, until the parts arrived from the Rolls Royce Company in England and the engines were repaired. But one thing led to another. Parts ordered were delayed in their delivery. Engineers needed to be sent from England because of complications with their installation. Bad weather limited testing. Then a bout of influenza intervened, and the stay became even more extended. Thirty guests, close quarters, four shared bathrooms, and a flu epidemic – that was a time to remember.

The British RAF airmen stayed with us for nearly three weeks, and we loved every moment. We were bone tired, always busy, and constantly entertained. I even hired Consolato again, this time assuming that if he knew how to wash the windows, he would be perfectly capable of washing the dishes. I am pleased to report that he performed this task with distinction. We were also able to employ some of our old friends, people who had worked in our household during the better times. Vincenzella helped with the ironing. Mariantonia helped with the laundry. My old maid, Celestina, helped with the cleaning. It felt good to have them back as part of our household. It was as if they had never left.

The men were divided into two groups, a day shift and a night shift. Half would stand duty at the Nisida fort, guarding and servicing the flying boats, while the other half would be at the pensione. This helped with overcrowding, but it also meant that we were busy both day and night. We served half the men breakfast in the morning and the other half breakfast in the evening. They also needed picnic lunches to be packed for when they stood guard at their base.

It felt as though we were slicing bread, preparing eggs, and making sandwiches twenty-four hours a day. Don Mario, Donna Peppina, and Vincenzella's father made daily visits to bring us needed supplies. There was a whirlwind of activity. The door was constantly being opened. Someone was always coming or going. I have never seen so much food consumed. It helped that we were serving the food family style. Consolato ran in and out of the kitchen, carrying food in large dishes with one hand and bringing back empty serving dishes with the other. We really were feeding an army. The elevator worked to perfection. Even our landlord, Signor Spinelli, made an appearance from time to time to inquire as to everyone's health and to take credit for how well the new kitchen worked. Fortunately, the cockroaches were respectful, and not a single one made an appearance. Just like that, in the course of those few days, the new and revised Pensione Alexandra became an overwhelming success.

The airmen were a delight, all polite, considerate, and respectful. They were an experienced career crew. Some were older, a few middle-aged, but most were under thirty, close in age to my boys. As the *madre della casa*, I felt like their mother and treated them as my own sons. They were a wonderful group of men and fine representatives of their country. If I had known how to reach their mothers in Britain, I would have written letters to each telling them what good young men their sons were and how proud they should be. We learned of their wives, their homes, their girlfriends, their families, their children, their country, and their dreams. We listened to their stories. We looked at their photos.

You can well imagine how thirty uniformed RAF flyers spending their free time in Naples might attract a great deal of attention along Via Caracciolo and throughout our neighborhood. Of course, the men followed strict RAF protocol when it came to fraternizing with the local citizenry, but they did have free days and nights to explore the sights of Naples. It was peacetime. You can be sure that there were many outings and party invitations. Several made new friends. I learned that a few developed local attachments. Given their situation, this was all quite understandable. I had three sons. I understood their interests.

When the men were not sleeping, eating, at the base, or out with friends, most spent their free time in the pensione quietly playing cards and board games or writing letters to friends and family back home. That was when we really got to know them. I took to teaching Italian phrases to one small group. Mela continued to improve her English and, despite her hobbled foot, traded all the modern dance steps with some of the men. Even Paul joined in, playing pinochle and other card games with anyone willing. Although Paul spoke only a few words of English, the cards and his cigars were a universal form of communication. It would be accurate to say that we all enjoyed ourselves. I hope you can see that, during those three weeks, we felt these men were part of our family.

On Thursday, February 14th, Valentine's Day, *La Festa Degli Innamorati*, the squadron received official word that everything was in order. The repairs were complete, and the engines thoroughly tested. Orders were issued for two of the flying boats and half the men to depart early the following morning. Their next stop would be the RAF seaplane base at Calafrana, Malta, as they hopscotched along their journey to Singapore. The other two flying boats and remaining men would leave the following day and rejoin the squadron in Malta.

As soon as the announcement was made, a big celebration was planned for the final evening. The men made all the arrangements and even recruited a replacement crew to handle their responsibilities at Nisida. A banquet was held at a neighboring hotel that had a large-enough room to accommodate all the guests. There was music and dancing. All the new friends made in Naples were invited to join in the festivities. Even Paul, Mela, and I were invited to be honored guests at their party.

We had a delightful evening. It was a wonderful farewell celebration. For three weeks, we had been busy day and night. It was such a treat to relax, to spend an evening out and away from the pensione, and to have no kitchen responsibilities. The men introduced me to all their new friends, and over dinner, I found myself engaged in many interesting conversations. Several of the men graciously asked me to dance. What a ridiculous sight that must have been. The jitterbug was definitely not like the waltz of my youth, and me, with my two left feet. Before the evening was over, the men even raised their glasses, and one gave a toast in the form of a poem thanking us for their stay at the Pensione Alexandra. I wish I would have written down his words. It was a wonderful gesture. I could feel the tears running down my cheeks.

How thrilled we were at the end of the evening, when Paul, Mela, and I walked arm in arm along Via Caracciolo and the seafront, back to the Pensione Alexandra. I could have danced the whole way. This was a night to remember. We were so pleased with our success.

Well before sunrise the next morning, Vincenzella's father delivered fresh bread, the man with the cow delivered fresh milk, and Mela and I prepared breakfast for the men. Everyone said their goodbyes. Mela and I hugged each of the men as they departed. They all vowed to return to Naples and stay with us again one day. Several promised to bring their wives and their families. They left as suddenly as they'd arrived. That morning, they were in a hurry to get to the fort to prepare the flying boats for their departure. Their schedule called for them to reach Malta no later than 11:00 am.

The two flying boats maintained visual contact as they flew together side by side on their route to the base in Calafrana. When they approached the Straits of Messina and began their flight over Sicily, visibility became limited. A large bank of clouds covered the mountains of the Peloritani Range, near the village of San Filippo del Mela. That was when they became separated. The thick fog made it difficult for the two flying boats to stay in close range and to maintain visual contact with one another.

Flying boat K3592 and her crew reached Malta a few minutes ahead of schedule, at 10:50 am. Ground command had already been advised that they'd lost visual contact with their companion at 9:00 am, as they were flying over Sicily in the thick fog. When that occurred, K3592 circled back over the Straits of Messina and the Peloritani Range in search of the other flying boat. Poor visibility hampered their efforts, and they failed in their attempt to re-establish radio contact. Due to a shortage of fuel, the crew of K3592 was compelled to resume their flight path to Malta. They had no further information to report.

Later that morning, RAF headquarters in Malta posted a radio alert and vainly sought news from all Sicilian wireless stations. Upon arrival, K3592 was re-fueled and ordered to turn back and to attempt another search. Weather conditions rendered these efforts fruitless. Without success, the crew of K3592 returned to the base at Calafrana with no sighting or additional information.

On the ground, near San Filippo del Mela, about 170 kilometers east of Palermo, a local witness reported seeing an aircraft strike the mountain and, upon impact, break into pieces. There were reports of a fireball and a terrible explosion. Information reported from the scene was that the intense heat from the fire made the crash site unapproachable. The witness reported seeing two half-burned men strapped into their seats in the front portion of the broken flying boat. Reportedly, medals and ribbons were visible on their chests.

Red Cross officials, police, firemen, and civilians were dispatched to the area of the disaster. However, continuous rains and the absence of roads in the mountainous area impeded the ability of rescue parties to reach the crash site. After a hazardous three-hour mountain journey, the rescuers reached the isolated location of the crash and were able to remove four charred corpses, including those thought to be the two officers seen by the witness.

Initial reports were unclear, but it seemed that the remaining bodies were apparently trapped within the buried hull portion of the flying boat. For several hours that evening, the firemen continued their efforts to search for survivors by torchlight, but rain forced them to abandon their recovery activities until the next morning.

Early that afternoon, we received initial word of a crash, only hours after serving the men breakfast before they'd left on their flight. No one knew what to think. Everyone was confused by the report. Our first reaction was one of disbelief. Obviously, this had been reported in error. A short while later, we received official confirmation that all nine, the pilot, co-pilot, and crewmembers, aboard RAF flying boat K3595 had been killed that morning when their flying boat had crashed into a mountain near San Filippo del Mela, Sicily and burst into flames.

That was nearly fifty years ago. At times, in my sleep, I can still hear the cries, the howls, and the sobs from the men who did not fly that day. We all were in shock. We all were heartbroken and devastated. I can still picture each of their faces. We still were in disbelief. These were our friends. These were their buddies. These were the men who reminded me of my boys. Try as we might, some memories never fade.

CHAPTER FOURTEEN

Some days, I sit and stare quietly at my hands, my eyes full of wonder and confusion. When did my hands suddenly change from so young to so old? These cannot be mine. When I was a young girl, my hands were soft, and the skin appeared so clear and unblemished. There were no wrinkles or scars. Now, in the daylight, my hands look so ancient, filled with the markings and crevices of each passing year, a roadmap of my life, all the bumps and, certainly, the bruises.

I suppose that is what life is, one moment happiness, the next moment heartbreak, bumps, bruises, and crevices. There really is no other way for me to describe what I felt that day. God works in mysterious ways. For many, belief comforts and consoles. I am happy for those who find explanation and solace in their beliefs. I wish that were true for me. My beliefs provide little comfort and even less explanation. At the time the men were killed, I was old enough to know that, sometimes, things happen for unknown reasons and that there are moments that never make sense no matter how far or wide one searches. Still, I was unprepared. I was really tested that day. No matter how strong my center was, I thought it might break. Nothing prepared me for those moments.

I was a grown woman, and this was the first time in my life that I'd experienced a tragedy as immense as this, a tragedy that seemed to surround me from so many sides. This was different from any loss I had known. The incident was so sudden and so unnatural. It seemed so unjust and so random. When the airmen were killed, I knew how to grieve. I knew what death was. I had suffered losses of those close to me in my life, parents and other family, but always in the natural order, never expected, but not unanticipated, not unimagined, sudden and sad, but not surprising. I could not begin to imagine the terrible grief that must have been felt by the airmen's parents, wives, and children when they learned of the crash. I could not begin to feel the depth of emotion that the remaining members of their squadron must have felt. I had only known these boys for less than a month. Their families had shared a lifetime.

I am thankful no photographs were taken the previous evening. Nine of the smiling faces would have disappeared less than twenty-four hours later. What an awful reminder that would have been. Yet there was nothing to hold onto, and what an awful reminder that was as well.

Mela was inconsolable and continued to be for many days. How could she understand? These were her friends, her older brothers, her tutors, her dance partners. Maybe one was something more. She never said, and I never asked. She had never witnessed anything like this before. There was little I could say or do. Paul and I really had no idea how to act and react. The reality for us was that our lives would go on just as they had before. We all knew that the lives that were lost would not. In so many ways, this gut-wrenching event was as simple and straightforward as that. For us, all that was left was emotion. We would wake up the next morning and turn to a new page.

The Pensione Alexandra would be open for business that day and the days that followed. Nothing about this tragedy would change that necessity. The nine men had been part of our lives for three weeks. When they'd checked out of their rooms, they'd left with their belongings. The rooms had been cleaned. The sheets and linens had been washed. Their bill had been paid. Now, they were gone, and their rooms would be filled by others. Like most of our guests, we would never see them again. The difference was that these boys had no choice. They could never return.

This flying boat crash was one of the most tragic and horrible days of our lives. I understand that it was the deadliest British Royal Air Force crash in many years. The next morning, personal messages were delivered to the pensione from King Victor Emmanuel III and Mussolini, and from British Prime Minister Ramsay MacDonald and King George V for the men who remained. It was such a solemn moment when the courier arrived. I felt so bad for all of them. They would travel the same path the following day. What would be in their thoughts?

There is one more thing I have to offer about this incident, and it is about life in a pensione. Guests arrive. Guests depart. Later that evening, we would have time to sit, to cry, and to continue to search our souls for answers. However, at that moment, I had no choice. I had rooms to worry about. I had bills to pay. There was little more I could do. I did what was required that afternoon. I went back to the train station to meet the next train and to hold my sign in search of our next guests. In another few days, Signor Spinelli would pay a visit to pick up the rent.

That was my reality. For me, this was a tough lesson to comprehend and absorb. I suppose I was like Mela. There were times I was in such a daze that I felt that my head was in the clouds. Just put both feet forward. Walk one step at a time. That is all one can ever be asked to do.

CHAPTER FIFTEEN

The loss of the RAF airmen was sudden, difficult, and heartbreaking. Understanding the realities of the world provided little relief to the emotion and pain we felt. It was one of those moments when there are no satisfactory answers to life's troubling questions. There is no explanation. The questions remain forever unanswered. The sheer randomness of the loss can only be endured.

That evening, we all sat quietly. I watched the confused faces and the suffering that Mela and the remaining airmen surely felt. I knew I was older, the elder in the room. I had no choice but to remain strong. That was my role as the mother of this house. All I really wanted to do was curl up in a little ball, like I had as a child when things did not go my way.

I would really like to tell you that this was the end to the incident, because these moments really were as horrible as I am certain they must sound. A steady flow of guests would visit the Pensione Alexandra and keep us busy during the days, weeks, and months that followed. And with time, we recovered as best we could from the tragedy of the flying boat disaster. But the truth is one never recovers. All one can do is let time give bad memories a chance to fade, a chance to let the memories be covered by better moments. These memories are never forgotten. Too many others know what I am saying. How can one forget?

Unfortunately, and as unlikely as it could be, there was more to this tragedy. And now I have to continue with where I began. This story was far from over. It would take another unlikely turn. This time, it would occur near a small village on the outskirts of London, more than fourteen hundred miles from Naples, in a place we knew nothing of.

On the morning of February 21, 1935, only six days after the flying boat crash in Sicily, two women booked the available six seats on a small commercial aircraft for a scheduled flight from England to France. This six-passenger airplane flew daily from the Stapleford Airport, near Essex, outside of London, to Le Bourget, near Paris.

The two young women, clad in expensive fur coats and holding a single item of baggage, were standing alone near the Kings Cross station in central London when the airline motor coach arrived to transport them to the airfield early that morning. They were expecting four others to join them on their flight to France. They asked the motor coach driver to wait for the remaining passengers before departing for the airfield.

After fifteen minutes, the others had still failed to appear. At the request of the driver, who was concerned that they might miss the flight, one of the young women went to a nearby telephone booth to place a call and inquire as to the whereabouts of the others. After doing so, she reported that there had been a change of plans. The other passengers would not be joining them. She told the driver that they should proceed to Stapleford. I should note that, days later, during the investigation that followed, it was determined that no others had actually been expected nor had anyone actually been called. This phone call and explanation were revealed to be a deception to prevent others from purchasing seats on the flight.

At the Stapleford airport, after paying for their seats, the two young women boarded the airplane and settled into the rear of the six-seater. The other four seats remained empty. The pilot had already filed the flight plan. He started the engines, taxied onto the grass runway, and took off into the air. Later, it was reported that the two girls were apparently heavy smokers, and shortly after the aircraft left the ground, they asked the pilot for permission to smoke. This request was denied, but the pilot did agree to their second request, which was to close the door between the cockpit and the main cabin as well as the ventilation windows to minimize the circulating draft. The pilot said that the women complained of the cold air.

Approximately forty-five minutes after the flight left Stapleford and shortly after crossing the English Channel, the pilot opened the door to the passenger section to inquire as to the comfort of his passengers. He was shocked and horrified to see that the rear of the airplane was empty. The passengers were missing. All that remained was their one suitcase. The pilot would later describe the exterior cabin door as apparently unlatched and partially open, actually moving slightly in the wind.

The pilot immediately reported the incident, turned the plane around, and returned to the Stapleford airport. Upon landing, he was to discover a lady's shoe, a partially empty whiskey bottle, and two sealed letters in the rear of the airplane. Other than the suitcase, these were the only signs left of his passengers.

A short time earlier, several minutes before the missing passenger incident was reported to local authorities, two workmen working in Upminster, England, near London, reported seeing what looked like two packages falling from an airplane overhead. Upon hearing a curious thud apparently only a short distance from where they were working, they ran to the nearby cabbage field to search for what had fallen. They were astonished to find the broken bodies of two well-dressed young women lying face down on the ground. According to one, "Their hands were clasped, and one had a tight grip on the other's coat."

As I said when I began telling this story, during the days that followed, this incident was thoroughly investigated. And as this was not an ordinary event, the front pages of thousands of newspapers throughout the world reported the sensational and mysterious details.

Even as far away as Naples, Italy, fourteen hundred miles from the site of the incident, we read the newspaper reports describing this horrifying event. And that was how we were startled to discover that the two young women were Elizabeth and Jane Du Bois, the twenty and twenty-three-year-old daughters of Coert Du Bois, the American Consul in Naples, two women whom we had been introduced to at a farewell party only one week before they'd plunged to their deaths. To be more precise, Mela, Paul and I, with others, had shared the same table over dinner on that particular evening.

Suicide notes, found within the sealed envelopes left in the main cabin, were opened during the autopsy that followed. The notes confirmed that the Malta-bound RAF flying boat that had crashed into the mountain near Messina only days earlier had triggered for the two women a bout of severe depression.

Further investigation confirmed that, indeed, the two women had been in Naples during the same time the RAF airmen had been staying at the Pensione Alexandra. According to the mother of the pilot killed in the RAF crash, two of the RAF airmen had befriended the two girls. For a number of weeks, the two couples had been seen together at outings, dances, and parties. During this time, sentimental attachments had reportedly been formed. There was even one report of an engagement. Another report speculated that a previous romance had been broken and rings had been returned. However, these details were never confirmed. Interviews with multiple sources revealed that the last time the two women had been seen in the company of the two RAF airmen had been at a hotel near the seafront in Naples, Italy, the preceding week, when a farewell dinner party had been held for the RAF squadron the night before the flying boat crash.

That was the night Mela, Paul, and I met them. They'd been our dinner companions. That evening we'd had a very engaging and entertaining conversation with the two girls, who had been introduced as Elizabeth and Jane. Both had seemed full of life and quite lovely.

I know I have said this before, but I need to repeat myself. Over the years we owned the Pensione Alexandra, I witnessed joy, love, sadness, passion, fear, tragedy, and struggle. I discovered emotions I never knew I had, emotions that I never knew existed. During the time we owned the Pensione Alexandra, I discovered myself, and I learned that we all share the same confusions.

CHAPTER SIXTEEN

Life does work in such strange and mysterious ways. I know this cliché is repeated too often, but there is an obvious reason. It is true. When I was a young child of six or seven, my father took me to a barrier island beach on the Baltic Sea near Kahlberg. There, we searched for the beautiful pieces of amber that were nestled between the rocks. I thought these semi-precious stones were the most exotic jewels ever discovered.

That day, Father and I spent several hours amused by the shore crabs picking their way across the amber stones and rocks. I always wondered what they were searching for. Did the crabs always follow the same path? Where did they start? How did they know where to go next? Did they ever need to turn around or change direction? Did they ever get lost? Did they ever fail? Were they in danger? How were they certain when they finally reached their destination? Was the end just the beginning?

Sometimes, I picture my universe filled with millions and millions of stars, each a small dot, just like the pieces of amber that appeared on the beach that day. I try to remember the path that has led me here to this place by the parking lot and school playground in Portland, Oregon. Now I know that my journey could never be repeated, certainly not in the same way. My path was so oddly connected at times that it seems impossible that I would ever find my way here again. I wonder if this was where I was always heading, whether Portland is where I was meant to go. How did I find the final destination, this place with the "lights out" rule, where I keep hoping to see the moon one more time?

Somehow, one dot led to the next: up, down, backwards, forwards. There was a certain order and, at times, a missed step. Was each step known before I started, or did they change as I moved from one to the next? At times, the dots were so close to one another that I remember tiptoeing between them. Sometimes, I ran. Sometimes, I walked. Other times, they were widely spaced. Those were times when I closed my eyes, clenched my fists, and took long leaps, hoping to survive the jump and land on my feet. What I always find puzzling, the question which continues to defy my explanation, is whether the dots became connected by random steps or by some invisible hand guiding me from one to the next, sometimes gently, sometimes forcibly, but always there. I pray for the invisible hand. How else would I have found my path? I find comfort in the thought that there is someone watching over me, making sure that I do not fall within the spaces that lie between the rocks.

During my childhood, I never imagined that there would come a day in my future when I would own a pensione in Italy. As a child, I never looked in the mirror and said confidently, "Elsa, someday, you will move to Naples, Italy, and become the proprietress of a pensione." Yet I am certain that those dots were always there. It's just that they were not connected. My question is: what made me go from one to the next? How did I reach this particular destination? Was it my luck, or was it my fate? Which side of the coin landed face up? Did it matter what I wanted, or was this all decided for me without regard for my opinion before I took the very first step? Was I chosen to live this life? I am not sure if any of this matters now. Yet I remain curious. For my one-hundredth birthday, I would like to know the answer. That would be a good gift. By then, I would have lived long enough to be deserving.

As a child, I am certain I had never heard of Naples, and even when I knew about such a place, I would never have dreamed of moving there or living there and raising my family. I was German. My family was German for as many generations as anyone could remember, and I was too. There was not one part of me that was not German. Germany was my home. It was where I was meant to be, where I belonged. Live in Italy? Become Italian? Why would I do that? Life would not be the same in Italy. Of all the things that I might do, that would be the least expected, a possibility never considered. If I'd made a list, this option would never have appeared. And if it had appeared, I have no doubt that someone would have crossed it out. I would have been told that it was not possible. I was a German. Why would I choose to live in Naples when I had everything I could possibly want in Koenigsberg? Italy was not Germany.

For me, it was such a remarkable change to leave my childhood home and travel to Italy. It was an unimagined adventure. In Germany, I had been surrounded by my parents, brothers and sisters, aunts and uncles, cousins and friends. They were all left behind when I caught the train to Italy. And when I waved goodbye to my family at the train station, I was comforted by the knowledge that my visit to Italy would be temporary, only three months; then I would return. Of course, when you are twenty-one, three months can seem like a lifetime. When I left that day, as is true so often, I had no idea that the next stop would shape my life's future.

I imagine that, by most standards, we were an exceptionally close family, and as a child, my three much-older sisters were my role models. Their paths were the three choices I was given to choose from. When the eldest was young, she wanted to be a doctor. I am told that Mother told her that if she didn't find a husband by her thirtieth birthday, she could ask Father to give his permission for her to study medicine. But this did not matter. She married before she was twenty-one. Her childhood dream was long forgotten and replaced before I was ever born. Instead of becoming a doctor, a path never encouraged, she became a wife and kept house, just as expected. She became a very supportive and devoted mother for her children.

My second sister was Mother's little helper, always by her side, very devoted and wanting to please. When she married, she did the same for her husband. She became her husband's little helper. Then, when her children were born, she became her children's little helper. And when they all died, there was no one else to help, and she became an old, quiet, and sad widow who dressed in black for the forty years that remained in her life. I once was told she'd laughed a great deal as a young child. I seldom saw her laugh or even smile as an adult. I seldom saw her happy.

The third was the most talented, the most critical, and the least ambitious. She was so talented that I am convinced she could have become a famous painter. She studied with one of Germany's most celebrated artists, a woman whose soulful works are displayed throughout Berlin and the world today. Jenny had the opportunities to do much more than she did, but she chose not to pursue them. The role she was given was to care for our aging parents, which she fulfilled precisely, as expected. I suppose she felt that she sacrificed her life for them in some way. Frustrated and unfulfilled, she was never motivated enough, and perhaps a little too spoiled, to follow her dreams. I know that some may take offense with my words but she remained an unsatisfied spinster for the rest of her life, always a bit untrusting of everyone's love. After our parents died, she became the old aunt we all relied upon. She was the one always asked to watch over everyone else's children and the butt of their jokes. She could laugh, but not so well at herself.

That left me. And for the first half of my life, I found my place somewhere within the boundaries drawn by these three alternatives. I really knew no other way. I don't say this to complain, because I was left with many wonderful choices. I simply was unaware of what I may have missed. I was much like a young child who fails to try a new food or who forms uninformed opinions because of what others may have said. I had no experience.

When I stepped off the train in Naples as an unmarried twenty-one-year-old woman, I felt as if I were standing on a ship cast out to sea. I was waiting for a lifeline to give me a clue, to tell me which of those fates awaited. It took time before I was able to find my sea legs. At first, I was homesick for my family and friends. My comfortable Koenigsberg life seemed, and was, a world away. I only knew what I missed. I only knew what I had heard. One thing seemed certain: Naples was definitely not Koenigsberg.

That is not to say that leaving home, foreign travel, seeing the world, and experiencing life in faraway places were altogether farfetched ideas. Quite the contrary. I was intrigued and interested. I was curious. As a family, we were not tethered to home, perhaps the girls a little more, but certainly not the boys. Each of us was encouraged to leave home and had been sent away for a worldly experience when we'd become a certain age. The sole exception was my sister Jenny, the unsatisfied spinster, who left only reluctantly after caring for our parents when fearing for her life became more necessary than staying home in Germany. We were a family of privilege. Even then, before the turn of the century, learning about the world was considered part of our education.

Our generation was not the first generation of privilege. Father had grown up in a quite well-to-do family and become a partner in a successful tea trading business. Before the turn of the century, he and several of his brothers had traveled extensively throughout the world by train and by ship. His business interests frequently took him to Russia and China. He was familiar with the entire European continent and had visited America on more than one occasion. My eldest brother studied business in London and worked in Moscow for several years. I was told that he would have remained in Moscow except that he was pressured to be baptized and abandon our Jewish religion. He refused and moved to America instead with another of my brothers and two of my sisters. My brother closest in age studied medicine and lived in Dusseldorf. We had cousins in France, England, and elsewhere throughout the world.

We learned much about the universe through our dinner conversations and over evening board games in the parlor. We all had received good educations and had been taught foreign languages. At a young age, I was taught to be conversant in German, French, and English. I could even get by in Spanish. Latin and Greek were always part of my studies, and I was told that I had a talent for learning languages. Unfortunately, when Mother suggested that I visit Naples and spend several months with my first cousin Betty, Italian had never been on my list of languages. I could speak only a few words and certainly not the dialect spoken in Naples, Betty was twenty years older than me, more like an aunt than a cousin. In fact, as a young child, when I first met her, she insisted I call her Aunt Betty. I suppose, in many respects, that was a reflection of her personality. She was that kind of person. When Aunt Betty married, she moved from London to Naples, as that was where her husband's export business was based.

In Aunt Betty's opinion, Naples, before the turn of the century, was a very poor and undesirable place, and a very big adjustment. The people and the language were unfamiliar. The food was not to her liking. She wrote Mother and told her that she found the stench intolerable and the people illiterate, not the best recommendations for sure. Naples certainly did not offer Aunt Betty the sophisticated cosmopolitan life of London. Mother was certain that Naples was the major contributor to Aunt Betty's poor health condition. Aunt Betty suffered from severe bouts of depression and rarely left the four walls of her home. She complained that she missed the companionship of family and close friends. Mother always claimed to be depressed after receiving letters from Aunt Betty. Months later, I would understand why.

My visit to Naples was Mother's idea. She thought that I, then idly sitting at the crossroads of my life, could bring joy to Aunt Betty and improve her condition. Mother also believed that the experience of living in Italy, away from home and immersed in Italian culture, would be a good education for me. I could keep Aunt Betty company. We could explore Naples together. This would give both Aunt Betty and me something worthwhile to do. As fate would have it, my planned three-month visit was to last nearly forty years.

CHAPTER SEVENTEEN

Although there were suspicions, I had little evidence of their conspiracy and no forewarning of its suddenness until I stepped off the train. Mother and Aunt Betty shared an additional reason in common for my visit, one that had only been vaguely hinted about and was only confirmed after my arrival in Naples. Apparently, Aunt Betty's husband, Arthur, had a thirty-one-year-old unmarried nephew who had moved from Stuttgart, Germany, to Naples years earlier to learn the inner workings of his uncle's business. Mother and Aunt Betty thought I was at an appropriate age to be introduced to this somewhat-unmotivated but handsome bachelor whom they concluded was clearly in need of a supporting woman by his side. While I would never change the result, I now know my future had been generally decided before I was ever asked to give my opinion. The dots were connected, and there were two people watching over me, giving me a gentle push. Mother and Aunt Betty were the guiding hands. All I had to do was put my one foot forward. They made it easy. I didn't even have to leap.

In Koenigsberg, I grew up in a very respectable, comfortable, and apparently affluent family. The seventh child of seven children, three boys and four girls, I was seventeen years younger than the oldest and eight years younger than the one nearest in age. That put me in a very exalted position. There was no denying that I was the baby of the family and the unanimous candidate to have "most spoiled and most stubborn" etched on my epitaph. Frequently, spoiled and stubborn are closely connected attributes. As a child, I am told that I always insisted on getting what I always thought I was entitled to receive. Years later, when I heard Father's voice in my head that day Mela suggested we buy the pensione, I knew he was right. I was spoiled, and I was stubborn. Moreover, I was very unknowing, particularly when it came to things that required experience, like operating a guesthouse. Stirring spoiled, stubborn, and unknowing together is not always a recipe for success.

By the time I was born and joined the household, the family had resolved most of life's significant questions. They were settled in their ways. Adding a seventh child to the existing mix of six changed little in the normal daily living habits of their home. With a half-dozen children preceding me, Mother and Father were both well practiced in the art of child rearing. Whatever parenting missteps they might have made when raising their first six had long been corrected by the time I came along. A certain way of life had been established. I was expected to fit in, but being the youngest made me frequently an equally loved and annoying addition to the family.

The difference in ages meant that, as I was arriving, the eldest was leaving, so finding a space in the family and a chair at the table was never a problem. And as for learning, there were certainly plenty of footsteps to observe. I was always encouraged to take steps of my own, particularly by Father. Mother had a different set of priorities, which were impressed upon me from the earliest age. She was more concerned that I learned the Victorian social graces, how to become a "lady," and that I marry well. Under her tutelage, I was taught how to manage a household and frequently reminded of the necessity to keep a husband happy. My personal happiness as an adult was seldom stressed. I was told it was secondary. In Mother's opinion, in order to be fulfilled as a woman, all I would need was a husband to take care of me while I raised children. If I was successful with that task, in later years, I could be assured that the children, in turn, would care for me.

In many respects, the gap in my brothers' and sisters' ages kept us all close knit and caring. Yet, there was certainly a pecking order that we were all mindful of. Those younger looked to those older with reverence, love, respect, and, from time to time, a little fear. And those older added comfort, support, love, encouragement, and, at times, a little intimidation for those who followed. My older brothers and sisters were my teachers, mentors, and much older friends. I never went to sleep without their goodnight kisses. And in one fashion or another, this continued throughout my life. Each, in their own way, kept their arms wrapped tightly around me. I could always count on them to never let me fail.

I imagine, as a family, we were similar to most established, upper-middle-class German families of that era. Strength of character, values, judgement, moral tone, and beliefs were guided by two wise, good-hearted parents who were married for life and who, throughout, wanted what was best for their family. They were able to provide well for their children. Mother and Father set high expectations, but they recognized that each of us had individual interests, abilities, and talents that needed to be nurtured. I believe that we all benefitted from this approach. Mother made it clear that she would not be swayed by what other families allowed their children to do. In our family, her word was the law. Father taught us the necessity of laughter.

We were a good, proud, and decent family. We children always knew we came from good stock. With many aunts, uncles, and cousins for comparison, to this day, I remain convinced that my parents had one of the happiest marriages of anyone I have ever known. They were patient, caring, and gentle with one another. By example, they taught us to be respectful of one and all regardless of our differences, be they race, religion, or economic circumstance. My memories of family life are all cheerful and happy, never somber or sad. By any measure, I had a very fortunate childhood.

Financially, we must have been well off. That was something I never thought about, and money matters were never discussed with children. As a child, I never found myself wanting in any respect. I never remember the family going through any difficult times. We were taught to be frugal, modest, cautious, and definitely not showy. There was always food on the table, a cook in the kitchen, and household help to mop, clean, and launder the clothes. Money never appeared to be a topic of worry.

Mother always insisted that our idle time be put to good use. We were taught that we need not concern ourselves with the work that others more suited might do. As the matron of the house, she refused to emphasize our training in domestic matters. I never received instructions on how to cook, clean, or iron. Instead, I was taught to plan menus and oversee the household help. I was expected to keep my hands clean, to never let them get dirty. Mother wanted her children educated, cultured, cultivated, well mannered, and well bred. The boys were educated for professions and business careers; the girls were educated in music, the arts, and etiquette. Time spent reading, painting, or playing music was considered time well spent. Mother believed that our educations should befit our place in the social order.

In later years, first, as a young housewife and, even later, when we first took over the pensione, I found myself feeling quite unprepared and inadequate, particularly when it came to marketing, cooking, and cleaning. Back then, I was thrilled to learn and master these tasks. How odd that these routine chores would give me a wonderful sense of accomplishment. Of course, the thrill and that feeling of accomplishment were short-lived and quickly faded. I learned that doing something occasionally for fun is much different than having to perform the same task day after day, much like learning that dreaming of owning a pensione is not quite the same as actually owning a pensione.

We had a large, extended family. It was almost impossible to know all the family members we had living in Koenigsberg and the surrounding region. Mother and Father each had twelve brothers and sisters. With that many aunts and uncles, there was a never-ending number of cousins of all ages and various generations, each with their own offspring. Birthdays, marriages, anniversaries, holidays, and such were much-celebrated family occasions, quite a contrast to when I first moved to Naples, where there were only Mother's cousin, her husband, his nephew, and their home, which was empty of children.

Father and his brothers took great pride in the family social status, and for some reason, the family name was often heralded. Members of the family had lived in Koenigsberg for many generations, and the family was well known. True or untrue, Father always claimed that our family was one of the leading families in Koenigsberg. My grandfather had been a highly regarded civic leader and one of the founders of many important projects like the city orphanage. Upon his death, Father's brother became the patriarch of the family. He was active in the affairs of the town council and served as president of the Jewish Congregation of Koenigsberg, the more reform-minded Jewish community of which we took part.

In retrospect, I believe that, to some degree, Father's generation continued to live off the family name. I imagine that many lived off of the accumulated family wealth as well. While Father and a few of his brothers were successful in various business endeavors and made their own contributions to the community, my impression is that a number of the others and their wives contributed little, but felt deserving of the respect due a well-regarded family name.

I suppose that way of thinking was a legacy of the era of royalty, nobility, and aristocracy. Claiming a certain social status has always bothered me. Mother would remind us, "Self-importance is not inherited and often exaggerated." I could never understand why one generation would believe they were entitled to take the credit for the accomplishments of another. That is a value I learned at a young age and that I have always held. It has formed the basis for many of my lifelong beliefs. I am sure there were times that way of thinking made me a bit of a renegade. And when we owned the Pension Alexandra, I believe that way of thinking challenged me to pick up a paintbrush and help paint the walls.

Koenigsberg, East Prussia, had always been the family home, and even today, although the Koenigsberg I knew as a child no longer exists, I still think of it as home. After I moved to Naples and raised my own family, I would return every few years to visit family there and to introduce my children at family celebrations. I always wanted to keep the family connection. While Italy became my adopted country, I remained German at heart. It was in my blood. In that respect, Italy never replaced Germany.

Koenigsberg was the largest city in the German state of East Prussia, on the Baltic Sea, not far from the Russian border, in the northeast of Germany. Koenigsberg was not only the East Prussian capital; it was a university city and the cultural and intellectual center. It was home to theatres, a renowned castle, an observatory, botanical gardens, parks, art exhibitions, and museums – and these were all part of my upbringing.

I grew up as a city girl, accustomed to and comfortable with the pleasantries a large city offers. Of course, back then, I had no idea that the world could be any different from what I knew. Years later, I would learn that the large cities of Germany had a particular way of life and, often, values and attitudes that were in stark contrast to Germany's country farms, small villages, and more industrialized areas. I suppose that was one of the reasons I found it difficult to understand what happened in Germany when the Nazis rose to power.

Sunny Naples aside, I hope you can imagine the metamorphosis I went through upon my arrival in Naples to stay with Aunt Betty and Uncle Arthur. Southern Italy was an entirely different culture and world for me. Not only was the language different, but every aspect of everyday life seemed unfamiliar. I felt like a young butterfly leaving its protective cocoon. My wings were in constant motion to keep me from crashing to the ground. The fact that I found myself on the arm of an eligible, handsome bachelor only made my wings flutter more. I learned a great deal about life's mysteries that first year in Naples.

CHAPTER EIGHTEEN

Knowing only the established order and German ways of Koenigsberg, Naples was like a breath of fresh air. Actually, fresh might not be the best description; foul would be better because the streets of Naples were smelly, grimy, and noisy, and the air was far from fresh. In 1904, the contrast between Koenigsberg and Naples could not have been greater.

Movement was everywhere: children, animals, peddlers, barbers, healers, knife sharpeners, storytellers, psychics, beggars, letter writers, vendors with their little carts piled high with whatever they might be selling. Everything was unfamiliar. Foods that I had never seen before were being cooked over buckets filled with burning coals spewing smoke, and they were served on street corners and in open air kitchens to people sitting on old wooden crates. It seemed that families lived their whole lives on the streets, laughing, crying, hugging, fighting, singing, drinking, shouting, eating, standing, sitting, running. Horse-drawn carriages competed with herds of goats and cows led through the main streets of the city by old men and young boys. And the churches! It seemed that there were churches on every corner.

Naples was a big city, but it was so different from the cautious, German, big-city way of life in Koenigsberg. I had never seen anything like this. My first impression was that Germans revered order and Italians relished chaos, and in Naples, it appeared that the more chaos, the better. And something else was immediately apparent: the way people met one another on the street. There was a difference in formality. In Koenigsberg, people would tip their hats and have brief exchanges, always stiff, formal, and certainly polite. In Naples, when people met, there was laughter and hugs and gestures – a friendly, open, welcoming informality. In Naples, no one seemed to encounter a stranger.

This was a distinction as different as darkness and light, night and day. When I left Koenigsberg, it was cold and wintry. Germany was like the moon, and Italy was like the sun. In a single instant, the moment I stepped off the train, I felt the warmth of the Mediterranean breeze and was basking in abundant sunshine. I had not imagined the beauty of Naples. It was breathtaking: the Bay of Naples, Mt. Vesuvius, and the surrounding hills. I found myself unprepared, amused, confused, aghast, frightened, and curious, if it is possible to have all of those competing reactions within the same instant – so many emotions and all at the same time.

Now, as I remember my first steps in Naples, I hesitate and wonder what I must have thought. Back then, I am certain my reaction could only have been shock and amazement. What kind of place was this? I was much too young and too serious to have learned to laugh at myself. I was far too concerned about my station in life, about the proper way for a lady to act, and about my appearance. I can tell you with absolute certainty that I had not been raised to live in a place like Naples. My eyes were as big as saucers, and my entire body was consumed with nervous excitement. I was about to embark on the adventure of my lifetime.

Frequently, the simplest things require even simpler explanations. With time, I would learn that the streets of Naples were black and appeared overly dirty because they had been constructed using the volcanic rock spewed for centuries by Vesuvius, that the streets were filled with people because, for far too many, the living quarters were too small for families with so many children, and that dwellings would stay cooler and free of the perils of smoke if the cooking was done on the streets. I would learn that goats, cows, and chickens roamed the streets because their owners sold milk and eggs from carts. I was unfamiliar with this type of existence. I could not imagine that people lived this way.

Thousands, perhaps tens of thousands, the city's poorest, the underclass, lived in *bassos*, windowless, often basement-level, four-walled ant-like hovels that were crowded and cramped and offered no privacy. Multiple generations of families might share the same small space side by side with their livestock. For the more fortunate, there might be a toilet in one corner, maybe a stove in another. Any passerby could peer through the open door, the only point for both ventilation and light, and see the entirety of the family's existence. The floors might be layered in a mix of mud and straw. Communal beds could be constructed with a few boards covered by rags. For decoration, there could be a flowerpot filled with herbs. This was a community of poverty-stricken and unfortunate people. The children who ran on the streets had no shoes and dressed in ragged hand-me-downs.

I would learn to love Naples, but it would not be on the day I stepped off the train from Germany. That day, everything was alien: the sights, the smells, the language, the noise, and, most importantly, the order.

I lived in Naples for nearly forty years and never stopped finding new discoveries that made it such a delightful and, sadly, unforgiving combination of special and natural. Coming from the more cautious and careful mannerisms of Koenigsberg, Naples became my personal adventure. Naples had a way of taking familiar sights, like children playing or the gardens or the markets, and making them all feel so unfamiliarly different and carefree. Every day, there was something new and unusual. And as beautiful as Naples was, its raw side of life was always exposed for all to see. I never reconciled how so many who survived in such miserable living conditions could be blessed with the childlike happiness of a simple life, and how our family could have so much, yet never experience the jealousies of those who had so little. How had the dots aligned themselves in quite this way? I was always amazed at finding undiscovered history, the remnants of antiquity, that had made Naples like this. Neopolis was indeed the new city, but when one looked carefully, it was as old as humanity. There were layers and layers of life within its foundation. It was complex, confusing, and colorful.

At first, I was fearful, and I was cautioned to never set foot alone on the streets. I rarely ventured beyond the boundaries of my comfort. I was afraid to be unprotected. But later, our children would have a way of changing things, as they so often do. Naples would be their home. It was where they were raised. They would understand its temptations. They would speak its language. They would embrace its wonder. They would become part of its mystery. Then, with nervous excitement and their urging, I learned to take small, cautious steps, and I was able to see Naples through their eyes, and it became something entirely different. And, finally, after many years, when we purchased the Pensione Alexandra, I learned that Naples was where I belonged and that I too could become a Neapolitan. That was when I was able to walk the streets of Naples with confident, purposeful strides. That was when Naples became my home and when it stole my heart.

One thing I knew from the first time I set foot in Naples is that it was a place like no other. Whether it was my cautious time, the time I explored, or my confident time, whether it was the day I first arrived or those final days before we departed, I could look out from my windows or stand motionless on the street and simply watch life being lived. For that was Naples. I was captured, captivated, and mesmerized.

Others would agree. Naples can seep into your senses and put its arms around you in an embrace when least expected. It is a place one can understand but that still makes little sense, a place where open doorways might bring delight in one moment and tears in the next. Where can an elevator work in only one direction, or a guesthouse be filled with stuffed birds? Where is a hospital built that has no toilets? Where can one build a villa that has no staircase to get to one floor from the next? In Naples, there was never a problem that couldn't be solved, whether adding turrets to a hospital to accommodate the bathrooms or adding a staircase in a parlor to get to the second floor.

I didn't learn this on the day I arrived, nor on the next, but I became convinced by the time I left. It was never the problems that defined Naples. It was the people, their delightful ingenuity, and their remarkable love for life, like the three workmen with their matching white caps, carrying their ladder on the way to the pensione, and my loyal old friend Consolato. That is what made Naples work. It was the sheer beauty of the place, the passion for what is before you, and the absolute certainty that life is too short not to be enjoyed.

Aunt Betty and Uncle Arthur were at the Centrale station to greet my train that first day. Moments later, we were in their carriage, shielded from the activity on the streets, and driven to their home. From my vantage point riding in the carriage, Naples seemed to be a happy, crazy, and strange place. Of course, I know now that some things were not exactly as they seemed. Much of what I saw that first day, I was incapable of understanding. Many of my initial impressions were mistaken observations. I confused happiness and sadness. I saw large crowds on the streets and didn't recognize that this was a reflection of the impoverished conditions of large numbers of people living in crowded spaces who were trying to make the best of their circumstances and destined to live difficult lives.

It had been a long journey, five days and five nights with many different trains. I thought the final portion, from Rome to Naples, would never end. The train stopped in every small village and station as it snaked its way through the Apennines Mountains. I was so excited with all the new sights before my eyes that I kept my head pressed against the window for nearly the entire trip. I am afraid that the lengthy trip as well as the soot and filth of the engines had taken their toll. My appearance, so tidy and proper at the start of my journey, had suffered greatly by the trip's end.

You can only imagine my embarrassment as I stepped off the train when I realized there was a third person in the company of Aunt Betty and Uncle Arthur. That was when I first met Paul.

CHAPTER NINETEEN

Were it not for Paul, I imagine my life would have turned out quite differently. After my three-month visit to Naples, I would have returned to my comfortable world in Germany, perhaps met someone else, and raised a family. I might have had a story to tell, but I imagine that it might have been entirely different. Even so, the world's events would not have changed. That part of the story would have remained the same. I am not certain how I would have fit in or what life I would have lived. I am sure that each would have had its own mystery and that the journey to connect them might have provided its own adventure. If I had not stayed in Naples, I like to think that I would have missed our time with the Pensione Alexandra. I certainly would have missed telling you this story. The simple truth is that you never miss what you do not know. Something else always manages to fill the space.

Courtship and marriage rituals have changed considerably since my arrival in Naples. But in 1904, these customs had changed little from the time when my parents had married a generation earlier. Within our social class, a young woman was never permitted to go out alone and meet a gentleman. She would always be accompanied by some elderly person who was known to have impeccable standards. In my instance, a chaperone was still necessary. A proper lady could not be in the company of a gentleman without watchful eyes observing. People were known to gossip. Rumors needed to be avoided. Proper behavior was required, and a chaperone assured one and all that an appropriate level of decorum was maintained.

Certainly, arranged marriages, alliances between families, and matchmaking were becoming traditions of earlier generations, but most parents remained consumed with the idea of finding the appropriate partner for their marriage-age children. Issues like family, status, connections, occupation, wealth, religion, and race all played their part. Depending upon one's place in the social order, love and mutual attraction were often secondary considerations. And the rules for young women were often crueler. No parent wanted their daughter to become a tired old spinster. Frequently, having a married daughter was more important than having a happy daughter.

Unlike today, when young people are apt to leave the family home soon after completing their education, most girls of my generation would reside at home with their parents until a suitable marriage could take place. Many formalities needed to be followed before a young woman might transition from the home of her parents to the home of her husband. The possibility of scandal was always a concern, and it certainly would become an issue were there any unexplained stops from one home to the next. One's moral history was always a consideration. It never struck me as fair that men were held to a different standard. I have always thought that what is good for the goose is good for the gander. However, for the men, fair or not, those interim stops were often viewed as simply part of their continuing education.

In my case, I think social class and family really were the most important factors for both Mother and Aunt Betty. I am not sure our religion was even considered. Having been raised in a Jewish family, I never entertained the notion that I might marry someone who was not of our faith. I can't remember ever knowing a young man who was not Jewish. It wasn't that I thought much about my Jewishness; I just had never had a reason to consider any alternative. Perhaps that was because my first teenaged imagined infatuation was with our rabbi. In Koenigsberg, we had always been part of the Jewish community, and I'd always assumed that I would continue to live that way of life, somehow associated with the nearby synagogue. It was never a matter of exclusion, but all our close friends were Jewish. No one asked for permission to marry outside the faith. It was always presumed that one would marry a Jew. I will never know if Father would have permitted me to marry someone who was not Jewish. I really have no idea, but it was such an unthinkable request that I cannot imagine ever asking.

It seems to me that, today, people who embrace their religion pay more attention to this issue. Many families prefer that their children marry someone who shares the same faith: Catholics marry Catholics, Jews marry Jews. Perhaps, today, this is a greater concern because young people have more freedom and opportunity to meet others and to venture beyond their community surroundings. In my time, at least within my family in Germany, marriage outside the faith was never an issue, because we really didn't know anyone who wasn't Jewish, at least no one I would marry. Nobody I knew concerned themselves with this, simply because it was never done. Later, I would learn that the regard for marriages between faiths was a major difference between Germany and Italy. It was a difference that changed the way people respected and treated one another. It was a distinction that influenced the way entire cultures acted. In Italy, mixed marriages were a common practice. And as a result, Jews were far more interwoven into the mainstream of day-to-day life than they were in Germany. Little of this mattered in my case, because Paul's ancestry was Jewish, although he chose not to practice the religion. This had never been encouraged, and he had no interest.

At the time I married, it was not unusual for marriages to take place between two members of the extended family, and Paul was my cousin's husband's nephew. Families were large. Family members were known. Families shared a commonality and common history. Often, young people were introduced to one another at family gatherings. To a great extent, family and community overlapped.

Society's constraints were not the only reasons marriages took place within families. Transportation and communications limited one's options. Family members were familiar and accessible. Within our own family tree, there were many examples of marriages between distant cousins and relatives of one sort or another. In fact, two of my sisters and one of my brothers married two sisters and a brother from another family. And there was plenty of precedent for this. Royal families were always arranging alliances through marriage. It would only follow that society's middle and upper classes would do much the same.

It was no surprise that my parents felt they shared the responsibility for helping me find a compatible and appropriate husband. I was twenty-one years old, the right time to be leaving the family nest. And that's what Mother did. Paul was identified as someone who was known through family and was someone of a similar social standing. He was trusted and familiar. We were cousins related through marriage and, thus, would continue that family connection. Although he chose not to embrace his religion, he had a Jewish ancestry and heritage. He was not known to have any defects of consequence. Moreover, he was the right age, eligible, and available. He had all the essential credentials and met all of Mother's and Aunt Betty's "suitability" requirements.

By parental arrangement, and under strict supervision, Paul and I were placed into a situation where we were left to decide the issues of love and mutual attraction. I know you might find it uncomfortable to hear these words spoken from a woman my age, but I admit that youthful curiosities also contributed. Often, what is denied is what is most desired. Attractions are not a modern phenomenon. Proximity provides the magic. That has not changed throughout history.

When I arrived in Naples, this was the stage set before me. Paul and I fulfilled our roles to perfection. We were gently placed into one another's arms. So, you may not find it surprising that, within a few short months, we professed our love for one another.

As society's customs are sometimes complicated, in our case, it became necessary to be married twice. First, we were married in a civil ceremony in Naples. Then, as a proper married couple, we could travel together without the need for a chaperone. Our honeymoon became the five-day, five-night train trip to Koenigsberg. There, a more formal wedding was held with my parents and extended family in attendance.

Conveniently, the wedding in Koenigsberg became a double wedding. My sister, Marie, who by that time was living in America, also brought her young man to Koenigsberg so they could be married. I never learned with certainty whether they, like Paul and me, had already married in a civil ceremony in America to avoid the taint of scandal. But I have little doubt they had already said their wedding vows to one another. Much older and still Mother's little helper, Marie was always one to abide by the strict Victorian standards and moral code.

You would be right to wonder about issues such as parental approval, permission, and suitability in Marie's instance, since she arrived with her chosen husband in hand. But all that had been long resolved. Her husband-to-be had two sisters who had previously married two of my brothers. Whether she knew it or not, Marie's union had been encouraged and approved years earlier. In fact, years later, I learned that was why Mother had sent Marie to America, for the same reason that I had been sent to Italy. Neither of our marriages had been left to chance. Both resulted from the careful hand of fate as orchestrated by Mother. Mother made certain that the path between those dots was well marked.

CHAPTER TWENTY

Those first months at the Pensione Alexandra loom so large when I think back upon them. They dwarf so many other, smaller memories. Now it seems that we hardly had time to learn how to walk before we were running as fast as our legs would take us. Experiencing the loss of the RAF flyers and the two Dubois sisters would not be the only twists of fate to be encountered during the years we operated the pensione. There would be others. Fortunately, all were not so tragic.

The simple lesson we learned again and again was that, each day, new guests would arrive and old guests would leave. Ours was a revolving door. Rarely a day went by when we would not greet someone new upon arrival and wish farewell to another upon their departure.

During the time they were with us, the guests shared our rather small common spaces: the breakfast room, the parlor, the dining area, and the balcony. Many became family. Some would enjoy the casual intimacy and reveal much about their lives and, at times, their most closely held secrets. Others preferred their privacy. They kept their doors closed throughout their stay and shared little about their activities or their lives. We respected both.

There were those we adored and wished would never leave. And there were the others, the ones who overstayed their welcome. We could hardly wait for their exit and for the door to close behind them. Many moments made me laugh and smile. Other times, I cried. There were many days I prayed, and other days I was anxious. Some days, all I could do was close my eyes, grit my teeth, and remember my manners. Few days were ever the same. One thing remained true. The sign near the door said "Welcome." Agreeable or disagreeable, we made it a point that everyone was welcome. There was never an instance when we turned someone away.

What our guests all shared in common was that their visits, no matter the length, were temporary. We were permanent. We stayed. They left. Most vanished from our lives, leaving little trace that they had been there. We were left with little idea of the fortunes and misfortunes that might await them. For some, we learned the outcome. They were the ones who wrote letters or returned to tell us their stories. For the remainder, we had no clue.

During the weeks and months that followed the flying boat crash, Mela and I continued our daily quest for guests. We visited the port to meet the ships from Genoa and Palermo, and went to Centrale to meet the trains from Rome. Even seaplanes began to arrive at the port, bringing more visitors to Naples. They flew their circular route six days a week, connecting Genoa, Rome, Naples, and Palermo.

I was pleased by the steady flow of guests to the pensione. Our friends in Naples helped too. They recommended the Pensione Alexandra to others they knew. The Marine Biological Institute, one of the best in Europe, had a well-known aquarium, and many students and professors, with grants from countries throughout the world, stayed with us when they came for their studies. An anthropologist from Bombay lived with us for three months while he taught a course at the University of Naples. Every day, our horizons were widened. We were able to get to know people from all walks of life, race, and color. Our dining room became the center of fascinating conversations. I was constantly challenged to learn more about Naples and to discover its mysteries. Every day, guests were asking my advice and recommendations for what they should do and see.

I cannot remember being filled to capacity the way we were with the RAF airmen, but the Pensione Alexandra seemed to always have enough guests to pay the bills. To our relief, we were even able to begin to chip away at our debts. With time, reputation and word of mouth became our best forms of advertising. Pensiones of similar style and value along the tourist routes began to recommend the Pensione Alexandra, and we, in turn, did the same for them. We found ourselves part of the young and growing tourist industry.

Gradually, our lives began to take on more of a daily rhythm and a sense of normalcy. I began to relax a bit, and Paul and Mela tolerated me. We learned that we could afford to pay the help needed to assist with the cleaning, the cooking, and the laundering. And when we were busy, Consolato was always available to wash the dishes and to help serve and clear the tables, tasks which he seemed to enjoy and had mastered.

All of this was a great improvement. Paul applauded our success, his reluctance slowly disappeared, and he started to take on more of an active role. He even began to claim some of the credit for making the decision to purchase the pensione. Each evening, with cigar in mouth, he would take care of the paperwork and bookkeeping, important contributions since numbers left me confused. As for me, with my newfound time, I was able to grow into my role as the *madre della casa*, the role I most cherished. I finally was able to sit down and visit with our guests, which is what I really wanted to do since the day we opened our doors. I could not have been more interested in their stories and observations. They gave me a firsthand view of the world.

One afternoon, I was sitting in the parlor, quietly biding my time, when there suddenly appeared a very tall, handsome, red-haired man with an extremely friendly smile on his much-freckled face. Today, I know that he could best be described as having an Irish complexion. Then, I had no idea. I had never met anyone like him before.

His was the kind of face that made you conclude that this person had never met anyone whose company he did not enjoy. Later, I would learn that he was a wonderful conversationalist, a bit of a raconteur with always a story to tell, and that he possessed a personality that always attracted and collected friends.

I remember this particular incident so well because, at the time, it struck me as so odd. One moment, I had been sitting all alone, quietly knitting and humming to myself, and the next moment, from seemingly out of nowhere, this man appeared before me. It was as if I blinked my eyes and he suddenly was there. I must have been napping. That was the only explanation I could imagine for his unexpected appearance. He didn't strike me as a man who could possibly be that quiet. It didn't seem to be his nature. If you had met him, you would surely know what I mean.

He politely introduced himself and explained that he was there to inquire about a room. He would require the room for six to eight weeks and perhaps longer, certainly an unusual request, since, other than the British RAF fliers or the students and professors, we had never had a regular guest stay longer than six or seven days, the typical length of stay for a tourist in Naples.

He also asked, on the basis of his proposed length of stay, to negotiate the price of his room, or, at least, when he could be expected to make payment. These requests were somewhat irregular, as, by law, the prices were posted on the wall for all to see and we had been cautioned about this practice of negotiating the amount charged for rooms by municipal officials, something to do with avoiding taxes. He apologized for his request and muttered a few words about a delay with funds he was anticipating and needing to conserve his money during the interim. Apparently, there had been issues with his spending habits. Perhaps his money problems contributed to his decision to seek a room at the Pensione Alexandra rather than one of the more highly regarded hotels in Naples that he might have been accustomed to.

I found no reason to question his claim when he told me he was a roving newspaper correspondent working on a book manuscript between writing assignments and in need of a place where he could sleep, write, and be left alone. He explained that he was under pressure to finish writing his book, tentatively titled *The Legend of Sanfelice*. A number of previously unanticipated excursions with a fellow writer living in Paris, who was confused by his unimagined literary success, had caused him to be behind schedule, presumably the explanation for the shortage of funds and for the rush to send the manuscript to his publisher in America.

Although he spoke the language beautifully, it was immediately obvious that he was not Italian; actually, very few of our guests were. And as he had said his publisher was in America, I assumed he was an American, which he was. He informed me that he had lived in Europe for much of the past decade and had traveled extensively, reporting on world events for magazines and newspapers in America.

As a brief aside, I have always been fascinated by the amount of information imparted by someone within five minutes of arrival, a phenomenon that happened repeatedly with new guests. For some inexplicable reason, upon their arrival, most people seemed anxious to justify their reasons for wanting to stay at the Pensione Alexandra. I have no clue as to whether this type of behavior is common when guests arrive at all places of lodging. In any case, this prospective guest proved to be no exception. There was a certain associated nervousness that I found amusing. As a rule, I found Americans to be consistently this way. They would often speak quickly. This is simply my observation. I draw no conclusions, as there were certainly exceptions to this mannerism.

The gentleman asked to see the rooms, expressing a specific concern about the furniture. I assumed he meant the beds, a concern echoed by many new arrivals. For various reasons, guests were always suspicious of the beds. I never knew what to make of that, nor did I understand what they would actually learn by using one hand to push on a bed to see if it bounced. Lying down on the bed would make more sense, but few possessed the self-confidence to do so. Most were embarrassed or were concerned about their shoes.

At times, I thought they were checking to see if a bed spring squeaked, which would be an understandable concern but difficult to determine with only a single push on the bed. Personally, I would have inquired about things like fleas, bed bugs, and window screens or mosquito netting, particularly during the mosquito seasons. The bath, meals, and drinking water are also good things to ask about. Incidentally, the drinking water is widely recognized to be quite good and safe in Naples, a result of hygienic measures taken following the cholera epidemic of 1884.

He expressed none of these concerns, and the bed was not his issue. He was interested in the tables and chairs. It seemed that he had a few minor requirements, the most important being the necessity for a large writing table and, as he put it, "a large, sturdy, comfortable chair with four legs of equal length." He expected to spend mornings in his room writing "with a great energy and intensity." He carried a typewriter with him specifically for this purpose. As for the balance of his days, he informed me that he planned to be out and about during afternoons and, depending upon his economic and other circumstances, might return very late in the evenings. He inquired as to whether we locked the doors at night and, if so, at what time and the procedure for getting into his room after the doors were locked. He used an expression that I had never heard before but have remembered ever since. He said he was known "to burn both ends of the candle." During this conversation, I failed to ask, but I admit to having been curious as to his experience with a chair with legs of unequal length.

That was how I was introduced to James Vincent Sheean. In his gregarious, laughing manner, he invited me to call him either Jimmy or Vincent. Apparently, his co-workers called him Vincent, and old friends called him Jimmy. He told me he could not account for the difference, had no preference, and would respond equally to either. We settled on Vincent, although within a few days, Paul took to calling him Vincenzo, the nickname we all adopted and he adored.

Vincenzo was our guest at the Pensione Alexandra for nearly two months. We wished he had stayed longer. Paul always enjoyed his company. Late at night, frequently, they would stand together on the balcony overlooking the Bay of Naples discussing the state of the world and predicting the next day's weather. The two would smoke their cigars and, as Vincenzo would often say, "howl at the moon."

I must say that I have never seen two grown men with so little in common spend more time enjoying one another's company and be more interested in discussing the weather. I often thought that it was the result of the wine and grappa consumed when they were together. Vincenzo was always fascinated with Paul's weather predictions and Paul's claim that Mt. Vesuvius was his barometer. Paul was convinced that the vapor issuing from the volcano's crater announced the weather in Naples twenty-four hours before changes occurred. When the cloud blew towards Capri, good weather was expected. When the cloud turned toward Ischia, it was a danger signal for pulmonary sufferers, and cold weather was on the horizon. And if the crater was concealed by a thick layer of clouds, Paul was certain that heavy rain was expected. These were hypotheses they thoroughly debated. I am certain that, somewhere in his notes, Vincenzo documented the results. He told Paul that he would refer to these predictions and give Paul credit in one of his future writings.

There remains one thing about Vincenzo that has always been curious to me. Many years later, I read somewhere that Vincenzo was said to have had a superior air and was very spoiled. I can't say that Paul and I ever found him that way. I suppose he may have changed – success can do that to people – but he never struck me as the kind of person who would change in that way. With us, he was always most polite, considerate, and down to earth. Perhaps what was written about him was by the person who supplied him the chair that had one leg shorter than the rest. I should have asked. Vincenzo was very clear that he had little patience for those he thought had "small and inferior minds."

That day, when he appeared before me in search of a room, I had no idea who he was, and neither did the world. Certainly, his name meant nothing to me. I had never heard of him. I just knew he was very tall, unlike anyone I had ever met, and that, in his amusing, self-confident way, he made me laugh. By the time he left to continue his lifelong journey and become one of the world's leading foreign correspondents, we learned that Vincenzo was a man who took great delight in patiently sharing his extraordinary stories peppered with fascinating amounts of detail. I have always been impressed by people who have the talent to paint exquisite paintings. They observe things most of us are unable to see, and they bring these observations to life in their works. There are a very few number of others who possess the special talent to do this with words. Vincenzo was one of those very special people. Before or after, I have never met anyone more talented with words than Vincenzo. He had an uncanny talent to find the perfect word to express what he wanted to say. He possessed the ability to make you feel that you were part of his moment. Mostly, he was the kind of guest we hoped would never leave. And when he did take his leave, we hoped he would return again and again.

CHAPTER TWENTY-ONE

That first day, when he arrived at the Pensione Alexandra with limited funds at his disposal, in search of an economical room, and carefully inspecting the furniture to find a proper writing table and sturdy chair, we could not have imagined that, during his stay, James Vincent Sheean, our friend Vincenzo the writer, would receive worldwide acclaim for the book he had published the preceding year. Less than two weeks after his arrival as our guest, a courier appeared at the door of the Pensione Alexandra with a telegram for Mr. Sheean announcing that his book *Personal History* had become number one on the New York Times bestseller list in America and been selected for the National Book Award as the Most Distinguished Biography of 1935. It would sell two million copies, a remarkable accomplishment at that time.

The other thing we did not know on that day he inexplicably appeared before me was that, on the evening the telegram announced his success, his friend and future wife, the fourth daughter of a renowned and knighted English actor, some would say the finest Hamlet of the Victorian era, would arrive with two bottles of Champagne and join the celebration. I can admit this to you now. That night, for more than one moment, I took my opportunity to join Paul and our guests on the balcony as they howled at the moon. It was a night to remember. Even Bertie Allen and her Ouija board could not possibly have made that prediction. The Pensione Alexandra might not have been fit for a queen, but within a very short period of time, we were fit for flyers from Her Majesty's Royal Air Force, and now were fit for one of her esteemed knight's daughters.

Here is how Vincenzo told us his story. One day in 1922, a twenty-three-year-old man from a tiny southern Illinois town in America walked into the Paris office of the *Chicago Tribune* searching for employment. He had failed to finish his studies at the University of Chicago, which had been interrupted for two years by service in the army. His previous job experience was limited and lacking. He had been employed for a brief period of time at the *Chicago Daily News*, where he had been fired for an undisclosed reason; spent a few short months writing a scandal sheet for the *New York Daily News*; and then made an aborted attempt to write the great American novel. For reasons that were never explained, but that were certainly understandable if you had met Vincenzo, the Paris office of the *Tribune* took a chance and hired him on the spot. Years later, he would write in his book *Personal*

History that was when "I became what was called a foreign correspondent."

What I have always remembered was that Vincenzo was a person who suddenly appeared before me, uninvited and seemingly out of nowhere. And before he left, he made a profound impression on my life. When I listened to his stories, I realized how little I knew and how enclosed my world was. For some, this may seem inconsequential. For me, understanding this was a revelation.

Until we owned the Pensione Alexandra, I had devoted my entire adult life to caring for my husband and my children. In all those years, I never took the time to stop and to consider much of the world beyond my own. I saw no reason. As a young girl, I had never been encouraged. While growing up in Germany, no teacher had ever taught me to do so. I had always been taught to listen and not to question, to learn from the wisdom of others who clearly knew more than me. In many respects, that was the German way. Vincenzo taught me to look beyond my own glass walls. He encouraged me to be curious, to question the truths I had always been taught, and to search for my own conclusions.

Today, I am no longer able to read books. My eyes prevent me from reading anything more than a card or a note, something I can only do by squinting carefully through a closely held magnifying glass. I miss reading. I have always been a voracious reader ever since I was a small child. What Vincenzo did in those weeks he stayed with us was change everything I wanted from books. Before, I was satisfied with stories that had good and happy endings, epic poems, and the classics. After I met Vincenzo,

I wanted to devour books about the world of places, ideas, beliefs, events, and people. I wanted to learn what the world thought. He posed questions, asked for opinions, and made me think about issues that had never entered my mind. I learned how to disagree. For me, this was a marvelous awakening.

Every few mornings, he would tire of writing and join me in the parlor for coffee and conversation. He would entertain me with his adventures. Vincenzo loved to talk. He loved to tell his stories. I suppose I was the perfect listener. I listened in amazement and rarely interrupted. I had no knowledge of his world. My formal education had ended when I was young. I'd never had the opportunity to attend a university like my brothers had. With Vincenzo, I had my own tutor, and I was able to sit and learn from one of the world's greatest foreign correspondents of that era.

He told me much about his book *Personal History*. I have read it since, but then I learned what it said from its author firsthand. I received an education about the world and its events and, for the first time, not simply with a bias favoring Germany or through the lens of Mussolini's Italian perspective. I learned from someone who was searching, above all else, for the truth in his story no matter how controversial it may be. He taught me that *why* is often the more important first word in a question than *what*.

As a foreign correspondent, Vincenzo had covered the Separatist revolt in the Rhineland, the League of Nations in Geneva, and the early days of Mussolini and fascism, and he had been arrested in Spain. To meet with the rebels in Morocco, he had donned a turban and, amidst gunfire, found passage through the French lines to Tangier. His stories never ended. He was in Persia for the installation of the Shah and in China when the Nationalists ousted their Communist partners. He was in Moscow when Stalin arrested Trotsky and in Palestine when the Arabs fought the Jews wanting to create their own state.

He told me stories of his days in Paris, his close friendship with Ernest Hemingway, and their escapades that had caused his shortage of funds. I learned that he had written articles for *The Atlantic Monthly*, *Harper's*, *Woman's Home Companion*, *Collier's*, *Century*, *The Saturday Evening Post*, *Commonwealth*, and *The New Republic* – magazines that I had not heard of and would not recognize until years later in America. How my world expanded in those few weeks he stayed with us. I really don't know why I tell you all these things. I am probably the only one who finds this interesting. At the time, all I could do was listen, absorb, smile, and nod. Now I can clearly see my evolution in Naples.

Many years have passed, and with time, I have learned to acknowledge that even one's sense of the truth is always subjective and that, no matter how objective one tries to be, perspective always has its own blemishes. Back then, I am sure that I failed to recognize that, sometimes, Vincenzo's self-confidence could be confused with self-righteousness and arrogance. He did have an inflated view of his own opinions. He always claimed his rightful place. I know that now.

But at the time, none of that mattered. It wasn't so much what he thought about things as much as understanding why he thought about things. What I learned was that facts mattered much more than the opinions of others and that, with knowledge, I could learn to have confidence in my own ability to make judgements based upon facts. This is a lesson that has served me well. Only with facts can someone form an informed and educated opinion. I also learned that facts can always be tilted in one's favor and serve one's motives, so we must always scrutinize and be vigilant and be prepared to change our views.

Today, not knowing this sounds preposterous, almost ignorant. But in the course of my lifetime, I have observed too many leaders disrupt the world by confidently portraying their opinions as facts and imploring and admonishing their faithful followers to agree. That was true when we watched the actions of Hitler and Mussolini, and it continues to be true. This is a lesson I want the generations that follow to know. Listen to others but ask your own questions and draw your own conclusions based upon knowledge and facts.

Vincenzo taught me that he had the right to his own opinions, but that right did not make his opinions necessarily right. It only made his opinions his own. I learned that I had the right to make my own assessments, that I was able and should possess enough self-confidence to come to my own conclusions and render my own judgements.

⇌ ⇌

Years later, I learned that *Personal History* had become required reading for incoming freshmen at Dartmouth College. If I had known that when he'd stayed with us, it probably would have meant little to me. Now, living in America, I understand the significance. Vincenzo really was my first college professor. Although Dartmouth will never have a record of my attendance nor any transcripts of my grades, I like telling myself that I took my first college class there and graduated with honors.

Vincenzo sold the movie rights to *Personal History* within weeks of his stay with us at the Pensione Alexandra in 1935. I imagine the ten thousand dollars he received was quite a sum for someone who was conserving his resources and trying to negotiate the price of his lodging only a few weeks earlier. Knowing Vincenzo, I am certain that if he was aware of this at the time he was our guest, he would have selected better-quality lodging (and insisted on a sturdy writing table and a chair with legs of equal length). Vincent Sheean continues to be heralded as one of the best journalists of his time. The movie adaption of *Personal History* was released in 1940. It was called Foreign Correspondent, was directed by Alfred Hitchcock, and was nominated for six Academy Awards.

CHAPTER TWENTY-TWO

From the day he arrived, the single topic Vincenzo really wanted to discuss was Italy's dictator, Benito Mussolini. Vincenzo was interested in what Paul and I thought about Il Duce. He wanted us to express our opinions, even more so when he learned of our Jewish backgrounds.

At first, Paul and I were reluctant. We chose to keep our opinions to ourselves. Talking about Mussolini was difficult and complicated. This was the kind of conversation we would typically avoid having with guests. We did live in a dictatorship. One had to speak carefully when talking about Mussolini. Freedom of speech did not include offering thoughts and ideas contrary to the national interest, opinions that could be considered anti-Fascist. Expressing any criticism of Il Duce could easily fall into that category. One could never be entirely certain who might be listening, who might repeat an offhand comment, or how something one said might be interpreted. There was always the risk of a telephone call being monitored or a letter being opened. We would never freely discuss our feelings about Mussolini unless we were among our family or with very close and trusted friends.

Late one moonlit evening, several weeks after he first arrived, Vincenzo joined us on the balcony. By then, we were comfortable having frank and honest conversations with one another, and Vincenzo knew he was free to ask questions. He was trying to understand. How did Mussolini's regime affect our lives? What did Paul and I really think? He had other friends in Naples, and they each had their own answers. Vincenzo couldn't comprehend why the international press was so enamored, why Mussolini continued to be praised by so many newspaper editors in America and elsewhere. Why did they refer to him as the divine dictator?

Vincenzo had strong opinions on this matter. He viewed Mussolini as anything but divine. He characterized him as a dominating dictator with an enormous ego willing to step over anything and anyone to get his own way. He was convinced that Mussolini would lead Italy into disastrous wars, that he refused to allow his advisors to have dissenting voices. He couldn't understand why Mussolini had not been stopped. Didn't others see this? Vincenzo thought Italians had been seduced by his rhetoric and charmed by his personality, that we worshipped him like a hero in a fanatical way. He warned that those who thought Mussolini was their friend would one day learn that he was their enemy, that he could not be trusted, that he possessed the cunning to betray his friends. He was convinced that there would come a time when Mussolini would be forced to join forces with Hitler. Mussolini was the only person who believed Italy would be strong enough to stand up to the power and might of Hitler and Germany. His ego demanded that. He was playing with fire. Mussolini needed to learn that he was not always the most brilliant and powerful person in the room.

Vincenzo had been following Mussolini for more than a decade, ever since Mussolini had risen to power. One of Vincenzo's first assignments as a foreign correspondent had been to take the train from Paris and report on the March on Rome. There, Vincenzo had witnessed the early rise of the Blackshirts, the militant wing of the National Fascist Party. Distinguished by their black uniforms, these volunteers had become Mussolini's enforcers, his gang of thugs, as he and the Fascists had taken control of Italy's government.

The Blackshirts included intellectuals, former army officers, and young landowners. They were vocal and convinced that they knew what was right. They had sworn an oath of loyalty to Mussolini and, throughout his regime, used violence and intimidation against their opponents. All of us living in Italy were aware of their presence. As we watched Mussolini's powers expand, so did the harsh measures used by the Blackshirts to control and eliminate his enemies.

When I first moved to Naples, Italy was still a relatively new country. It had only been forty years since Giuseppe Garibaldi had hailed Victor Emmanuel as the king of a united nation. Italy was still struggling to find its sense of national direction and still lacked a sense of national unity. The government was always in turmoil. Many ambitious plans and programs were initiated, but few were ever finished. Little was accomplished. Often, the leaders seemed to change from one day to the next. Each promised to overcome the failures of their opponents. Few Italians actually believed that the government could get anything done. While northern Italy improved, the politicians only talked about helping Southern Italy, which remained in terrible shape. The differences between the north and the south were apparent to all. The bad conditions I saw in Naples were only the tip of the iceberg. More than half the population was illiterate. There were many critical problems: cholera outbreaks, natural disasters like earthquakes and landslides, unemployment, poverty, organized crime. Even starvation was an issue in certain areas. Parents worried about opportunities for their children. Thousands of Italians left Italy every year hoping for a better life in America.

In Italy, politics was a very messy business. People made fun of the politicians and held out their hands asking for money in exchange for their votes. It was like a national sport. Everyone knew that games were played with the voting and that there were lots of bribes and such. Before Mussolini took control, our old friend Consolato told Paul about how people in the wealthy areas were encouraged to vote and, in the poor areas, people were intimidated not to vote. Paul always said that Italian politics was corrupt. It wasn't like Germany, where the rules were followed and taxes were paid. In Italy, Paul would tell me that the politicians only cared about lining their own pockets. As far as our family was concerned, the less the Italian government had to do with our lives the better. Nearly all of our friends felt exactly the same way.

World War I was the breaking point. The politicians had promised too much, and the Italian people paid the price. Italy had sided with the Allies against Germany and Austria-Hungary in World War I, but despite being victorious, most Italians believed that Italy had been treated very badly at Versailles. Nearly half a million Italians had died in the war. Italy had been promised lands along the Adriatic coast, but when the Treaty of Versailles was signed, Italy was ignored, and we learned that promises made were promises broken. Then we all suffered again with the crazy inflation and unemployment that followed. Italians were searching for a strong and decisive leader, someone who would take charge and stand up for Italy, someone who would bring order to the chaos.

Benito Amilcare Andrea Mussolini, an Italian World War I veteran and journalist, and his newly formed right-wing organization, the National Fascist Party, boldly stepped in and promised to fix the mess. Mussolini relentlessly criticized the Italian government for its weakness, argued for a strong sense of Italian nationalism, and opposed social class discrimination. He was portrayed as standing side by side with the common man, who had long suffered at the hands of the wealthy. The masthead of his newspaper read "He who has steel has bread." Mussolini believed in only negotiating from strength. Even the word "Fascism" was derived from the Latin word "fasces," which was an ax tightly wound with sticks that symbolized strength and power through unity. Some said he always made sure that he was the bully in the room. He was a talented orator and a wily politician, and he possessed an overwhelming amount of self-confidence.

At every opportunity, Mussolini confidently promised to raise Italy to the level of its great Roman past, to create the new Roman Empire. With the help and strong-arm methods of his loyal and enthusiastic Blackshirts, Mussolini and the Fascist Party emerged from obscurity in the 1921 elections. In 1922, after failing in his attempt to be part of a new compromise government and fearing a Socialist takeover, Mussolini and thirty thousand of his followers, his Blackshirts, in a demonstration of power, led a march on Rome. The following day, he took control of Italy's government and was appointed prime minister by Italy's weak and indecisive King Victor Emmanuel II. Within three years, he had dismantled Italy's democracy, eliminated his enemies, and, aided by his brutal police organization, taken the title Il Duce and declared himself dictator of Italy. He was convinced that his destiny was to become the Roman Empire's next Julius Caesar.

CHAPTER TWENTY-THREE

You may be surprised to learn that Mussolini was one of the first rulers in history to take full advantage of the electric loudspeaker to amplify his voice. He was a brilliant public speaker. When we first heard his name, it was when people referred to his speeches. That was what everyone talked about. He had the ability to capture the Italian spirit and imagination. He would excite the passions of his listeners. He made people proud to be Italians. It was a message of "All for one and one for all." He would appear before enormous crowds. He went from standing on soapboxes and giving speeches on street corners to becoming the leader of the Italian people. He was in power for twenty years, and for much of that time, the Italians stood with him. Despite his enormous control and power, I believe he was dictator because most Italians wanted him to be dictator.

His picture was on posters everywhere. Fresh posters for the regime were put up all the time. In Italy, there were so many illiterate people, and the posters could be easily understood. They were all attractive and portrayed Il Duce as a great man who was doing so many great things for Italy. They always conveyed a simple message. People could take one glance at the posters and immediately know that their leader was always working for their interests. I will always remember the posters. He was a mastermind of propaganda.

Not long after he gained power, he started broadcasts on the radio. I think the Fascist party had a program on the radio for two hours each day. Mussolini wanted everyone in Italy to own a radio. He wanted us all to hear his voice and his admonitions. At first, very few could afford radios, but he insisted that his government find a way to produce less expensive radios so everyone could listen. The National Fascist Party always broadcasted his speeches. Group listening was promoted. He was very confident, and people were attracted to his confidence. He was always talking about service to the nation, that Italians had to put the national interest above their own. He likened Fascism to a religion. We all needed to believe. He would lead, and everyone should follow. I suppose, in some ways, he was a genius. Many followed him as if he were the Messiah. Whether you cared for him or not, we all had to listen.

Before we owned the pensione, I paid as little attention as I could to politics and the Italian government. I had no interest. Paul felt the same, but the truth was that the Italian government was impossible to avoid. We were living in Italy, and one just had to accept Mussolini and his government. That was all we could do: live our lives and go about our business.

Some things were complicated. We knew many Fascists. There were many brilliant thinkers in Italy who supported Mussolini. At first, an acquaintance of Paul who lived in Naples, Benedetto Croce, the well-known philosopher and historian, gave his support. He thought Mussolini would keep the more rabid Fascists in check, that he was more moderate. Later, after the Socialist politician Matteotti was assassinated, Croce opposed Mussolini. Croce was convinced that Mussolini had not discouraged the violent act. After Croce withdrew his support, he was constantly threatened by the Fascists.

To gain support from the Roman Catholic Church, religious education was made compulsory in all elementary schools. Although he was an atheist, Mussolini and the Catholic Church worked arm in arm throughout the 1920s. He understood the Church's immense influence on Italian society. He increased clerical salaries and restored the crucifix in law courts and schools. His first three children were baptized, and he even re-married his wife in the church ten years after their initial civil ceremony.

People from all walks of life supported the Fascists, even many Jewish leaders. Race and religion were not part of the Fascist platform. Jews were part of Mussolini's government. It was said he had a Jewish mistress. The rules for Jews would change when Mussolini formed his partnership with Hitler, but that would come much later, not for the first sixteen years of Mussolini's rule. Italy was not Germany. Even if one did not support Mussolini, most Italians felt that Mussolini would not allow Italy to become like Germany. He would not banish the Jews from society.

Once Mussolini became dictator, even though, by then, Paul and I had both become Italian citizens, we weren't allowed to vote. Actually, only a small number of people were able to vote. In the 1929 election, voting was restricted to only his supporters, men who were members of a trade union or an association, soldiers, and members of the clergy. Voting hardly mattered. The only ones on the ballot were members of the Fascist party, and they always won.

We did see some of his staunchest supporters, the Blackshirts, walking on the streets at times, but we stayed far away. We didn't see them often, mostly at patriotic events like parades or rallies. I always thought they were a bunch of self-righteous thugs. We were never bothered, nor were the children, although I must say the Blackshirts were an intimidating presence, particularly at large public gatherings. It was better to remain quiet and mind one's own business. This was a society where you kept your opinions to yourself, especially on anything involving Mussolini or the Fascists.

As for the Fascist party, unless you wanted a certain type of employment because of the unions, wanted a job working for a government-controlled industry, or needed government assistance, there really was no reason to join. It was encouraged, but we were never required. I suppose those who did join learned they had to do other things in support of the regime. With regard to our family, Paul dealt with whatever the government asked for and usually didn't tell me. I was happier that way.

Vincenzo's question was a good one. The truth was, even if one did not want to pay attention, Mussolini did affect and influence our lives. When Mussolini proclaimed that Italy was the most powerful Mediterranean country and that the countries that surrounded the Mediterranean should belong to Italy, he spent our government's resources to build up a powerful navy so he could control the Mediterranean Sea and the Adriatic coast. When he lectured us about *mare nostrum* and told us that the Mediterranean should become *our lake*, he required us to pay taxes to support his dreams. His grand ambition to recreate the Roman Empire, his plan to grow the population by encouraging girls to have more babies, and his requirement that boys join the army affected every family. None of this could be avoided.

As dictator, all of what he did furthered his ambitions and affected our lives. Many things were important and good and improved our lives. I am sure that is why many of those outside of Italy referred to him as the divine dictator, at least during his early years of power. He was decisive and was able to get many things done, often by the sheer force of his will. Italy constructed a major transportation system of highways and roads, repaired bridges, and built new train stations to replace those that were old and crumbling. The Fascists spent money on new schools and other public buildings. They worked to improve working conditions and work hours. One thing was certain: you could be sure they would name the building or

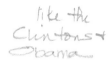

there would be a sign nearby proclaiming their accomplishment. The Fascists knew how to claim credit.

But at the same time, there was no question that Mussolini and his followers silenced their detractors. He and the Fascists often made unilateral decisions and informed the public only after they were made. Things got done because he required that they be done. And while he demanded loyalty from others, he did not always return his loyalty. On any given day, he could turn against his supporters. He was a pragmatic politician who formed new alliances and coalitions whenever it served his purpose. If he had a moral code, I am not sure what it was. His ambitions came first.

Mussolini had an uncanny ability to rally the masses, and as he did, the Fascist party found its way into nearly every aspect of our lives. Work, play, rest, and worship all were influenced by Il Duce and his followers in the years of the Fascist regime. The customary handshake was replaced with the Fascist salute. A Fascist calendar, which began counting the years after the 1922 March on Rome, was introduced. The Italian language was changed, substituting the informal for the polite in the form of address. Individual movement was controlled by the right to review and cancel passports, to fire on persons attempting to leave the country illegally, and to deprive Italians abroad of their citizenship and property if they openly criticized the regime. There was little question that we lived in a dictatorship. We had no choice but to follow their rules.

Mussolini sought to mold the Italian population to serve his grand plan. With propaganda, he tried to transform the Italian people into militant Fascists. The Fascist Party created youth organizations to train boys and girls from age six to twenty-one. Public schools featured instruction on Fascist principles and the glorification of Mussolini.

There was little Paul and I could do to keep our children away from these types of influences. I think the older two were affected more than the twins. Fortunately, their private school had an international following, and they had several teachers who refused to change their curriculums to accommodate the Fascists. Those teachers were concerned about the quality of their education and chose not to waste valuable classroom time teaching propaganda. Others less fortunate did not have the luxury of private schools, and Fascism was all those children learned.

The Fascists took charge of most leisure-time activities. You could not play bocce in the park or take a hike in the countryside without encountering Fascist propaganda in one way or another. Sometimes, one was required to join a team or belong to a club. If you went to the movies, the first thing you saw was a newsreel extolling the successes of Il Duce. The Fascists controlled theaters, athletic and sports clubs, sporting events, sports teams, choral societies, bands, night schools, libraries, and pleasure clubs. Even travel and tourism was affected. Special tours and train rides were frequently organized. Card-carrying Fascists could always obtain special discounts for any of these activities. One could find many reasons to support and become a member of the Fascist party.

For our family, because we were foreigners, we managed to keep much of our independence. We always kept our German identity. Some of that would change with the pensione, but there was little we could do to change our accents. In one way or another, we were always outsiders. Of course, the children grew up in the Fascist environment, but I like to think having Paul and me for parents helped. Their wonderful teachers sheltered them too, particularly when they were at impressionable ages. Most of their friends were raised in homes where the thinking was similar to ours. Somehow, our children grew up to form their own opinions.

As for Paul and me, until the time we began operating the pensione, our circle of friends was almost entirely German. We were active members of the German community. While I believe we were always respectful of our surroundings and our host country, we were never particularly interested in what Mussolini had to say. We just tried to keep to ourselves, go about our business, and stay out of his way. All that would change, but that would come later.

CHAPTER TWENTY-FOUR

Paul and I were sorry to see Vincenzo leave. Vincenzo did send me a letter from Vienna that summer, and we were able to learn a little about what came next. He wanted us to know that he'd married Dinah, his friend from London who'd joined us that night when we'd howled at the moon. Vincenzo wrote that they had been attending the Vienna music festival with friends when they'd received word that Dinah's father would visit them the following day. For some reason, her father was under the impression that they had already married. He would not approve of them living together under any other circumstance. With less than twenty-four hours' notice, Vincenzo had been forced to appeal to the American consulate and the Bishop of Vienna to bend the rules and arrange for their immediate marriage ceremony. Knowing Vincenzo, I could imagine his troubles. Vincent Sheean was certainly one of the more interesting guests to walk through the Pensione Alexandra's doors.

As Vincenzo was leaving, he gave me a copy of *The Atlantic* magazine published the previous October, which carried a story he had written. He wanted me to read it. I will never forget his parting words: "Pay attention to the Nazis. Too many Germans have never met a Jew." The article was titled "My Friend the Jew." It was about an experience he'd had as a young student in college.

Vincenzo's story told about the many students he had met who had formed opinions about the Jewish race. Most knew no Jews and only repeated the words that had been said by others. Vincenzo observed that many false impressions and images had been passed from one generation to the next. He found that, for many, these impressions had become truths. Why was he told that he would be excluded from certain campus activities if he had a friend who was a Jew or if he joined a Jewish fraternity? Like many other underclassmen, he had never met a Jew before he attended the university. And when he did, he couldn't understand why there were so many popular students who felt Jews were somehow inferior or undesirable. Vincenzo worried about this accumulated prejudice. He found it to be an unconscious form of anti-Semitism.

Vincenzo's magazine article left quite an impression on me. It made me consider what I knew about the differences between Germany and Italy. And the more I thought, the more I worried.

CHAPTER TWENTY-FIVE

When I first arrived in Naples, there was one aspect of my journey that seemed oddly familiar. It was the way Aunt Betty, Uncle Arthur, and Paul lived. It was as if they had never left Germany. For that reason, in many ways, I barely noticed my transition from Koenigsberg to Naples. Despite the physical differences between the two cities, and the contrast between the organized way of life of Koenigsberg and the chaotic life of Naples, I went from the protection of one cocoon to another. I left the secure and comforting life of my family in Germany and joined the sheltered lives of Aunt Betty, Uncle Arthur, and Paul in Italy. Sitting in one house was not altogether different from sitting in the other. I found that for Aunt Betty, Uncle Arthur, and Paul, nearly everything in Italy remained German. Within their house, we spoke German, ate German foods, and shared German culture. All of their friends were German. Only when I ventured beyond the sheltered four walls of their home was the difference between Naples and Koenigsberg so startlingly apparent.

One aspect of their life was a big change for me. In Koenigsberg, our family life was centered within the Jewish community. We belonged to the local synagogue, lived in a Jewish neighborhood, and observed Jewish customs, traditions, and holidays. Our extended family and all of our friends were part of this larger Jewish community. Most of our family's activities were associated with the synagogue in one way or another. We always went to Father's brother's house on Friday evenings, lit two white candles, closed our eyes, and recited the blessing before the family meal. Saturdays were quiet family days.

That was not how Aunt Betty, Uncle Arthur, and Paul lived in Naples. They were not part of the Jewish community. They did not attend the synagogue. I had no idea if any of their friends were Jewish. I only knew that they were German.

I imagine my family was like many other reform-minded Jewish families in Koenigsberg. Our race was Jewish, our religion was Jewish, and our nationality was German. There were other Jews in Koenigsberg, but we really did not know them. They came mostly from small villages in the east. Although we shared a common religion, we tended to feel that they were different. They spoke their own language and lived off to themselves. Many of them were older. They dressed more traditionally, the men wearing caps and the women often covering their hair with kerchiefs. We considered ourselves more modern, more assimilated.

I think the distinction is important to understand because it did frame some of our thinking. We did not live in a completely closed or closeted world inhabited only by Jews. We dressed in a modern style, and my generation was the first of the newly created German empire. By law, Jews were as German as any other citizen. Little kept us from enjoying society's pleasures. However, the life we lived was mostly among other Jews. They knew us. We knew them. I suspect some of this is human nature. We were more comfortable being surrounded by others like ourselves.

In Germany, we had assimilated in our own way. Although most of us found shelter within the Jewish community and chose to live our lives primarily with other Jews, many of our fathers and brothers had broader business interests and ventured out into the greater community. They were merchants, bankers, professionals, and teachers. As children, we attended public schools. It was not an exclusive world. We were not kept apart unless we chose to. We were not segregated or confined in a Jewish ghetto. Those rules were long forgotten. However, in Germany, there was a past and an attitude that hadn't always been accepting. German Jews tended to keep with their own. For us, we found that was a better way to live.

German laws did not erase one's memories or change one's beliefs. German Jews remained wary of Germany's varied history. Vincenzo was right. Most Germans had never met a Jew. Centuries of accumulated prejudices had left many with misguided opinions.

When they first arrived in Naples, I know it would have been difficult for Aunt Betty, Uncle Arthur, and Paul to immerse themselves in the Jewish community or become part of the synagogue. Italian Jews spoke Italian. Aunt Betty, Uncle Arthur, and Paul were foreigners. They spoke German and hardly a single word of Italian. And when I stepped off the train in Naples ten years later, this was still true.

Language was not the only reason Aunt Betty, Uncle Arthur, and Paul chose to live their lives differently in Naples than we did in Koenigsberg. In Italy, Jews felt little necessity to live apart. There was little need to find shelter or protection or to congregate only with other Jews. My observation was that Italy's Jews were more fully assimilated and integrated than in Germany. Without prejudice, they fully participated in the mainstream of everyday life. The tiny Jewish population, far less than one percent of the Italian population and ten times smaller than the Jewish population in Germany, was totally involved in all aspects of society – commerce, politics, the professions, education, government, and the military. Jews had intermarried for generations.

I read once that more than one-half of the Jewish marriages in Italy were mixed. In Germany, less than one in ten Jewish marriages were mixed, and many Germans disapproved. In Italy, nearly everyone had a friend or someone in their family tree who was Jewish. Italians rejected the notion of anti-Semitism. Italy was a melting pot of tribes and races. This attitude was part of the Italian culture.

In Naples, as there were few compelling reasons for Aunt Betty, Uncle Arthur, and Paul to become part of the Jewish community, they chose the German community.

They found comfort being with their fellow Germans, a rather small and close group in Naples. They were Germans, and that is where they felt they belonged.

I did observe that neither Aunt Betty, Uncle Arthur, nor Paul appeared to be as "Jewish" as we were in Koenigsberg. I really don't know why. Their Jewishness seemed to have less to do with their religion as it did their race. They chose not to observe Jewish customs and traditions. They never denied their heritage, but they didn't embrace Judaism as we had in Germany.

Birds of a feather flock together. I suppose this was as true in Koenigsberg as it was in Naples. Only, in Naples, I learned that I was to become part of the German community instead of the Jewish community. This didn't trouble me. It made me feel comfortable. Many things were familiar. I had only planned to visit for three months and was not concerned about practicing my religion or attending the synagogue. This was a new and different way to live. It was the first time I was on my own, and I felt the freedom to make my own choices.

⇒⇐

During those first months in Naples, nearly all of my hours were spent sitting with Aunt Betty in her home as her companion. Even if I had wanted to, there was no time to visit the synagogue or join in the activities of the Jewish community. As it was, I found little opportunity to explore the streets of Naples or learn about its culture. There were many things to see, but leaving the house was discouraged, and I was not confident enough to explore

Naples on my own. The people I met were all Germans, friends of Aunt Betty, Uncle Arthur, and Paul. I rarely met an Italian, and I made no genuine Italian friendships. It seemed that Naples was quite a different adventure than I'd anticipated when I'd first left Koenigsberg.

Poor Aunt Betty continued to suffer from depression. She was unhappy with how her life had turned out and seemed unable or incapable of changing it. She found herself married to a much older husband who appeared to enjoy his work and his German friends more than he enjoyed the company of his wife. Uncle Arthur and Aunt Betty could be kind and generous in their own way, but they had no interest in Italian life. They acted as if they were visiting. I know I repeat myself, but I cannot understate the significance of this. They preferred everything German: language, food, friends, and customs. They stayed within their German community, rarely mixed with others, and were unwilling to change their ways. The only Neapolitans they appeared to know were the household help, and even with these workers, they seemed to have no interest in engaging in anything beyond the basic pleasantries. As Aunt Betty made no effort to find her own friends or create her own life in Naples, she spent her time suffering from boredom in her house each day.

Honestly, I can't say I felt that sorry for Aunt Betty. She certainly had the ability to open her windows and doors and enjoy the Neapolitan life, but she sat all day, idle and often complaining, waiting for the world to come to her. I never could determine whether she was simply lazy or lacked the ambition and interest necessary to do most anything. Unfortunately, as a twenty-one-year-old woman, there was little I could do to change the habits of my much older cousin/aunt who was quite set in her ways and not particularly interested in hearing my opinions.

My time was spent by her side listening to her unhappiness, not the most pleasant way to spend one's time, day in and day out. I counted the minutes until I could spend time with Paul. His and my friendship continued to grow. I suppose you could say that Aunt Betty sent me into Paul's arms. The difficulty was that Aunt Betty also chaperoned most of my time with Paul. Under her stern supervision, I found it next to impossible to be in Paul's arms.

I was thrilled when Paul asked me to marry him. There was so much new and exciting to look forward to, and I was content to go along with the way the others lived. I was young and impressionable, and I acted the way I thought one was supposed to act. True to how I had been taught, when I married Paul, his habits became my habits. I adopted his version of Jewishness. His way of life became my way of life, and the German community in Naples became my community in Naples. I suppose one way to look at this was that I was German first, Italian second, and somewhere in the mix, I still remained Jewish. One thing was certain: my Jewishness would no longer be as prominent in my life as it had been in Koenigsberg.

CHAPTER TWENTY-SIX

You may remember that one of the extravagances we were forced to give up when our financial situation became difficult was our membership in the German club. Perhaps you found that odd, but what I neglected to emphasize was how important the German club was to our way of life. Paul and I never considered the German club to be an extravagance. It was the center of our German community. All of our friends were members.

Paul was one of its founders and had been a member for forty years. It began as an informal gathering for the few German men living in Naples. They could get together in the evenings to visit, play cards, smoke cigars, and drink beer. Later, the club became more organized. It expanded to include wives and children. Dues were collected. Events were planned.

When Paul first arrived in 1894, Naples was a lonely place for a twenty-one-year-old from Germany. It was natural that the small number of Germans living in Naples would gravitate toward one another. They had much in common. Like most others, Paul didn't speak Italian. He was unacquainted with the Italian customs. He was unfamiliar with the Italian food. Everything was foreign. These Germans living in Naples did not understand Naples, and Naples did not understand them. Indeed, they were strangers in a strange land.

Germany was spreading its influence and economic interests throughout Europe and the world, and Naples was a major seaport on the Mediterranean Sea. It was not surprising that Naples would attract a small number of German merchants and businessmen. Some, like us, were there for their careers and would make Naples their home. Others would leave as soon as their work was complete. Some were single. Others were married. Some had families.

There were a few who tried to adopt the Neapolitan lifestyle, but most of us chose to keep our German ways. We had little interest in becoming too Italian or venturing too far from our German customs and culture. Personally, I liked being the *Signora forestiera*, the foreign lady. It gave me greater freedom than the Italian women, who, I found, were very restricted in their lifestyle. Perhaps I felt a bit aloof and superior, an attitude I do not care to admit. There was no denying that we were Germans. That was our upbringing. We certainly had a German outlook and believed that our way of life was better. We were convinced that Germany offered the best of everything. Most of us saw little reason to change our habits just because we were living in Naples.

Life in Naples had its own set of rules. For a German, it was difficult to be accepted. As friendly as everyone was on the streets, families in Naples were often large and complicated. Many preferred to keep the company of their own. I think foreigners face these issues throughout the world. Naples was not all that different. Even if one wants to integrate, sometimes, it takes years to fit in.

When the club first formed, the members were mostly young men who shared this common German bond. It was only natural that these bonds would grow to become lifelong friendships. After Paul and I married, his friends and their wives became my friends. We cherished these friendships. We knew their children. They knew our children. We celebrated family events together, and together, we shared our family losses. This was our community in Naples, and it all seemed perfectly natural. This was how we lived. We kept with our own, cared for our own, and mixed with our own. It was our home. These were our friends. This was where we belonged.

With our lifelong ties to the German community and friends who participated in the German club, it was devastating to realize we could no longer afford the membership dues. After having enjoyed the good times, Paul and I found it very difficult to admit our financial downfall. I don't think anyone likes to share their failures with others. Learning of our situation, one dear and close friend went to the others and made arrangements allowing us to continue our membership. They told us to repay the club when times were better, an act of kindness among friends. They valued our friendship and wanted us to belong.

That act of kindness three years earlier and these lifelong friendships made what happened all the more difficult to understand.

⇒⇔⇐

It was a wonderful early summer evening. The Pensione Alexandra had consumed every moment of our time for months. We were ready to take time for ourselves and be with our friends. Paul and I took the night off and left Mela in charge. The German club had scheduled a party, a celebration, something to do with the new stadium being built in Berlin for the 1936 Olympics, which, I believe, was to be the largest in the world. Germany was extremely proud of its selection to host the 1936 Olympics. I knew nothing about the Olympics, but our group rarely needed an excuse for a party. The club was social, and we enjoyed spending time with one another. We hadn't seen our close friends for months.

That evening, as we entered the hall, we immediately noticed that something was different when we were greeted with a life-sized portrait of the führer, Adolf Hitler, which had been hung by the entrance. Later that evening, when everyone stood and sang the German national anthem, we watched as our friends raised their right arms in the Hitler salute.

Moments later, I overheard the conversation. Our old friend who had so kindly arranged for us to continue our membership in the club was speaking to others. I can still hear his words: "If a Jew enters this hall, I will be forced to leave."

It is frightening how much can be turned upside down in the briefest of moments. I remember saying to myself, *He cannot be talking about us. He must be speaking about others. He knows us too well.* But then our friend turned and stared.

Paul looked at me, and I looked at Paul. In that single instant, we both recognized that the world had changed. We were not about to deny who we were. Until that evening, we'd believed that, because we lived in Italy, our family was sheltered from the evil that was spreading throughout Germany. Now we considered the possibility that Italy's broad shoulders might not be big enough. Germany might be pointing its finger at us.

CHAPTER TWENTY-SEVEN

Even today, I am unsure how to react to that evening. I always thought we belonged, that those were our friends. I believe all human beings crave that feeling of belonging in one way or another. I certainly do even today. I cry because it hurt. This was a betrayal, and I became angry because of the arrogance. I was confused because Germany had always been my home and I'd always considered myself German. I weep for the friends and family members who were later lost in the madness. I bleed for all those who suffered. I am tired because I have thought about this for far too long. Incomprehensible. I think that is the word I am searching for. It was all so incomprehensible that I hardly know where to start. My feelings remain unchanged. What had made my blood less German? How had I become suddenly less German than others?

As soon as we heard the remark that evening, we left and never turned back. We severed our relationship with the German community in Naples and walked away. The comment marked the end of so many forty-year friendships. Others heard it when it was said. No one chose to stand with us, at least not on that night. Some would later. That night, they all watched us leave. No one apologized. No one asked us to stay.

The wife of the man who had spoken was one of my closest and oldest friends, a friendship that dated to my first months in Naples, a friend who had shared so much with me. We had cared for one another's children. We had consoled one another when our parents had died. A few days later, I learned she'd been told by her husband to never see me again. I ask you, who can defend this behavior?

Now I can see that this was our first warning. Perhaps we should have heeded it at the time and left for America. But that is hindsight. At the time, I was hurt. Something having little to do with me had made me lose my friends. I was angry because this was not the silliness that happens among playmates, when one-day friendships shift, when some are in and others are out. This was hatred and cruelty and arrogance. I was stung, hurt, and disappointed. For my entire life, I had always been a German Jew. I was a proud descendent of German Jews. Who had the arrogance to claim that Jews could not be German?

Anti-Semitism was not new to Germany or, for that matter, Europe. For centuries, Jews had been blamed for everything from the plague to economic disasters. My parents had taught me this history. As far as I was concerned,

Hitler was one more in the long line of politicians who had painted Jews as the scapegoats for Germany's troubles. But like many, I could not believe that others would allow this madness to continue, that others would embrace this way of thinking. Throughout the modern world, Jews had been emancipated. It was 1935, and my entire adult life had been spent in Italy. It was different here. Mussolini rejected the notion that Jews were any less Italian. Jews could be Italians. Why couldn't a Jew be German? Who had the right to think that way?

What made this remark at the German club so uncomfortable was that it had been said by someone who had always been a trusted friend, someone who knew us well. What had changed? How had the air become so poisoned? How dare a German living in Naples say such a thing. Hadn't we all learned better?

There was little Paul and I could do that evening except choose not to go where we were not welcome. The words had been said. They could not be taken back, and I would remember. I had little time in my life for this nonsense, and I certainly had little patience for fools. One thing I knew was where I belonged. I was the proprietress of the Pensione Alexandra. There were rooms to fill and a pensione to run.

CHAPTER TWENTY-EIGHT

That fall, we started to experience something new and different from earlier in the year. The nationalities of our guests were changing, and more guests were arriving. More languages were being spoken. This was very apparent in the breakfast room each morning. Through the spring and summer, most of our guests were British or American. That made sense. For years, guidebooks and booking agents had characterized the Pensione Alexandra as English-speaking. But I had tried to change this. I'd hoped that by expanding the list of languages, we would be visited by more guests. Now it seemed that these efforts were producing results.

I wanted tourists to know that a German family was operating the Pensione Alexandra and that we were able to communicate in German, English, French, and Italian. There had been only one issue, a time when I had been at the train station and Paul had been the only one available to assist the guests. A French couple had been staying with us. When they'd asked for his recommendation as to where they might go for an ice cream, he'd gone to the kitchen for ice. This confusion had been temporary and quickly resolved.

The other news was that an extra pair of hands joined us to take more of the burden off me, a much-appreciated improvement. Consolato was a big help in the kitchen, and the workers I hired to handle the other daily chores, like mopping the floors and making the beds, had made a huge difference, but I still remained terribly busy. I never imagined that there were so many things that could go wrong at the same time or so many places I needed to be at the same moment. With thirty guests, someone always needed something. Guests would appear in the front room at all hours of the day and night. Managing the pensione remained a twenty-four-hour-a-day job, seven days a week, with no time off.

Mela was capable and had been an enormous help, but Mother was right, Mela had her own life, which by now included a boyfriend and all the associated parental worries. He seemed like a nice boy, but one never knew. Once again, Mela's head was in the clouds. Paul was concerned, forever reminding her to keep both feet on the ground and discouraging her from listening to too much Mussolini on the radio. To Mela's credit, she was learning about life. We were happy for her.

Between running to and from the port and the train station, holding my little sign in search of new guests, and manning the front, taking care of the needs of those who stayed, I had little rest or time for myself. Someone was always asking for a tour guide, or I had to find Mariantonia to make a clothing repair, or a picnic lunch was needed because someone was taking the boat to Capri. Guests were always checking in and checking out. There were days I yearned for my old life, when I could just hide in the bath with a good book and soak in the tub. Once again, I was reminded of the difference between dreaming of owning a pensione and actually operating one. I suppose one good thing was that I was so busy with the pensione that there was little time to think about the incident at the German club, which always made me sad and angry.

Lotte was the perfect solution to my problem, and she could not have arrived at a better time. What was even better is that we all fell in love with her from the moment she stepped off the train.

Only the month before, I had received a letter from Germany, from an old childhood friend, Trude, who still lived in Koenigsberg. Trude asked if her daughter, Lotte, could come stay with us. She described their situation. Despite what we might have heard in newspaper reports to the contrary, it was clear that, every day, Jews were more and more excluded and shoved aside. Yes, there were days when it seemed that the Nazis talked more than they acted, and she was still able to go about her business without too much concern. But this was in the neighborhood where everyone was known and where all the Jewish businesses were located. It was different when she ventured near the main square, by the park. Near the square, there were a few troublesome people who were beginning to make life difficult. However, she did say she was not yet concerned for her own safety.

Trude's words were that, at times, it felt as if there was a "foul odor in the air," the sense that it had become acceptable to treat Jews in unacceptable ways. Rude behavior, particularly by young people, was replacing respect. One of her friends had been frightened by the taunts from a group of young men standing at one street corner. There were signs in certain shops saying that Jews were not welcome, but these were shops they avoided anyway. Anything they needed they could find in Jewish-owned shops. In general, when going out, it was better to stay in the company of others.

The more important issue was what might be next. There was a lot of talk, much speculation, and no one really knew anything for certain. Right now, people were talking more about the Olympics in Berlin and Hitler's plans to rebuild the army and air force. The Jews seemed to be the only people worrying about the welfare of Jews. It was a confusing situation. What concerned her most was the filth that the young people were being taught. That scared her. They were brainwashing these children. She was glad that her children were grown. One of her neighbor's children had some issues at the school. Intimidation was a problem. People were being told how they should act, even good people, people who should know better. But even the good people were afraid. They were being told it was better to be against the Jews. It was their patriotic duty to keep Germany for Germans.

She'd heard others say it was time to leave. "Why should we live where we are told we don't belong? But where would one go? What is happening in Koenigsberg must be happening in Berlin. The Nazis are spreading this garbage throughout Germany. You can't just pick up and leave. It is not that easy, particularly if one's parents and children and sisters and brothers all remain. Little makes sense. We are Germans. Our husbands and fathers were soldiers and fought for our country. Many lost their lives. Hitler says he wants to reunite all Germans, to rebuild the German empire. And then he has the arrogance to say there is no room for us."

Trude wrote that her son planned to move to Australia, to be as far away as he could be. She was not concerned for herself, but she wanted a future for her daughter, Lotte, who was now twenty-one and still unmarried. As long as the Nazis remained in power, one could never be certain as to what they might do next. Trude asked if there was room in our house for Lotte. Could she send Lotte to stay with us in Naples until things in Koenigsberg were sorted out?

By a stroke of luck, Trude's letter arrived on the same day that Mela came home and excitedly announced that she had found a full-time job. She had been hired to be a clerk in the children's department at a bookstore. She would be the reader, reading books out loud to children of all ages. But she was worried about her tutoring. Mela would need to give up her part-time job teaching German to the two children who lived on our street.

I had the perfect solution. I immediately wrote back to Trude. Of course Lotte would be welcome. We had a spare room. This could be a wonderful opportunity for Lotte. She could spend two hours each day tutoring German to the two children in the neighborhood, and she could help me in the pensione to pay for her room and board.

⸻

Now that so many years have passed, I am able to admit that luck is not the only reason moments like these occur. Sometimes, luck happens when one picks up two coins and rubs them together, something that, I admit, might have been true in this particular instance. The letter from my old friend Trude might not have been entirely a surprise and was not unprompted. I misstated the facts when I told you that Trude had asked if Lotte could come and stay with us. In fact, it was actually Trude's response to a letter I had written earlier inviting Lotte to come to Naples. I'd written my letter on the day my friend, the bookstore owner, had told me that a new clerk was needed in the children's department. She'd asked whether Mela might be interested.

I had my reasons for this deception. I remembered how my mother and Aunt Betty had nurtured my relationship with Paul. Now it was my turn to do the matchmaking. Alex, my twenty-five-year-old unmarried son, had just finished his two-year obligation to the Italian army and was now living with us until he could find his future. Alex was a wonderful son. He reminded me of his father, who, at a similar age, had been searching for his future. When Trude wrote back, she concurred with the arrangement.

One More Moon

We agreed to rub these two coins together to see what might happen. Neither Alex nor Lotte had any idea.

That was why Mela and I went to the Centrale station to greet Lotte as she stepped off the train on that particular afternoon. Some days, there is no need for a pigeon to do its business on one's head to bring good luck. And that day, no one had to know that luck doesn't always happen entirely by accident. Sometimes, it just takes a little encouragement, a gentle push by an invisible hand.

CHAPTER TWENTY-NINE

Lotte had been living with us for less than two weeks when she heard the front desk bell ring one afternoon. When she went to explore, she found a rather distinguished, gray-haired older man wearing a beret standing in the reception area. He was well dressed except for a rather annoying smudge of bluish-green paint that was very visible on the lapel of his jacket. It was the sort of thing that would be noticed if he were standing in a crowd, particularly in Naples, where proper people were expected to be properly dressed.

He was somewhat hurried and distressed, actually a little fidgety, as he explained that he and his wife had arrived in Naples only a short time earlier in the day. They were tourists in need of a room for ten days. He was very polite and apologized for not having made a reservation, an oversight. He spoke German, but it was much different from the East Prussian German we were accustomed to hearing. He was clearly an educated man.

One thing that made this episode odd was that, although his language was German, his papers were French, a question quickly resolved when he disclosed that they had not travelled from Germany. Apparently, they were living in France and had taken the overnight train from Paris. He explained that he and his wife were actually on a honeymoon of sorts. All this was imparted rather quickly to Lotte, who had not been expecting a guest to appear and had been on her way out the door when the bell had rung. She was in a hurry. The two young girls who lived down the street were waiting for their German lessons, and she was late.

Lotte found me playing solitaire in the kitchen and quickly relayed this information before she left. When I went to the front to greet the honeymooners, I was surprised to see him but not her. Her absence was quickly explained. She had been left sitting on a bench near the fountain on the grounds of the Villa Comunale two hours earlier while he went in search of a room. Unwittingly, he'd left her longer than intended. After a somewhat frustrating search, he'd asked a man sitting on the front stoop of a nearby apartment building for advice. The man, who'd seemed rather bewildered at first by the interruption, had kindly pointed to the Pensione Alexandra. In the meantime, she had stayed in the park, standing guard over his easel and painting supplies as well as their luggage. He would go and fetch her once a room had been secured for their stay. He was reasonably certain that she would still be there. Where would she go? He could not imagine that she would be elsewhere.

When he returned an hour later, he was accompanied by a young woman who appeared to be about the same age as Mela and Lotte, and who most assuredly was his daughter, not his wife. I apologized for Lotte's confusion and explained that she must have been thinking about the German lessons she was about to give and had misunderstood his requirements. I had not been told that his daughter was accompanying them. Clearly, they would need two rooms, not one, one for him and his wife and the other for their daughter.

As soon as I said these words, I was struck by one phrase Lotte had used as she'd run out the door, "a honeymoon of sorts," and, in my moment of clarity, I considered the question: *Who would bring a twenty-year-old daughter on their honeymoon?* Unfortunately, this moment occurred only after I had spoken.

You can imagine my embarrassment when he responded that there was no mistake. There was no daughter. This was his wife. And that is how I met Herr Doktor Josef Samson and his much younger wife, Kaethe, a very quiet and reserved girl in her early twenties. As I stood there recovering from my mistake, I observed a very refined-looking, well-dressed, and well-groomed young woman, quite attractive, with excellent posture and a long neck that gave her a very graceful appearance. I still remember saying to myself, *My gosh, he is as old as Paul, and she is as young as Mela. Paul better not get any crazy-in-the-head ideas.*

That day, when we first met, I had no idea that Josef and Kaethe would become two of our most favorite guests at the Pensione Alexandra. They would return each year, usually for the last ten days in September and always with his easel, paints, and brushes. In 1939, they surprised us with an unannounced spring visit. Then, after that visit, after they left Naples to return to Paris, we lost all contact. At the time, it seemed as if they had vanished from the face of the earth.

Of course, on the first day they appeared, I had no reason to imagine how close and special our friendship would become. That day, all I knew was that they were a bit of a mystery, and I was curious to know more of their story. Why would an elegantly dressed German-speaking man wearing a beret and with a paint smudge on his well-tailored jacket, a man who appeared as old as Paul and who was accompanied by his German-speaking wife, a very refined, well-dressed, quiet and reserved girl with a long, graceful neck and excellent posture, who seemed young enough to be his daughter, travel from Paris to Naples for a honeymoon of sorts carrying two suitcases, a painter's easel, paints, and brushes? Who were they, and what were they really doing here?

With time, we would learn many of their answers. That night was like most others at the Pensione Alexandra. After our dinner, Paul fell asleep on the balcony. Mela, Lotte, and I stayed up and speculated. Mela wondered whether they were foreign agents in the same way she'd convinced us to wonder about the man from Vienna. Today, as I sit here, I am reasonably certain they were not. That evening, it was late when the girls left for bed. But I stayed up later. I quietly sat by myself for an hour, watching the moon as it rose over the Bay of Naples. There was too much to think about.

CHAPTER THIRTY

Our guests were frequently a puzzle. At the Pensione Alexandra, we rarely knew who to expect or when they would arrive, and we always enjoyed the mystery of the unknown. Each morning, I woke with the anticipation that someone with a new story might be about to walk through our doors. Sometimes, we knew who would arrive, but typically, we had no idea and would find ourselves amazed. Herr Doktor Josef Samson and Kaethe were two of many who surprised us when they suddenly appeared on our doorstep.

Mela was always trying to unravel the mysteries. She loved looking for conspiracies and creating stories that matched the circumstances. When the three nuns from Rome arrived, Mela was certain that the pope had banished them to Naples and that there had to be a very good reason. When the man from Vienna came to visit, she convinced us that his accent was wrong, that he could not be from Vienna, and that he was most certainly a spy.

But it wasn't only the puzzles. Each day, I learned a new lesson, as in the case of Josef and Kaethe, when I opened my mouth to solve a problem before a question was even asked. And with each day's lesson, I gained more experience and became more confident. I was becoming comfortable with my role as the *madre della casa*. Paul told me my personality had changed, that my shyness had been replaced by a stubborn determination. To this day, I am not sure what he was trying to tell me or whether that was a compliment. I only know that what he told me was true. Each day, I was learning new things and seeing the world through different eyes. Each day brought a new challenge and gave me a sense of accomplishment.

One lesson I learned many times over was that it is better to respect a secret than attempt to unravel it in public. Privacy is more than a desire. When people open up their hearts or unburden themselves of their secrets, they don't expect to hear their innermost thoughts repeated. Sometimes, it is best to keep one's privacy to oneself. That lesson has served me well in life.

And I didn't need to own a pensione to learn another important lesson. Most people enjoy telling their story, particularly to strangers they may never see again. I never knew what prompted them to act this way, but it would happen time after time. Usually, all that was required was a pair of willing ears to sit patiently, listen, and not judge.

Herr Doktor Josef Samson and his much younger wife, Kaethe, were two people who valued their privacy.

They divulged little. It is fair to say they kept their secrets where they were most protected. They chose to keep their secrets to themselves. I always felt that they both thought that the world would gain little by learning too much about them. They never seemed to think of themselves as deserving of attention. Their desire for privacy appeared to be more a function of their modesty and the nature of who they were than a deeply held desire to keep secrets that no one else would discover.

I say this to you so you will understand that what we knew about them and what I am sharing with you took several visits and a number of years to learn. I have always tried to respect their privacy and have refrained from telling others much of their story. Of course, now so many years have passed. Perhaps it is time to tell you more about them.

Over the course of their visits, Josef and Kaethe became dear and close friends, and much of what we learned about them was through observation, not words. There were no boasts or claims. They did not like to talk about themselves. They were distinguished by their personalities and character. Today, I can't imagine what they would think of me telling you all of this. It was so long ago when our lives intersected that they would be mystified as to why I would bother to remember them now.

One question was easily answered the very next morning. Who was the man sitting on the stoop of the apartment building the previous afternoon, the man who'd recommended the Pensione Alexandra? Even before putting on his apron to wash the breakfast dishes, Consolato asked for a referral fee. He had been sitting with a friend, enjoying his afternoon wine, when the older gentleman had stopped and asked for a recommendation. Consolato assured me that he was always looking out for our monetary interests.

CHAPTER THIRTY-ONE

Josef and Kaethe came into our world at the beginning of such a dreadful time. We were all drawn together by mutual confusion. We had been tossed around, and each of us was beginning to learn that we had little idea as to which part of the world we belonged to anymore. I believe that was something we shared in common. Just as we'd had the incident with our former friends at the German club, Kaethe had experienced a similar encounter with her brother in Germany, although she chose never to share the details or explain the circumstance.

Josef had had his own experience. We were never given the complete explanation of what had caused him to so suddenly leave Germany and move to France. We never determined whether he had walked, run, been chased, or what he might have left behind. All he divulged was that he'd arrived in Paris in 1933, within days of the Reichstag fire in Berlin, just one month after Adolf Hitler had been sworn in as chancellor of Germany. I have never thought there was any connection to the firebombing of Germany's Parliament, but often, I have wondered whether there were enemies Josef might have left behind in Berlin. As open as he became on most things discussed, on this topic, he was closed. Paul always thought he was protecting Kaethe from something or someone. This was a mystery never revealed.

Josef was fifty-seven years old when we met him. Born in Berlin in 1878, he spent the first fifty-five years of his life there, moving to Paris only two years before he arrived at our doorstep with his much younger wife, Kaethe, on their first visit to Naples. He was a true Berliner, accustomed to the pleasures of big-city life and a patron of all its offerings, particularly the arts. He maintained a large, well-furnished twelve-room apartment in the heart of the city. In Berlin, whether he sat at restaurants, cafés, or the theater, or stood at museums and galleries, he was always accompanied by his prized wirehaired pointer, Herr Heinz, for many years a much-beloved member of Josef's household.

By profession, Josef was a physician, a doctor of internal medicine on the staff of Berlin's largest hospital. With an office at his apartment, he also maintained a successful and busy private practice. From what I gathered, he authored papers, presented lectures, taught courses at the university, was quite active within the medical community of Berlin, and maintained a wide circle of interesting friends.

He had been torn by his choice of career. Josef's first love was painting, and he'd initially chosen to study at Berlin's prestigious Art Institute, but he'd quickly switched to medical school after a professor's realistic evaluation of his talent and a critical self-assessment of his ability to earn a living while standing in front of an easel. Medicine had been a rewarding choice, allowing him to continue his interest in painting during his free time. Painting became a lifelong hobby, and he was an excellent artist. Some of his works attracted attention of patrons and even today are displayed in homes and buildings in America. His early friendships and training with a number of Berlin's rising young artists resulted in the walls of his apartment being adorned with fabulous paintings.

Music was another of his passions. Josef's interest in music, both piano and flute, was encouraged by his mother throughout his childhood. I have no memory of ever hearing him perform, so I cannot comment on his talent, although Kaethe told me that he was very accomplished and that, in Paris, he rose early each morning to practice his skills.

He truly was what I would call a renaissance man: educated, sophisticated, talented, active, and always serious about his passions. He liked to travel and explore. He was fond of hiking and spoke often of his walks in the Swiss and Austrian Alps. He loved to talk about visits to northern Italy and Switzerland, hikes in the Dolomites, stays along Lake Maggiore, and particularly the walks near Lugano which he seemed particularly attracted to.

Throughout his travels he rarely ventured far without his easel and paints.

Josef had been married before, right after the turn of the century, about the same time Paul and I were married. His first wife was an American from a wealthy San Francisco family. She had been studying in Berlin when they'd met. They did not have children. Tragically, ten years after they were married, she died of complications following a surgery. I learned this from Kaethe, who told me that Josef's apartment in Berlin had remained unchanged. Josef never spoke one word about this matter.

Neither Josef nor Kaethe shared any information about the ensuing fourteen years, the time between the death of his first wife and when he met Kaethe. All I could deduce was that he'd continued to live the life he had always lived, busy with his medical practice and enjoying his free time hobbies. This was simply a time he neglected to talk about. As he was a widower during those years and Kaethe was still a young child, it could be that he had no interest in sharing the details since they certainly had nothing to do with Kaethe.

Kaethe was twenty-five years old when we met, that day I mistook her as Josef's daughter, close in age to Mela and Lotte. Like Josef, Kaethe was also born in Berlin, but in 1910, thirty-two years later. She had two older brothers. One died of tuberculosis following World War I. The other was married, had two daughters, and lived in Germany. There were also a number of cousins. Kaethe had developed a warm relationship with her young nieces, but apparently, her family connections had ceased when she'd moved to Paris to be with Josef. The only exception had been her father.

Kaethe's mother died when Kaethe was twelve years old. By all accounts, she must have had a difficult relationship with her mother, but I have no idea if that was a result of her mother's illness. I did form the impression that Kaethe had more of her father's personality than her mother's. On numerous occasions, Kaethe mentioned that her mother had been demanding and critical, often berating Kaethe's appearance and ability when she practiced ballet. With her father, it was quite the opposite. Kaethe was very close to her father, a man nearly the same age as Josef. Sadly, Kaethe's father had died the preceding year shortly after visiting Josef and Kaethe in Paris.

Now, as I tell you this, I realize we know more of Josef than of Kaethe. I suppose that is a function of his longer life and the result of Josef's broad array of interests. As for Kaethe, despite having spent many hours in conversation with her, I never learned of any hobbies or interests she may have had. I was left with the distinct impression there were none. In fact, I cannot give you an account of anything she did with her time other than that she kept house and devoted all of her energies to Josef.

Kaethe and Josef's relationship developed in late 1928, when they both lived in Berlin, when she was eighteen years of age and he was fifty. I have always wondered but never was told how they met. As best I know, even from the photographs she showed me of their Berlin apartment, when Kaethe entered his life, Josef changed little to make room for her. She brought few things of her own when she joined Josef's world. I believe this was quite understandable. He was quite settled in his ways, and she was quite young.

First impressions can be misleading. If you have pictured their relationship as an older man preying upon the charms of a young woman, or a charming young woman seeking the fortunes of a much older man, disregard either impression. Nothing could be further from the truth.

⁂

Throughout the entire time Paul and I knew them, we were continually struck by how different Josef's personality was from Kaethe's. In so many ways, they seemed like opposites pulled together from the extremes of two different sides. He was active, talkative, informed, opinionated, and outgoing. She was reserved, somewhat reticent, cautious and quiet, rare to differ or venture an opinion. Later, I learned that Kaethe did have opinions and they could be expressed in private moments. However, in unfamiliar company, she maintained her distance and chose to keep her thoughts to herself.

Josef and Kaethe were both exceedingly polite. She, in particular, was very respectful. Her behavior might have resulted from the fact that Josef, Paul, and I were of one generation and she another. But I doubt this was the reason, as her manners seemed part of her demeanor. She seemed very well bred. Other than the rare occasions when she was with Mela and Lotte, I never saw Kaethe interact with any others her age, but I assume she would have been equally polite and respectful. She never spoke of having any close friends.

Kaethe would listen carefully before she ever spoke. She would never dare to interrupt anyone else while they were speaking. And if she was ever impatient, it was a side of her that never showed. Only once or twice did I see her angry, but even that was closely held. You had to watch her face for the sign; it was such a momentary flash in her eyes. In conversation, I never saw her hurried. Her hurry was something that one noticed only in her steps when she walked.

As different as their personalities appeared, it was clear that Josef and Kaethe were exceptionally close, as close as anyone I had ever met. Their arms were always linked, and they watched over one another with endearing care. When you were with them, whatever differences they might have had disappeared. They were a curious couple to be with. Many times, in their actions, it appeared their ages had reversed. I would think that she was much older and he was much younger. The impression left was that they were quite happy to have met one another somewhere near the middle. They were very protective of each other.

Their religions were different. He was Jewish. She was not, and they shared a time when others made that an issue. It was clear that what others thought made no difference. To them, their religious beliefs seemed not to matter. They seemed to have little interest. They knew who they were. I never saw either pray. I know they never went to the synagogue or attended church. If they expressed any belief, it was in one another, and if they observed any customs, the customs were their own.

Some of their differences were not so easily discerned and left me confused. There was never a question about Josef's education. He was a student of everything and well trained in his field. Gaining knowledge seemed his goal. Curious and inquisitive, he was committed to studying and learning. With Kaethe, one was never quite certain. Her silence masked much. With regard to schooling, Kaethe had little. Whatever formal education she received ended early, when she was no more than sixteen. Yet when she spoke, her lack of education was well hidden. Her intelligence seemed always apparent, and whether true or not, she gave one the impression of having a kind of wisdom that was well beyond her years. She always conducted herself in a very mature manner. It was easy to conclude that Kaethe knew much more than she revealed.

Josef was clearly a student of politics. Many of our conversations were laced with his conclusions and views. He could have been an activist of some sort or involved in some type of intelligence service. Although I never was able to confirm how active he might have been, I was always left with the impression that he had played a significant role in opposing Hitler's rise to power. As for Kaethe, I have the impression that she had no interest in any of these matters. I can't recall a single instance when she disclosed her opinion on any political issue or expressed support for one side or the other. On these topics, I have no idea what she thought.

While Josef's talents for painting and music were often put on display, Kaethe was his opposite. When he painted, she chose to sit silently and watch or pose. How long did not matter. She could spend the day and not care. When he performed, she preferred to listen to his music and would patiently turn the pages.

He had traveled the world. She had not. What she knew of places, she had learned from him. His curiosity and resources would take him wherever he wanted to go. She appeared perfectly content to follow his lead. She enjoyed the scenery. Her role was to sit by his side.

Neither appeared moody. They knew how to laugh with others and how to laugh at themselves. They both had a sense of humor. But neither were funny, and they never acted that way. Both took life seriously. I would not characterize either as emotional. Both seemed to consider before they acted, Josef because he was trained in that manner. It was Kaethe's silence that made her appear that way.

Physically, they were an attractive couple, he not overly handsome, she not overly beautiful, but beautiful and handsome nonetheless. It may have been the way they carried themselves, with good posture, good bearing, and grace. He appeared his age and never seemed wanting to be something he was not. She dressed with maturity, classic and timeless, and was always well groomed. Dignified and refined, I never thought she desired to appear older; it was simply the way she conducted herself naturally.

I am certain that it would be easy to conclude that he was the father figure to her and she was the daughter figure to him, but I actually never was given that impression. Their relationship was something different. I always felt that they filled a space quite well together, he doing his part and she doing hers. If that left little gaps between them, these did not show. Any openings were sealed with caring and respect. It was as if they loved one another so much that they refused to waste any time with those things that did not matter. Maybe their difference in years made that so.

So, for me, I am sure you can see that Josef and Kaethe made quite an impression. The more we knew of their story, the closer our friendship became. I believe they would have said the same of us. There are some friendships one never forgets. And even with the closest of friends, sometimes, there are secrets that will never be divulged and mysteries that always remain unanswered.

CHAPTER THIRTY-TWO

We saw little of Josef and Kaethe during their first days in Naples. Josef had a lengthy list of things to be accomplished. At breakfast each morning, he was busy consulting his much-worn copy of the *Baedeker's Guide* to Southern Italy. Many pages were dog-eared and marked, and he always had a list filled with questions to ask us. Then they would set off for the day, and we would seldom see them until late afternoon.

    I imagine they visited the typical sights: the Museo Nazionale, the Aquarium, the triumphal arch in the Castel Nuovo, the Porta Capuana, several of the churches, I assume the Cathedral, Santa Chiara, San Domenico, and Monte Oliveto. I doubt they missed the view from the belvedere of San Marino and don't recall if they took excursions to Vesuvius and Pompeii or Sorrento or Capri. But I would presume they did as most tourists, splitting their time between the sights of the city and excursions to ancient ruins and the Amalfi coast. If one of our guests asked for a suggestion along the coast, I always recommended my favorite, Ravello, where one can take a lovely hike down the steep hill to Amalfi for a rewarding midday meal at a seaside café. The return hike to be taken up the hill is the perfect excuse for a delicious and rich dessert.

What I do remember is that their afternoons were reserved for Josef's paintings and that they always ate their evening meal early at the pensione. Then they would walk along Via Caracciolo and the Bay of Naples to the Aquarium and back after their dinner. I do recall that, early in their first visit, they dined out one evening at a local restaurant that we'd recommended but Kaethe found the food to be not to her liking. After that experience, they always chose to dine in. I always found her a bit peculiar in that regard. The only Italian food she seemed to enjoy was my gnocchi, which, to me, was more German than Italian.

Each evening, once they returned and after I finished organizing the next day's breakfast and the kitchen was closed, Paul and I would join Josef and Kaethe on the balcony for conversation. One night, we told them about the incident at the German club. I wanted to hear Josef 's perspective. I couldn't comprehend how Germans were attracted to Hitler. I was struggling to make sense of the events that had overtaken Germany. It wasn't that we were unfamiliar with the news. We had all heard stories, but my visits to Germany had stopped after my parents had died. I was unable to understand how Hitler and the Nazis had been allowed to come to power. Who were his supporters? How was it possible that, within such a short period of time, Hitler could destroy Jewish life in Germany?

Josef was able to give us his firsthand account, and it was much different from the occasional sentences in letters written from family. He was in close contact with friends who remained in Germany. With Josef, I was able to ask questions. His perspective was totally different from Vincenzo's. Josef had spent his life in Germany. He was Jewish. Josef could understand things Vincenzo could only observe. I remembered Vincenzo's lessons well. He had taught me to be a keen listener, to gather my facts before stating my opinions. Once again, the Pensione Alexandra became my perch to listen and learn. It was my window to the world. Here is what Josef told us that week.

He began with an unusual observation, one that I have never heard since. In order to understand what most Germans believed, Josef suggested we pay attention to the words in the first verse of "Deutschlandlied," the song of the Germans, which was adopted as the German national anthem in 1922.

From the Meuse to the Memel,
from the Adige to the Belt,
Germany, Germany above everything.

He reminded us that every German knows these words by heart. Every schoolchild in Germany has been taught to memorize and sing these words, and every German believes these words. One needs to understand what this verse says. It is a patriotic call to all Germans to build and

1922

unify their nation. It was written in a time when there was no real German nation, only many small states with German people living in them. These small, independent areas were generally within the borders of the four rivers in the verse: Meuse, Memel, Adige, and Belt. The verse is an appeal, a call to action, to all Germans to join together in one nation, the real Germany. Josef told me I should not be mistaken: "Hitler and the Nazis won't rest until Germany expands its borders and gives a home to all Germans. They will use their power to take the lands needed to support and protect the German people. They believe that is their righteous cause."

When "Deutschlandlied" was adopted as the national anthem, all Germans were reminded of what had been lost in World War I and what the Treaty of Versailles had taken from Germany. Germans believe that their lands needed to be recovered and the German people reunited. Josef said that to understand Hitler and the Nazis, I needed to know that this belief was in the hearts and minds of most Germans. Every time Germans stood and sang the national anthem, they were reminded.

In 1920, following Germany's defeat, the Treaty of Versailles, drafted by Britain, France, Italy, and the United States, severely punished Germany. Germany and her allies were forced to accept responsibility for the war. Germany had to give up her lands. Germany was permitted to keep only a small army with no modern weapons. The reparations Germany was forced to pay crippled the German economy and led to mass unemployment.

Josef suggested that it should come as little surprise that the German people were angry when the terms of the treaty were signed. Ordinary Germans were forced to pay the price for the actions of an unrepresentative government. The treaty restrictions on the German military meant that Germany was stripped of its ability to unify the people and lands that belonged together.

There were many who argued that the provisions of the treaty were too harsh, that the burden on the German people was too great, and that German pride would require that they fight to recover what they had lost. Many reasonable people agreed with that assessment, including Josef and a number of his closest friends.

In Josef's opinion, America's President, Woodrow Wilson, was naive when the Treaty of Versailles was signed. When America, France, and Britain redrew the map of Europe after World War I, they thought they could force people to change their history, one that spanned many generations. They thought they could redefine borders with the stroke of a pen. Now, having watched the wars I have seen in my lifetime, I have often thought that Joseph was right when he told us it was foolish to believe that people would forget where their ancestors had lived and what they had fought for.

After World War I, until 1933, Germany was governed by the Weimar Republic, an ambitious group of reformers who hoped to create a modern democracy. The first years were unsettled and marked by international isolation, attempted revolutions, hyperinflation, and mass unemployment as the government struggled under the pressure of the Treaty of Versailles. Street protestors blamed the leaders of the Weimar Republic for accepting the terms of the treaty. Threatening incidents and extremist uprisings brought the government to near collapse.

At one point, the Weimar Republic was teetering on the verge of disaster. It was saved when a coalition of moderate parties took control and gave Germany a government that could successfully govern. This started a period of stability and success, and by the mid-1920s, Germany entered a time when the economy and cultural life flourished. For Josef and Kaethe, Berlin was a wonderful place to live during those years.

Unfortunately, the good years did not last. By 1930, Germans felt the impact of the Great Depression. Josef thought it was far worse in Germany than what we experienced in Italy. Foreign loans collapsed. There were runs on the banks. Millions were unemployed, and Germany's economy, for the working class, was a disaster. Adolf Hitler's National Socialist German Workers' Party, which had been roundly defeated in the 1922 elections, took to the streets and, with angry rhetoric, redoubled their protests. Hitler boldly promised to restore Germany's eminence in the world order, to reunite the German lands and people, to make Germany great once more.

He promised more jobs. He vowed to defy the Treaty of Versailles and institute a draft to create a larger army and a navy and air force. Hitler argued that a larger military would create more jobs and reduce unemployment, making him popular both with the unemployed and the military. He promised a strong and stable government, widely supported by industrialists, who were terrified of the left-wing unions and communism.

Hitler had a strong message and the skills to deliver it. He gained a large following, particularly among those who had been hurt by the economy. The worse the economy became, the more he gained in popularity with ordinary Germans looking for confident leadership.

No one should be surprised that the German politicians exploited the anger of Germany's citizens. All the politicians did to one degree or another, and many were right. Things did need to change in Germany. Hitler, with his fiery rhetoric and the gangs of thugs who followed him, was more successful than the others, particularly those in power, who were forced to defend their actions.

Hitler blamed the current leadership for not being strong enough, for not doing enough for the German people, for not acting decisively and fast enough. And then he pointed his finger at the very tiny Jewish segment of the German population, less than one percent. They were to blame. They were the ones responsible for Germany's economic collapse. They had stolen Germany's wealth. They had filled jobs needed by the German people. They had profited at Germany's expense. They were the reason Germany had lost World War I. His message was that Jews had never belonged in Germany. They were not real Germans.

In 1932, Hitler's Nazi Party did not win a majority, but they captured one-third of the vote for the German Parliament, more than any other party. By January 1933, Hitler had consolidated his power and was named Germany's chancellor.

I will always remember Josef's final comments. "If you fill a room with one hundred people from Germany, only one will be a Jew. That is how small the number of Jews are in Germany. Most Germans have never met a Jew. All most Germans know about Jews is what they have been told. Most Germans have no Jewish friends. The Jews in Germany have kept themselves apart and been kept apart. You ask: who are the supporters of Hitler and the Nazis? You are asking the wrong questions. You should be asking: who in Germany supports the Jews? Who are their defenders?"

⇌

As we spent our evenings together during that first visit, our friendship continued to grow. Slowly, we discovered our common histories. We found that we shared many of the same questions and searched for many of the same answers. On issues like religion, race, and nationality, none of us questioned who we were. But we knew that others did, and that left us confused. What kind of Germans were we? Who was entitled to make that decision? What part of a Jew will forever be Jewish? What part of our religion still belonged to our race? Could one be German if one was a Jew? Could one be Jewish if one was a German?

And before their ten-day visit to Naples was over, just as Vincent Sheean had become Vincenzo, they asked that we call them Josef and Kaethe. We, in turn, asked them to call us Paul and Elsa. It is funny how little things set people apart. Vincenzo had insisted that we use first names on the day we'd first met him. With Josef and Kaethe, that level of informality did not occur until the end of their first visit. I have always wondered if this was a function of culture, the difference in the way Americans and Germans handle these things, or a function of trust.

As for Kaethe, she never felt comfortable calling us Elsa and Paul. Perhaps that was her way of saying that she wanted something more in our friendship or because her own mother had died when she was so young. Maybe this was because her father had died the year before. So, for Kaethe, I became Mamarella, the nickname Paul and my children always used for me, and Paul became Papa. Paul always felt that Kaethe saw us more in the light of parents and that she wanted to belong to a family.

When they were leaving, Josef presented me with a wonderful watercolor he had painted. He called it *One More Moon*. It was the view of the Bay of Naples from our balcony. Josef knew how much I enjoyed watching the moon. He'd worked on it late in the evenings after we had all gone to bed. It was one of the most beautiful paintings I have ever seen, and it became one of my most cherished possessions.

On their way out the door, he mentioned one last thing. It was the reason he'd referred to their visit as a *honeymoon of sorts*. Ever since Kaethe had joined him in Paris, for various reasons, he had never found the time to gather the papers necessary for a marriage ceremony. He assured me that they would marry sometime soon. I laughed and told him I thought Kaethe was *crazy in the head* to put up with such an old man who was becoming so forgetful. He was lucky to have her in his life.

CHAPTER THIRTY-THREE

It was only a few months following Josef and Kaethe's visit, early in 1936, when I received a postcard from Dusseldorf, Germany. My brother, Martin, had written and summarized the new Nuremberg laws adopted by the Nazi government. Martin began by saying he would describe the laws in the way he would explain a medical condition to one of his patients. This was his clinical observation, perhaps not what I wanted to hear nor what he wanted to say, but his most honest objective assessment of the situation.

1) By law, Jews were no longer German citizens. All rights to citizenship had been revoked. Jews were now state subjects, excluded from the workforce, economy, and most aspects of society, and encouraged to leave Germany.

2) German citizens were being given the jobs and positions Jews once held. Jews were being forced to sell their businesses to German citizens at unfair prices. Employees of these businesses were being replaced with German citizens.
3) Support for Hitler and the Nazis by German citizens was growing throughout Germany. Hitler was doing what he'd promised. No one should be surprised. He was reclaiming and rebuilding Germany for the Aryan race. He was creating the German empire.
4) Martin's conclusion? There was no place for Jews in Germany. Unless the situation changed, there would come a time when the Germans would not know what to do with the Jews who'd refuse to leave their empire.

He'd added a postscript: "Please write Jenny in Koenigsberg. She remains as stubborn as she always has been and refuses to leave Mother's house. Tell her to leave for America at once."

—❖ ❖—

In 1936, none of us could imagine how true Martin's conclusion would become.

CHAPTER THIRTY-FOUR

Martin's postcard was abrupt. His message was frightening, and his prediction terrifying. What haunts me is that an entire country knew this and no one prevented his warning from actually becoming true.

When I was growing up, I was taught that Germany was the center of the universe. We were all taught that. It was the German way of thinking. We were always competitive. All things were compared to Germany. Who was bigger? Who was better? Who was stronger? Who was more advanced? Whose lives were richer? And the conclusion was always Germany. We were taught to be proud Germans. And we were proud. We all believed that the German people were the finest people on earth.

We never thought ourselves arrogant. It was simply our view of the world. Now I know better, and I understand how this arrogance must sound to others. But then, arrogant or not, that was our attitude, and we all accepted it as truth. I suppose that when pride is added to nationalism, the result is patriotism. Now I know that, without proper checks and balances, patriotism can become a powerful force of evil.

When Vincenzo had stayed with us, he had warned of this German sense of superiority. He felt that Germans had been taught to be loyal followers, that we had been taught not to question the belief that Germans were better or to question our leaders. He'd told me that, in his travels and reporting, he had seen what can happen when one group of people is taught that they are better and more deserving than another.

For the first thirty-five years we lived in Naples, our friends were all German. We all had been taught that way of thinking. We were fond of Italy and enjoyed its people, but we were convinced that our German way of life was better.

That night at the German club was the first time I had a taste of what it is like to be on the other end of this attitude. Others throughout the world have known this their entire lives and have experienced a level of pain, suffering, and discrimination that I will never know. I suppose we all are products of what our parents and teachers have taught us. I refuse to believe that people are born to think this way. We are all God's creatures. Why else would a nation of people show such a total disregard for the lives of their fellow human beings? There is a very fine line between arrogance and hatred. Germany's Nazis may have chosen to cross it, but an entire nation of more than sixty million people chose to follow.

≕ ⇌

In the months after Martin's postcard telling us about the Nuremberg laws, we heard many other rumors and reports about Hitler and Nazi Germany. It was clear that Germany wanted the Jews to leave their borders and that the German government was making life miserable for Germany's Jewish population who'd chosen to stay.

Jewish officers were expelled from the army. Jewish university students were no longer allowed to sit for doctoral exams. Jews were being forced out of their businesses, and the new owners were dismissing workers and managers. Jewish lawyers were no longer allowed to practice the law and appear before courts. Jewish university professors and teachers were being fired or forced to retire. Jews were being fired from lower-status government jobs like messengers, street cleaners, and train and postal workers. Quotas were being placed on the number of Jewish students who could attend schools and universities. Jewish patients were no longer admitted to municipal hospitals. Jewish doctors and dentists were excluded from the national health insurance system.

I believe most Jews in Germany recognized that they needed to leave. But recognizing and acting are two different things. It is difficult to leave a country that has been your home for generations and where you believe you belong. It is heartbreaking to leave a country when family members are left behind. It is nearly impossible to leave if you are frail or weak or if you don't have the resources or the energy or the strength that it takes. And hope and denial can be terrible curses. Far too many waited too long believing that this crisis would pass.

CHAPTER THIRTY-FIVE

I remember how thrilled we were to learn that Alex and Lotte had decided to marry. They were so excited to announce their news. Mela could not have been happier. Lotte was the sister she had always wanted. And me? I could not imagine having a more wonderful daughter-in-law. My matchmaking skills had worked. Just as my friend Trude and I had planned, by placing the two dots near one another, we'd only needed to wait for fate and magnetic attraction to perform their magic.

They would have a small civil ceremony, held in the afternoon. That was what they wanted. Paul, Mela, and I would be the only ones there from our family. Theo was busy in Milan. Arthur had found work in Bolzano. The times were just not right for anything more. There were three others who joined us. Two of Lotte's oldest friends from Koenigsberg travelled to Naples by train. And as a surprise, they brought Lotte's mother, Trude, my old childhood friend. It was so good to see her. I learned that just as I had been renamed Mamarella by my family, Trude had been renamed Mutti. Alex teased us endlessly, Mutti and Mamarella, what a fine pair of old ladies we were. We laughed so hard. The wedding could not have come at a better time. We all needed some happiness in our lives.

Lotte's old friends George and Nina were a delightful young couple. Nina was Lotte's maid of honor, and George served as Alex's best man. George and Alex had never met before, but it was easy to see that they would form a lifelong friendship.

Although the ceremony was held in front of a magistrate at the municipal building, I think we all found it perfect. I had never seen my son Alex so serious, almost scared. He had always been the silly one, everyone's favorite, always happy and funny and without a care in the world. Now, no matter how hard he tried, Paul couldn't even get him to crack a smile. He looked so grown-up in his dark suit with his hair brushed back, him so tall and Lotte so short. It was easy to see how much he loved her. His chin wouldn't stop quivering as he tried to get his words out. I didn't think Mela would ever stop crying. It was the kind of wedding ceremony I like the best: simple, serious, and full of tears. Who could ask for more?

To celebrate, Paul insisted that we all go to a restaurant in Posillipo. During dinner, George suggested we avoid any conversation about the situation in Germany. He was right. They were glad to get away from Koenigsberg. Why spoil such a happy event with depressing thoughts? As for

Nina, I found her very engaging, and we had a delightful time visiting with one another. She had been trained as an artist, a sculptress, and her passion for her work reminded me of my sister Jenny. I had never met someone with this type of training before and found myself curious. Ever since I was a young child, I have been impressed with people who can mold art with their bare hands. My feeble attempts were limited to trying to create puppets and stuffed animals when the children were young. I always found those efforts challenging, far exceeding my powers of observation and beyond the ability of my less-than-nimble fingers.

I think one has to focus, observe, and understand so much more in order to add a sculptor's depth and dimension to something created. It requires skills much more complex than sketching on a flat piece of paper. On my better days, I believe that I possess a modicum of talent when it comes to small bits of drawing, a hobby that I pursue in only my most private moments. This is an interest that is seldom shared and limited by my lack of self-confidence. I can't begin to imagine molding something from clay or casting a figure in bronze. I told Nina of my fascination with the street scenes in Naples, children playing in the street or in the parks, and that I thought it would be challenging to create a sculpture of two children on a seesaw. I can imagine it, but I would never have the nerve, the ability, the training, or the confidence to attempt to mold it with my hands. I remember suggesting this piece as an idea for her portfolio one day.

The wedding party ended almost as quickly as it had started. Alex and Lotte left on a brief honeymoon in the company of Nina and George. Alex wanted to share some of the Amalfi coast with them. He had fond memories of Sorrento, where we used to take a small house for a week in the summer when the children were young. I loved visiting with Trude, but there was never enough time, only the evenings on the balcony. With Lotte away, I had more work to do. As for Paul and me? We rejoiced in Alex and Lotte's happiness. Then we went back to our daily life. I was short one pair of hands. There were rooms to fill, and I had a pensione to run.

CHAPTER THIRTY-SIX

For four years, Hitler planned and promised to use Germany's strength to expand its borders and reunite Germans across the German empire. And as Josef suggested, reuniting Germany was not only Hitler's dream. This had been the patriotic dream of much of the German population years before he came into power, ever since World War I had ended. Resisting the Treaty of Versailles, Germany began rebuilding its military not long after it was signed. Germany stretched the rules. Submarine crews were trained abroad. Pilots practiced using civilian planes. When Hitler became Germany's chancellor in 1933, he instituted a far more ambitious and secret program. In direct violation of the treaty, within two years, the Nazis had twenty-five hundred warplanes in its air force and had built an army of three hundred thousand men, three times the size allowed.

In 1935, Hitler made his plans public. He unilaterally canceled the military clauses of the Treaty of Versailles and defiantly announced that he would reinstate compulsory military conscription. The army would be increased to 550,000 men. By 1937, new weapons were being manufactured day and night. Industries had been transformed, and Germany's youth had been molded into soldiers. Unemployment problems had been solved, and the German economy was booming.

During the months that followed, Hitler engaged in heavy-handed diplomacy and bluffed, bullied, and threatened as he pursued his plans. One of his first targets was Austria, a country torn from within by conspiring Austrian Nazis and whose external borders were threatened by German troops amassed to make it appear that an invasion was imminent.

In early 1938, Austrian Nazis attempted to seize the Austrian government by force and unite Austria with Germany for the second time in four years. In Vienna, political unrest caused economic panic. People withdrew their money from banks. Business was disrupted. Tourists stayed home. Learning of the conspiracy, Austria's leaders met with Hitler in the hope of maintaining their country's independence. Instead, they were met with defiance. Hitler insisted that Austrian leaders be replaced with Austrian Nazis. Hoping to resolve the question of a union with Germany once and for all, a national vote was scheduled. But before the vote could take place, Austria's Chancellor resigned. He pleaded for the Austrian military not to resist a German advance and avoid the carnage that would result.

One issue remained for Hitler. He wasn't certain how Mussolini would react to a German invasion of Italy's neighbor. An emissary was quickly sent to Rome to ask for Mussolini's approval. Some say he carried a letter containing the false claim that Austria was plotting to attack Germany and that Hitler's forces would defend Germany. Mussolini gave his consent.

The following day, Adolf Hitler accompanied German troops as they roared across the German-Austrian border in tanks and armored vehicles. He was met by enthusiastic crowds. They met no resistance and, in most places, were welcomed like heroes. Hitler appointed a new Nazi government in Austria, and Austria was incorporated into the German Empire.

Without firing a single shot, Germany gained seven million people, an army of one hundred thousand, and steel and iron ore to add to its empire. Neighboring Czechoslovakia recognized that it was surrounded on three sides by the German Army. And Hitler and the Nazis began considering their plans for the occupation of Czechoslovakia's Sudetenland, home to about three million ethnic Germans. Hitler was fulfilling his promise. He was rebuilding the German empire for Germans.

When news of the invasion reached Britain and France, their leaders did nothing. In France, internal political problems prevented any military response. French politics were in turmoil. Two days earlier, the entire French government had resigned. France was in no position to oppose the invasion.

Britain was having its own political problems. The foreign secretary had resigned over the prime minister's decision to open negotiations with Mussolini. In Britain, there was no political will to oppose Germany. For most, the unification of Austria and Germany was not seen as a threat to Britain. Both nations were German-speaking, and there was no good reason why Austria and Germany shouldn't unify. Most of the world paid little attention to these events and thought this was an internal matter far away in a foreign country that they need not meddle in.

In Germany, Nazi newspapers printed a fictitious telegram saying that Austria had requested help from the German government because of rioting in Vienna and street fights involving Communists. Hitler told the world that the Austrians themselves, desperate to restore order, had requested military assistance from Germany.

CHAPTER THIRTY-SEVEN

This was such a strange time, and we had little factual understanding of the events that were taking place. We received little news, and the news we received was tightly controlled. Unless personally affected, most of us had little interest in what was going on elsewhere. Only weeks after Germany captured control of Austria, large headlines in our papers announced that Hitler would be making a state visit to Italy. Hitler wanted to thank Mussolini for supporting the German army and their efforts to contain the rioting in Austria. [handwritten annotation: staged & paid for by Nazi's — just like Obama did in Charlottesville, DC, etc]

Newspapers in Italy told us that Germany's resolution of the Austrian crisis was a mission of peace widely supported by the Austrian people. The upcoming visit would cement the bond of friendship between our two countries. Major preparations were underway in Rome for a tremendous welcoming ceremony for Germany's leader.

Within days, in the most unusual way, I learned that a visit to Naples was to be included on Mussolini's itinerary.

On that particular morning, I was returning from the Porta Nolana fish market and walking down Via Caracciolo along the waterfront, not far from the pensione, when I happened upon our old friend Professor Renato Caccioppoli, the brilliant and celebrated mathematician who taught at the University of Naples. We had known Renato and his family for years, ever since he'd attended primary school with our eldest son, Theo. His father, Giuseppe, was a surgeon who had treated Paul once. I can't remember what his ailment was.

Encountering Renato on Via Caracciolo was not an infrequent occurrence. Nearly every day, he would pass by the Pensione Alexandra when he walked his little dog along the seafront promenade. Often, he would stop to visit a fellow faculty member who had rented a room from us at the pensione, a very nice man, I believe a professor of economics.

What made this particular morning unusual was that Professor Caccioppoli held a leash in his hand but was not walking his dog. I had to look several times to be certain I understood what I was seeing. That morning, I was more than a little astonished to see a rooster proudly strutting on the other end of Renato's leash.

I suppose those of us who knew Professor Caccioppoli would not find this moment as odd as it might first appear. Many of us were accustomed to his strange and peculiar behavior. Renato was legendary and not only for his inventive mathematical concepts. Perhaps a function of his genius, he did have a history. He was known to make bold and outrageous displays of protest in public. His nonconformist temperament was well documented. Once, he tried living as a vagrant and was arrested for begging. That morning, it was obvious he was staging another form of protest.

In the rather lengthy and prolonged conversation that followed, as I tried to keep my distance from the rather frightening-looking rooster, Renato told me he was quite upset. He explained that he had tied the rooster to his leash to protest Hitler's upcoming visit to Naples. The Fascist party had recently advised men not to walk small dogs, like his chihuahua, because it was considered not very masculine and not a display of virility. To show his dissent, he had decided to walk with this rooster on his leash.

That morning was the longest time I have ever spent in the company of a rooster, and I never understood the mathematical sequence in Renato's mind that connected Adolf Hitler with a rooster. In any case, my chance meeting with Professor Caccioppoli was how I learned that Adolf Hitler, accompanied by Mussolini and King Victor Emmanuel III, would be including Naples on his state visit. I suppose that, even in a dictatorship, one is entitled to a little harmless resistance.

CHAPTER THIRTY-EIGHT

Mussolini and Hitler had met on two other occasions: first, in Venice in 1934, and then, three years later, after Mussolini had declared that all countries would rotate on the Rome-Berlin "Axis," he'd travelled to Germany to sign the Anti-Comintern Pact, a major step in forming the aptly named Axis alliance of Germany, Italy, and Japan.

Much has been written about the relationship between Mussolini and Hitler. I have found that most people think of the two as staunch and inseparable allies always working in close cooperation. Vincenzo and Josef had very strong opinions about both men. Having observed their behavior and actions, my own view is that their relationship was more complicated than might first appear and that it changed considerably with time. These were two men with overly developed egos, dreams, and ambitions.

I believe their alliance was a marriage of convenience, expedience, and, at times, necessity.

Some argue that they had different moral codes, that Mussolini was the more tolerant, which was certainly true for Jews in Italy during the first sixteen years of his rule. Personally, I believe that neither man had any moral code. If they swore any allegiance, it was to themselves. I firmly believe that, in the end, they both were tyrants and evil men.

I doubt that, in private, either had any trust in the other or, for that matter, even liked or approved of one another very much. Their egos would never have allowed it. Even when they became military allies, they often worked at cross-purposes, were secretive, and remained wary of one another's ambitions.

By the time Hitler rose to power in 1933, Mussolini had ruled Italy for eleven years, and he'd had dictatorial powers for the last eight of those years. Most describe Hitler as an admirer, an apprentice, that he deferred to Il Duce, the more senior dictator of the two. Hitler often acknowledged that Italian fascism was the elder brother of Nazism. Some suggest that the Munich Beer Hall Putsch was Hitler's failed attempt to copy Mussolini's March on Rome. Others note similarities between Mussolini's Blackshirts and Hitler's gangs of thugs.

I imagine part of their kinship was the distance both felt from Great Britain and France. In his fight to recreate the German Empire, Hitler relentlessly blamed Britain and France for the Treaty of Versailles and defiantly rebuilt his military power. When Mussolini invaded Ethiopia in his initial effort to rebuild the Roman

Empire, he found Germany and Italy shared a mutual disregard for the League of Nations. The Spanish Civil War also brought them closer together. They had a common cause, supporting Franco's nationalist forces and upending Europe's democratic order and fighting the spread of communism.

I believe that, by the time Hitler arrived for his state visit to Italy in the spring of 1938, their relationship had mostly tilted in Hitler's favor. By 1938, Hitler did not need Mussolini as much as Mussolini needed Hitler. Hitler's military was far more prepared for battle. Mussolini knew that his army would not be ready for several years. In 1938, when Hitler came to Italy and Mussolini put his army and navy on display, he wanted to impress Hitler. He wanted to convince Hitler that Italy remained a powerful and equal partner.

CHAPTER THIRTY-NINE

In early May of 1938, Hitler's entourage of three bomb- and bulletproof trains filled with some five hundred party officials, diplomats, security guards, and journalists, who were dressed in matching uniforms of a light brown tunic, black trousers, and black peaked caps, arrived in Rome at a train station specially built for their six-day visit to Italy. Even the sendoff in Germany had been spectacular. In Berlin, all government offices and businesses closed early that day in honor of Hitler's trip.

Upon arrival in Rome, the visiting Germans were greeted by Mussolini and King Victor Emmanuel, and Italians and the world were treated to a lavish spectacle, a magnified example of Fascist propaganda, and a massive display of Fascist power. In Rome, thirty-five thousand torchlights illuminated the colosseum. An improvised stadium was built to seat fifty thousand. The welcoming celebration included 11,500 performers and forty-five bands. The prisons were filled with persons of suspicion. Italian authorities took no chances with security. All possible enemies of the state were put under lock and key.

On the day the train approached Naples and Hitler and his party saw their first glimpse of Naples Bay, they were greeted by a gigantic sign hung on the slopes of Vesuvius that read "Heil Hitler." At the train station, which was decorated in Nazi and Italian Fascist symbols, thousands of Neapolitans stood to welcome the visitors. One thousand young Fascists drew their sabers and saluted as the motorcade left the station to begin the parade. The papers reported that half a million people lined the parade route that day.

Large Italian and German flags were draped from all the buildings along Via Caracciolo and the Naples waterfront. Security was everywhere. Armed guards in black shirts joined us on our third-floor balcony, and as we watched from around the flags, we had a bird's-eye view of the motorcade as it slowly passed by the Pensione Alexandra and turned around. I can't imagine how one could have a better view. Hitler stood in an open car and saluted and waved to the cheering crowds. It was as if he were looking directly at us. His ministers and other dignitaries rode in the cars that followed. We had never seen anything like this. Even the crowds for the Piedigrotta, the feast of the Madonna, when it seemed that every person in Naples spent the night on the streets with their trumpets and noisemakers, were not this large. I could not believe the number of people standing in front of the pensione that day.

Later, the official party boarded the battleship *Conte di Cavour* and reviewed the Italian fleet in a seven-hour exercise the newspapers described as the greatest naval demonstration in the world and the largest number of warships ever gathered in one place. Fourteen passenger ships lined Naples Bay, each filled with leaders of Italian society who had been invited to watch.

Under the clear skies and on a calm sea, nearly three hundred ships were involved. Forty-eight sea planes were launched from the decks of warships, and more than seventy others were sent aloft from land bases. Huge crowds of onlookers stood on the shoreline to watch the naval maneuvers. The review included all of the Italian Royal Navy's submarines, more than one hundred, doing a nautical ballet: submerging, emerging, firing salvos, submerging, all in unison, acting as one unit.

I don't agree, but the newspapers informed us that the highlight of this very lengthy demonstration of Italian force was the target practice with live shells against the *San Marco*, a ship controlled by wireless. From the Pensione Alexandra, we could only hear the explosions. All we could see from the balcony was the smoke. There was so much smoke in the air that we had no idea if the sun was shining or if the sky was clear.

Actually, I thought the day's highlight took place later that evening. We learned that our friend, Professor Caccioppoli, was at it again. He'd managed to convince an orchestra at an open-air restaurant to play the French anthem, "La Marseillaise," and then he stood up and made a speech against both dictators. As you can well imagine, he was quickly arrested.

I am certain his life was spared when he was able to avoid trial by a special political court instituted by the Fascists against their opponents. With the help of his aunt, a chemistry professor at the University of Naples, Renato was declared mad and eventually sent to an asylum. Later, he was allowed to live in less confined quarters, where he continued his writings. From there, he was able to submit his works to a journal published in the Vatican state away from the strict control of the Fascists.

CHAPTER FORTY

We should not have been surprised when the *leggi razziali*, the comprehensive set of Italian racial laws patterned after Germany's Nuremberg laws, were approved and announced by Mussolini's regime. There had been plenty of forewarning. That summer, not long after Hitler's visit to Italy, the *Manifesto Degli Scienziati Razzisti* was published in the newspapers. Signed by forty-two eminent Italians and embraced by Mussolini, the *Manifesto* presented a scientific explanation and justification for racism in Italy. It concluded that the civilization of Italy was of Aryan origin and declared that Jews do not belong to the pure Italian race. For the first time, the Italian people were told to be concerned about race. A continuing drumbeat of supporting propaganda emphasizing racism and slandering Jews continued in the newspapers all summer and fall.

like our media toward the Right.

There had been so many signs. I remember my son Arthur telling me that we should have listened when Mussolini had told the chief rabbi in Rome that there were no ill feelings about Jews in Italy and that Italy had no racial problems. Arthur never trusted the Fascists and wondered why Mussolini found it necessary to make such a statement. And there was the time after the invasion of Ethiopia, when we heard Mussolini warn Italians to not fraternize with the Ethiopians, when he was concerned that they, too, might infect the Italian race. Hitler's visit should have been the most important sign. The strength of the Italian army had failed to impress the Nazis. By now, we all understood what they were doing in Germany and Austria, and we began to recognize the threat to Italy.

What was surprising to most of us was the abrupt change in Mussolini's public behavior. Just as Vincenzo had predicted, Il Duce broke his promises. Throughout the years of his rule, Mussolini had consistently voiced the view that Jews living in Italy were not a threat and should be left alone to live peacefully and in harmony. Unlike Germany, Italy was a country that didn't discriminate against Jews.

Mussolini had many Jewish friends and acquaintances. Jews had helped him found the Fascist movement, and many had joined and given him their support. Jews had fought for their country and held important positions in the government. For sixteen years, Mussolini had told us that anti-Semitism did not exist in Italy, and Italians had embraced that belief. While Jews may not have been his biggest supporters, many of us believed that Mussolini would shield Italian Jews from Hitler's hatred. We hoped that Mussolini was our protector.

But now, with these new laws, everything changed. For the first time in Italian history, Jews were defined in racial terms instead of religious ones. Children of Jewish parents would belong to the Jewish race no matter their religion. A special census was established to make this determination.

We were such a small number. In Naples, there were perhaps a few thousand Jews out of a population close to one million. Why would anyone want to or need to concern themselves with the Jews? Perhaps it was different elsewhere in Italy, in places like Rome, Florence, Milan, or Turin. But even if you took all the Jews in Italy and stood them together, there were less than fifty thousand, hardly more than one tenth of one percent of Italy's population, one Jew in a crowd of one thousand. Why would a country of forty-four million people suddenly concern themselves with such a small group of people who had contributed so much throughout all aspects of Italian society and posed no threat? Naples? In Naples, the anti-Fascists were more of a threat to Mussolini than the Jews.

I suppose, at first, we didn't want to believe what we read. It made no sense. What caused Mussolini to so abruptly change his behavior? Once again, denial was a dangerous excuse. What should have alarmed us when the *Manifesto* was first published was that the newspapers claimed that it was embraced by Mussolini. We should have paid more attention. We all knew that the Fascist newspapers were Mussolini's propaganda machine. The *Manifesto* should have been the sign. We should have understood that Mussolini wanted us all to know that the rules were about to change. From a distance, we had watched Jews lose any semblance of a normal life in Germany. We should have considered that Italy might be next. We should have known that Mussolini cared more about his nation as a whole than any small number of people. Nationalism was preached in every one of his speeches. And we all knew that Mussolini was capable of saying one thing and doing another. Yet while we were always suspicious of the Fascists, we never were the subjects of their discrimination. In that regard, Italy had never been like Germany.

First reactions are sometimes hard to explain, understand, and are often mistaken. At first, I thought this could not possibly have anything to do with us. Why would it? Of course we were Jewish, but we were fully assimilated into Italian life. We had become Italians. I thought they must be talking about others, people who looked and acted different from us. Please don't misunderstand. That did not mean that I wasn't upset or that I didn't care. It was simply that I refused to believe that this could be about us.

The truth was that Mussolini sacrificed the Italian Jews. Mussolini's highest priority was always to protect his empire. We all knew this. We were pawns in a much larger calculation, and issuing the racial laws was about political expedience. Mussolini's invasion of Ethiopia and support for Franco in the Spanish Civil War had left Italy isolated from much of the rest of the world. Italy's closest ally was Germany, which had already demonstrated its growing military presence and the extent of its power.

Hitler had carefully watched the Italian army's ineptitude in Ethiopia. He was aware of the shortcomings of Mussolini's forces. Mussolini needed Hitler to remain his friend. He did not want to become Hitler's enemy.

Hitler had already thumbed his nose at the Treaty of Versailles and defied much of the world. Germany had taken Austria. Hitler could do the same with Italy. Now Germany's reach was expanded, and Austria was no longer the buffer to keep our countries safely apart. What better way was there to show Hitler the bond of Mussolini's friendship than to institute anti-Semitic racial laws in Italy just as Hitler had done in Germany. Italian Jews were becoming too vocal. They were voicing their objections to Italy's relationship with Germany. They were critical of Hitler. If removing this objection was at the expense of the few Jews in Italy, Mussolini found this a small price to pay. This was his gift to Hitler. I believe that Mussolini chose to make this trade. He demonstrated his loyalty to Hitler and the Nazi regime by banishing the Jews from Italian life. Better to strengthen his alliance with Hitler than to become the target of Hitler's ambitions and put Italy in his crosshairs.

Did it matter whether the *Manifesto's* scientific explanation for racism in Italy was false or dishonest? Not one bit. The *Manifesto* gave Mussolini and the Fascists the justification they needed to put in place the racial laws separating the Jews of Italy from normal society. The range of the regulations affected every part of our lives. The laws deprived us of our livelihoods.

One regulation required foreign-born Jews granted Italian citizenship after 1919 to leave Italy. Fortunately,

Paul and I had become citizens well before then, so this did not apply, but my heart went out to those forced to leave their adopted home. Many had been Italian citizens for most of their lives. Other regulations banned Jews from jobs in government, banking, insurance, education, law, and a variety of other professions. Jews were forbidden to hire non-Jews. Jews were banned from teaching at or attending educational institutions. Marriage was prohibited between Jews and non-Jews. Businesses and property were confiscated. Jews were prohibited from serving in the military.

I know others will have their own reactions. I can only speak for myself and our family. We felt betrayal, disbelief, and disappointment. We were rejected and humiliated. We were angry. We were unable to be defiant. Can you imagine what this was like for the children? They were adults. They understood what this would mean for their lives. Whatever opportunities they had worked so hard to achieve were being taken and denied. They had been promised a future. Alex and Theo had completed their service in the Italian army. Now they were told they were no longer Italians. We had been loyal and faithful to a country that had suddenly stripped us of our civil rights.

The harsh truth is what we thought and how we reacted really didn't mean very much. We were in no position to change things. None of us were. We lived in a dictatorship.

Vincenzo had taught me that *why* was the important question to ask. But now my Dartmouth education failed me. Why something happened, no matter the debate, was not nearly as important as what these new laws might mean. Now I learned that asking why is the luxury of philosophers, observers, and teachers. It is the virtue of a democracy. When you are forced to live in a dictatorship, *what* becomes the most important question. That was the reality of our world.

CHAPTER FORTY-ONE

I believe it was our son Arthur, Mela's twin, who was the first of our four children to decide to leave Italy and emigrate to the United States. The others made their decisions in quick succession. They were all adults, and we encouraged them to each decide for themselves. Theo was in his mid-thirties, living in Milan with his wife and son. Alex was nearly thirty. He and Lotte were living in Naples in a small apartment not far from the pensione. By now, the twins, Mela and Arthur, were in their early twenties. Mela had always lived at home. Now she was very busy with her life. Arthur had left when he was fifteen to work in the north.

Our connection with America was very strong. America was a very familiar place. Nearly all the extended family had moved there years earlier, and we had considered moving to the United States many times. Both

both of Paul's brothers had lived in the U.S. for over forty years, most of their adult lives. The children knew their uncles well. They had often come to visit. Even Paul's mother had lived in America for many years before Paul brought her back to Naples to live out her last years with our family.

With the exception of my brother Martin and my sister Jenny, my brothers and sisters were there too, all busily engaged with their lives and families. Martin and Jenny were making arrangements to leave for America as soon as they could. Although none of our children had traveled across the Atlantic, both Paul and I had visited America. Two years earlier, when my oldest brother had celebrated his seventieth birthday, the family in America had sent me a ticket, and I'd spent the month visiting family in Boston, New York, and Chicago.

I remember that visit well. Lotte had done such a good job managing the pensione while I was gone. I left my worries behind and was so impressed with everything American: the houses, the highways, the skyscrapers, the appliances, the washing machines, the grocery stores, the refrigerators, the gadgets. Everything was so shiny and new, so different from most things in Italy. It is funny how impressions are formed. In Italy, we had always heard that American children had no manners, that they refused to listen to their parents and misbehaved. But I saw no evidence of this. They were just like the children in Italy. When it comes right down to it, we are all the same. I had no doubt that America would be the right choice for my children and grandchildren. In America, they would find their opportunities.

You would be right to ask why Paul and I chose to stay in Italy when everyone else moved to America. The truth was that Europe was our home and we had never found a good reason to leave. There had always been better reasons to stay. Somehow in Italy we had become Neapolitans. We'd never planned it that way. And despite the Nazis, you might find this strange, but I will always feel German. It doesn't matter what Hitler said about Jews; being German is in my blood. I am a product of generations, and little can ever change that.

Naples was just where the dots had led us, and it had become our way of life. Even if I hadn't become Italian at first, time changes things. Events do too: raising children, the pensione, the experience of the German club and losing our friends. If it hadn't been for Hitler, Mussolini, and the war, I am convinced that Paul and I, and the children, would have stayed in Italy for the rest of our lives. Why would we leave? We all loved Italy. I loved the Pensione Alexandra, and Paul did too. We could have lived out our days operating the pensione and playing with our grandchildren. That would have been a very fine life. We would have all been satisfied.

Arthur telephoned and told us of his decision to leave only days after Mussolini announced the racial laws. He was living and working in Milan at the time. Through his work, he had met an older man, a Jew, whose family owned a very successful and large manufacturing company in Germany. When the laws were unveiled restricting Jews, this man had taken Arthur aside and described how terrible the situation in Germany had become. He'd convinced Arthur that the same could very well happen in Italy. Mussolini was placating Hitler, and that would not last. He'd told Arthur to leave while he could. He should not wait any longer. America should be his future. Italy should be in his past. Who would stop Germany? The world had hardly noticed. Unless Germany's ambitions were thwarted, the Nazis would destroy life and opportunity for anyone in their path who had Jewish blood flowing through their veins. Forget Mussolini. He would do whatever he was told. Hitler and the Nazis were in control.

When Arthur called that day, he told us he had been fired from his job. The reason? He was Jewish. No other explanation was needed. The firm he worked for did business with the government. They had been ordered to fire any Jews on their payroll. That same afternoon, he went to the United States consulate in Milan and began the process of applying for a visa. Then he went to see Theo and urged Theo to do the same. Within the week, when he returned to Naples, he encouraged Alex, Lotte, and Mela to leave. That is when they made their decisions.

Knowing that our children all planned to move to America, Paul and I agreed that it was time to consider our future. I remember that evening so well. We sat out on the balcony and enjoyed the crisp Mediterranean breeze rising from the sea. It was the kind of special evening that I loved most at the Pensione Alexandra, the kind of evening that always enchants and that one always remembers. The sky was perfectly clear and filled with stars. Later, the moon appeared and was nearly full. I don't know why, but the city seemed quiet that night. For that one evening, the entire world seemed at peace.

We sat silently as Paul enjoyed his nightly cigar. I thought to myself how much the pensione had changed our lives and how it had changed me. I thought about Naples and how it had taken time, but it had captured my heart. We stayed up most of the night talking and listening to one another. It was not a difficult decision to make. We both wanted to share in our children's lives. We recognized that this chapter of our life was about to end, and we understood that, at our age, there was little chance we could start over again.

The following morning, we told the children. As soon as possible, we would leave for America too. Oh, how I cried. How dare Mussolini and Hitler destroy our dreams?

CHAPTER FORTY-TWO

Those decisions were made late in 1938, and as each day passed, more restrictions were issued. It became more and more clear that Mussolini's Italy would deprive us all of any possibility for a future. The fear of Nazi Germany hung over our heads, particularly when we learned the truth about Austria, what our newspapers had failed to mention.

We had never been told that the German army had simply marched into Austria and taken control. The papers had never reported that the Nazis had not been asked or invited. Now there were those who said that, when Mussolini honored Hitler's request and made no effort to stop him, he had been misled. He had been duped by Hitler. Others warned that the Italian army was not strong enough to stop the Germans and that Mussolini had no choice. One thing remained true: Hitler was rebuilding the German empire for the Aryan race, and Mussolini had become his partner.

We learned that the campaign to rid Austria of its Jews had begun immediately. Jews were paraded through the streets of Vienna. Synagogues were destroyed. Jewish men and women were detained at random by Nazis. Thousands were jailed for no reason while police allowed open looting of Jewish homes and businesses. Days later, when Nazi officials realized Jews in Austria would pay just about anything to exit the country, the newly created Office for Jewish Emigration extorted money and valuables from Jews in return for their freedom. It was so successful that it served as the model for Germany.

I remember when Arthur told us what it had been like in Milan the day that Germany had invaded Austria. During the takeover, it was as if Milan had stood still. Everyone had been holding their breath. Nothing had moved. If Mussolini failed to resist Hitler's invasion of Austria, then Germany would be at Italy's border, and Mussolini would become mostly a captive in his own land.

After word was received in Milan that Austria had been invaded, militant young Germans in Milan began celebrating. Arthur had been quite shaken. He said that, in front of the Leonardo monument in the Piazza della Scala, the Germans were yelling at the top of their lungs, "Today Germany and tomorrow the world!" Some of the militants were shouting about "using bayonets to cleanse the countries with Jewish blood."

CHAPTER FORTY-THREE

As unjust as the situation might have been, we all were convinced that, for our family, we had made the right choice. The sooner we could leave the better. There was no second-guessing. Hearing the stories of what had happened in Austria was frightening. How could we know whether this might be repeated in Italy? We did not think so, but one could never be certain. Oddly, despite the racial laws now in place, we still felt under the protection of Mussolini. In some ironic way, Mussolini's partnership with Hitler was keeping Hitler at bay. How long this allegiance would last would be the question asked throughout our remaining days in Italy. For now, as long as Italy's racial laws did not put us in harm's way, we would go about our business and leave for America as soon as it could be arranged.

We had watched others try to leave, so we had an idea of how difficult emigrating to America might be. Yet just as when we'd purchased the Pensione Alexandra and I'd learned that dreaming of owning a pensione was not the same as actually owning a pensione, I quickly learned that dreaming of moving to America was not the same as actually moving to America. There would be obstacles. It was a difficult process.

One of the first things learned was that there were different rules for the children than there would be for Paul and me. This difference was very significant. Entry to the United States was not based upon country of origin, citizenship, or passport, but rather country of birth. There were quotas, limits on the number of people who could legally enter the U.S. as immigrants in any given year. These quotas had been set for each country in the early 1920s. Despite the current events in Europe, American immigration law had not been changed. I was told that President Roosevelt had been asked to consider special quotas for Jews fleeing the Nazi horrors, but had refused to consider the request.

Under the rules, our children would be subject to the Italian quota, which, while limited in number, did not appear to pose a significant problem. Paul and I, however, were subject to the German quota, and the numbers were staggering. There was a long wait. There were many ahead of us waiting in the same line. The line? The line appeared to stretch for miles and miles. We were cautioned that it could be as long as two and a half years before we became eligible to have our applications reviewed and considered. Even then, there was no certainty they would be approved and entry visas issued.

I have no aptitude for numbers and always have had a strong distrust of statistics. Nonetheless, others have told me that the quotas allowed for fewer than six thousand Italians and twenty-six thousand Germans to emigrate each year to the United States. I have no idea how many of these openings were actually filled. I do know that many applications were denied. Someone told us that there were three hundred thousand Germans trying to leave Europe and, for most, the first choice was the United States. Even with my mathematical aptitude, I did understand that twenty-six thousand openings was a small number compared to three hundred thousand people in need.

Few of us had any idea that immigration, allowing people to enter, was such a controversial debate in America. Why would we? This didn't make sense to us. We'd all heard the words beneath the Statue of Liberty: *Give me your tired, your poor.* We thought America was the land of opportunity. It shined like a beacon. Now we learned that moving to America was not that simple. There were very many complicated issues. Immigration was a very divisive topic. America's politicians had many strong opinions.

Nationalism, the desire and responsibility to take care of one's own citizens first, before allowing and inviting newcomers, was the political debate then just as it has always been. And in many parts of the world, including the United States, anti-Semitism and the attitude towards Jews remained widespread. It was much the same story as my old friend Vincenzo had written about. Most people had never met a Jew. Generations of misleading images and misconceptions had nurtured the politics of anti-Semitism. Too many people believed only what they had heard and were not interested enough to learn for themselves.

In the U.S., despite the compassionate and genuine concern of countless Americans to assist Jewish refugees fleeing Europe, there was vocal and persistent opposition. Many Americans were not prepared to give jobs to immigrants at a time when there were not enough jobs available for American citizens. They used the arguments that immigrants would compete with Americans most in need for low-paying jobs, and that younger, educated Americans beginning to enter the labor market would have to compete with immigrants who could perform the same work and would be willing to be paid less. Others were afraid that enemy agents might pose as refugees.

There were those who voiced the fear that impoverished refugees would require government assistance and resources for their care and feeding. We all knew that was an ill-informed excuse. Every one of us was required to find able and verified sponsors to guarantee that government assistance would not be necessary. Those wanting to leave were resourceful, educated, and productive. Most had been denied the opportunity to earn a living. Refugees were penniless because of what they were forced to leave behind, not because they did not want to work.

Only later would I learn that apathy and disbelief played a big part in this debate. Many people had little interest in what was going on in Europe. Many others refused to believe what Germany was doing to Jews. Since I didn't live in America at the time, I wouldn't know, but I can see how this would be possible. Apathy and disbelief are not uncommon anywhere. It rarely matters what the topic is. Most of us are too busy trying to take care of our own lives, let alone worry about others.

I know that there are many differing opinions about these matters, and I suspect that these types of issues will always be debated as long as we have a world where some have more and others have less. People will always seek to migrate for safety, security, and opportunity. That is human nature. All I can say was this was the situation we found ourselves in. We were a successful, good, decent, and proud family living in Italy. We were Jewish, and we were German, and we wanted to move to America to keep our family together. We never thought of ourselves as refugees. Those were others. They were not us.

CHAPTER FORTY-FOUR

We resigned ourselves to wait. There was little more we could do. The application process for entry visas was lengthy and demanding, and many details would have to be handled when our quota numbers were called. Nobody could tell us with any certainty when that might be. Then there would be interviews and a long list of items to be submitted: certificates of good conduct from police authorities, medical examinations, bank information. In the meantime, we took care of the things we were able to, like arranging for family members in the United States to sponsor each of us. While Paul and I already had passports, the children needed to apply so theirs could be issued in time. What became immediately apparent was that nearly everything would require a bureaucracy to act and the patience to wait outside offices for doors to open.

In the meantime, Italy's racial laws changed many things for us. It was clear that we needed to be inventive and cautious in how we conducted our lives. In Naples, there were always ways to beat the system, and most of us looked for the means to survive within the rules. Thanks to the kindness of Signor Spinelli, we were able to change the ownership of the Pensione Alexandra to his name, allowing us to keep the doors open. Now he owned the business, and we became his employees. We agreed that when we departed for America, he would take possession of whatever was left behind. By then, the stuffed birds would be in need of another dose of his cologne. Times were different, and tourism in Naples might not have been what it once was, but most importantly, we were able to continue to receive some income from the pensione, and Signor Spinelli would continue to receive his rent every month.

Many good, decent people stood by us, helped us, and watched over us during this time. These people didn't care if our ancestors were Jewish. My impression was that most Italians rejected the notion of anti-Semitism and believed that Mussolini was doing Hitler's bidding when he unveiled the racial laws. It wasn't in the blood of Italians to treat Jews differently from one day to the next. I don't know about other places, but that was certainly true in Naples. Of course, our old friends, members of the German club, may have felt differently, but we were no longer part of their social circle, and I no longer cared what they might have thought. Good riddance. This was not their country. They weren't Italians.

All Jews were required to register with the authorities and carry an identification card. The most significant rules, like the ban on mixed marriages or excluding Jews from public schools, did not affect us. Restrictions on where Jews could work limited opportunities for the children, and there was a growing list of things we could not do: visiting certain beaches and popular vacation spots; placing advertisements and death notices in newspapers; owning a radio; having our name listed in the telephone book; entering certain public buildings. But Neapolitans were never too good at following rules they could not understand, and often, these dictates were disregarded. I can't remember that Paul or I were ever questioned or asked to show our identification. I can't speak for the children. If this happened, they never told me.

We just had to stay on guard. We avoided the troublemakers as much as we could and never openly disobeyed any important rules. And we clearly heard the message. When it came to public life in Italy, Jews no longer belonged.

Paul, Lotte, and I continued to take care of the pensione. Mela had changed jobs and no longer worked in the bookstore. For the last year, she had worked as an interpreter for German and Czech engineers in a glass factory. But like Arthur, she was fired. Then she found work caring for some children who lived nearby.

Arthur was the most inventive. He found a job at a family-owned vegetable warehouse in Torre Annunziata, a small village twenty miles south of Naples, at the foot of Mt. Vesuvius. His journey to and from work was complicated, but late at night, he regaled us with his stories about the people who worked there and the customers. He told us his employers assumed he was Catholic and never inquired or asked whether he was Jewish. He was always bringing home the most wonderful fruits and vegetables – huge artichokes, wild strawberries, enormous lemons, and fresh asparagus. I don't remember what kind of work Alex found, but we all did what we could to support ourselves. We stayed busy all the time.

CHAPTER FORTY-FIVE

It was not only our personal life in Naples that was unsettled. Each day, it appeared that the world was spinning out of control. As soon as one crisis was resolved, another one erupted. The Nazis kept pursuing their ambitious plans, and Hitler continued his strongarm tactics, taking every opportunity to test how far he could push the European powers. And at each turn, they chose to back down and appease him.

For months, ever since Germany had taken control of Austria, Hitler had threatened war unless Czechoslovakia surrendered the Sudetenland to Germany. Italian newspapers heaped praise on Mussolini for brokering an agreement between Italy, Germany, Britain, and France to avert the crisis. In exchange for Hitler's promise of peace, Germany was allowed to annex the Sudetenland.

This was only a negotiating ploy by Hitler. The Sudetenland gave Germany's war machine most of Czechoslovakia's manufacturing resources and left them vulnerable to complete German domination. In the spring of 1939, Hitler and the Nazis marched into Prague and proclaimed their bloodless victory. A short time later, Hitler and Mussolini signed the Pact of Steel, formalizing the political and military alliance between Germany and Italy.

CHAPTER FORTY-SIX

There were so many things going on in our world that spring that I find it hard to remember many details. We were all busy trying to adjust our lives to the new rules. We were all trying to understand what was going on in the world. Mostly, we were just trying to survive. Perhaps that was why this event was so unexpected. How could we have imagined that Kaethe and Josef would show up on our doorstep in the midst of this madness? But that is exactly what happened. Out of the clear blue, Kaethe and Josef arrived for a ten-day visit.

We'd had no idea they were on their way. There were few tourists in Naples. Needless to say, it was a very strange and confusing time for a visit. So many people were desperate and searching for safety. Others were living their lives as if nothing had changed. It was as if there were two different worlds. We had no idea how Josef and Kaethe had made their way to Naples. We knew that many border crossings had become difficult with the events that had occurred. Who would choose to travel now?

And once again, Mela began speculating. She always had questions about their visits. She was always trying to unravel their mystery. I just laughed. It was wonderful to see them again. That was good enough for me. We needed a good visit to brighten our lives, and I didn't mind having a few more paying guests. They seemed just the same as they had always been, although Josef did pull me aside to assure me that they were now married. I told him it was about time. It had taken much too long, and he wasn't getting any younger. We had been waiting for years.

Some things don't change. Habits are hard to break, and I suppose that was true for Kaethe and Josef's visits to Naples. Following breakfast, they spent their mornings sightseeing. Josef always had a long list, and he claimed that the sightseeing was now even better. There were fewer visitors and shorter lines. The guides had more time to answer his questions. Their afternoons were devoted to his painting. On this visit, he was interested in setting up his easel near the port. He wanted to paint pictures of boats and such. When he told me this, I could hear Mela in the back of my head telling me, *I told you so. He must be a spy.*

By dinner, they were always back at the pensione. Despite their many visits to Naples, Kaethe still had not developed a taste for Italian food. She found the sausages and cheeses to her liking but could not accept the idea of a dinner without meat, potatoes, and some kind of vegetable that had been grown under the ground. Of late, she did seem to have developed a fondness for dark chocolate and cheesecake. At least that made the meals a little more interesting. Josef had always been the more adventuresome of the two, but on matters of food, he always deferred to his wife.

Following their meal, they always went walking, but on this visit, they varied their destinations. I assumed they were simply tired of always taking the same walk along Via Caracciolo to the Acquario and back. But again, Mela found it curious that they were seeking new destinations.

One thing did not change, and that was our evenings together. They always were back in time to join us on the balcony, and that was where our friendship continued like it had never been interrupted. Each evening, we sat together and tried to understand the events that were shaping our world.

What I remember most of that visit was Josef's preoccupation with appeasement and the British. Josef was so adamant. It was as if the British government was not listening to him. He could not understand why the world was failing in its obligation to stand up to Hitler. He said this made little sense. Couldn't the world see what Hitler was up to? He praised the British Secret Service but blamed the British politicians. They need to listen to what their intelligence officials were telling them. Why did the politicians think that, if they gave Hitler a little, he would not insist on more? How many times did that lesson need to be repeated before the world would understand?

I remember having a terrible argument with Josef one evening. I don't know who started it, but I do recall telling him that he was so focused on Hitler that he failed to concern himself with others. He needed to stop and look around and try to understand what Mussolini was doing in Italy. He was not always right. He needed to ask why his favored Switzerland was not taking a stand. He needed to explain what was wrong with America. We had such an argument that evening, and I was so tired of all this bickering that I just went to bed. Paul just watched in amazement. Later, he asked me what had happened to the sweet young girl he'd married. That night, I just rolled over and cried myself to sleep. I just could not understand the world I lived in anymore. Sometimes, too many cloudy days makes one sad and angry. That is how I felt too often that spring of 1939. I was glad our friends were with us, but I was tired of what the world was making us become.

I suppose sunshine cures most headaches, and that was true the next day. I do recall that it seemed that everyone walked on their tiptoes around me that morning. I was reminded of the days when we'd first purchased the pensione, when the construction had been underway and everyone had avoided me. For a short time, I enjoyed my exalted position. Then everything returned to normal, and we all got along as if nothing had ever happened. I imagine we all go through these moments in life. I just learned about them at an older age than most.

One day, Josef and Kaethe insisted that Paul and I join them for an excursion to Sorrento. Everyone said it was time for me to take my apron off and go. You may find it odd that we could do this given the various restrictions on Jews, but there were no rules to prevent this, and there was no one to stop us, so we just went. We packed a picnic and took the ferry to Sorrento, a one-hour journey. It was a wonderful day and just what I needed. We walked the streets and sat on the beach. It brought back so many memories of days that had been less complicated, when our biggest cares had been so little.

It seemed their visit ended as quickly as it had started. That morning, we went to the train station to see Josef and Kaethe off. None of us knew when we would see each other again. We all knew the world was changing before our eyes and that there was little we could do to stop it.

Josef always sent us a card upon their return to Paris. Kaethe always enclosed a long letter. They did this after every visit without exception. This time was different. After their visit, we didn't hear from them again, no card, no letter, no word. I always wondered and worried why. I knew that some guests arrive and others depart, but Josef and Kaethe were different. I wrote them one time, but my letter was returned. What had happened to them? Where had they gone? We had no answers. It was as if they'd vanished into thin air.

CHAPTER FORTY-SEVEN

Suddenly, late that summer, everything seemed to happen at once. Arthur received word that the applications for Alex, Lotte, Mela, and him were being processed by the American consulate. They would soon be called for interviews and physicals. Officials in the United States were verifying their sponsorship paperwork. They were also informed by the Italian authorities that each would need to be granted a *Nulla Osta*, the official document stating that the Italian government had no objection to their leaving. We all found ourselves a bit confused by one issue. It was like the problem of the chicken and the egg. There was a question of which came first, the visa or booking the passage on a ship. There were different interpretations of the rules. Navigazione Italiana, who would book their ship, advised them they needed visas before berths could be reserved. A friend of Arthur's told him that the ship needed to be booked before other necessary documents could be issued.

Throughout that summer, much of the world watched events unfold as they appeared to plunge faster and faster towards war, but the news in Italy was tightly censored. We had little information. Despite the rules, we kept our radio and sometimes heard reports from BBC broadcasts or Spanish radio if we could receive the signal. All we knew was that Germany had its eyes on Poland and there continued to be a great deal of speculation about whether a peaceful resolution could be found. Some said negotiations were underway. There were also rumors that Britain and France had given assurances to Poland. We understood that, if Poland were attacked, Britain and France were prepared to step in and stand by Poland.

As I tell you this history, I realize that sometimes I get confused with what we knew at the time and what we learned later. There really was limited information, and the news we did receive was often unreliable and incomplete. In Italy, all that was really known was that Germany and Italy had formed their alliance. None of us knew what commitments and guarantees each country had given to the other. If it came to war, would Italy be drawn in? If Germany invaded Poland, and Britain and France rose to her defense and declared war against Germany, the question that remained was what was Mussolini obliged to do? What commitments had he given to Hitler?

On September 1, Germany invaded Poland. News reports gave conflicting stories. One report said that Germany reacted to Poland's attack on German troops stationed at the border. Another report claimed that

Sept 3, 1939

Germany had attacked first. Two days later, honoring their guarantee to defend Poland's borders, Britain and France responded by declaring war on Germany. That day, the world learned that World War II was underway.

Ironically, that very same day, we received word from the American consulate that immigration visas for Alex, Lotte, Arthur, and Mela had been approved. Lotte's visa had been a major concern, but since she was married to Alex, her visa was processed as part of Italy's quota.

Unfortunately, the declarations of war complicated everything. Although Italy was not party to the war and Mussolini had not taken any action, we worried that time might be running out, preventing anyone from leaving. Another problem was that, even after nine months of waiting, Italian officials had still not finished processing the passport applications. Arthur and Alex had taken turns sitting and waiting at the passport office but they'd been unable to receive any assurance as to when the passports might be issued. Without passports, the immigration visas would be of no use. And now, with the war underway, the persistent question regarding Italy's involvement made matters even more confusing.

We continued to be confronted with issues. As soon as one was resolved, another would appear. Three days after the visas were issued, we learned that the ocean liner S.S. *Rex* was scheduled to cross the Atlantic direct to New York. This was the first vessel to leave the port of Naples for the United States in several weeks. Everyone was excited. Arthur thought berths might be found and booked. Then the excitement suddenly faded. Despite their promises, we were informed that the passport office still needed one more day to complete their work. As it turned out, it didn't matter that day. No berths on the ship were available.

Finally, the very next day, after nine months of waiting, the passports were issued. Everyone went to meet with the chief of police, who had to stamp their papers. Their next stop was the American consulate, where their passports were signed and stamped granting permission to immigrate. Now all that remained was to find a ship that would take the four of them to America. Then they would be on their way.

Once again, excitement turned to anxiety. That same day, within hours of receiving their passports and having their visas stamped, Italy found it necessary to close all shipping lanes in and out of the Naples harbor. All ship traffic was blocked until further notice. No ships could leave, and none could arrive. There was no additional information. No one could say whether this might be for days, months, or even years.

Imagine their disappointment. Paul and I felt so bad, but there was nothing we could do to change their predicament. Mela was so upset and bewildered. She showed her emotions more than the rest. We knew how anxious they were to go forward with their lives. They were so close. Now they had no idea if their efforts were in vain. Again, they chose to take turns waiting, this time in the ship terminal offices in six-hour shifts. If something were to change, they wanted to be first in line.

Seven days went by before they heard any news. It was Arthur's turn at the ship terminal early that morning when he learned that the *Conte di Savoia* was tentatively scheduled to leave Genoa later that day. If she were given permission to depart, the shipping lanes in Naples would be temporarily reopened, allowing the ship to enter the harbor and pick up passengers the following day. Though the ship was fully booked, there was a reason to be hopeful. If other passengers failed to board before she left Genoa, additional berths would become available. This was a very real possibility. With so many trying to leave Germany, passengers were frequently delayed at border crossings, preventing them from reaching Genoa in time for their scheduled departure. More would be known once the ship left port and a count of passengers and a check of cabins could be made.

Shortly after noon, Arthur was informed that the ship had departed and that four berths were available in an inside cabin without windows on the lowest deck of the ship. He didn't wait to hear from the others. He accepted the offer and was told that the tickets would be issued as soon as the funds were received. They would leave for America in the morning.

Everyone was thrilled. Pandemonium and panic erupted at the pensione that afternoon. After months of waiting, suddenly, they had less than twenty-four hours to pack and cut all their ties with Italy, their friends, and their past. This was such a bittersweet moment. My emotions were complicated. I was so happy they could finally begin their adventure and go forward with their lives. I was so sad that my babies would be leaving. That afternoon, I had a smile in one eye and a tear in the other.

Within the hour, we were confronted by the next issue. Another crisis erupted. There was no time for emotion.

The shipping agency called to advise that, as a result of the war, fares had increased and had to be paid in American dollars. Everybody stopped packing. We did not have American currency. We couldn't pay for the tickets.

CHAPTER FORTY-EIGHT

We all bit our nails as a barrage of transcontinental cables were sent to the family in America asking for loans and for the funds to be wired so the cabin would not be lost. Once again, my family put their arms around me. They always watched out for their little sister. By evening, we received confirmation, and the tickets were purchased. In total confusion, the four terribly excited young people packed their life's belongings while drinking Champagne with their friends.

Paul and I joined the celebration, but my heart ached too much to stand with them on the balcony later when they howled at the moon. That night, I felt that I could watch them forever as they sat in the center of the room with their suitcases. They'd always been so young, and now they were so grown. They were so happy and excited, but it was all so sudden. I wondered what fate would bring. Would our dots connect? I found it impossible to sleep that night. I prayed we would all be together again soon.

The following morning, at 6 am, the carrettiere came with a two-wheeled horse-drawn cart to collect their luggage. They would follow by taxi. They wanted to take the lovely trip along the Bay of Naples, past the Villa Comunale, and past the Acquario one last time. Paul and I stood on the balcony and waved goodbye with our white handkerchiefs as we watched them leave. We weren't allowed to accompany them to the ship. War precautions were underway, and the port was off limits.

And so, on the morning of September 16, 1939, under a smiling blue sky and with our old friend Vesuvius watching, the anchor was lifted, and our children left for America. It seemed as if they had been part of our lives for only an instant. One day, they'd been born. Now they were gone. I will never forget my tears.

CHAPTER FORTY-NINE

For me, everything about our life changed after the children boarded their ship that day. If I'd had any reservations about leaving, they disappeared in that instant. Paul and I knew that America would be next for us. It was where we were supposed to be. We just didn't know how or when we would get there. A few guests remained at the Pensione Alexandra, but it felt empty and hollow. It couldn't be the same without the children.

I know I refer to the four as children, but I believe that is how mothers always think, no matter the age of their offspring. When they left for America, they were grown adults: older, wiser, more experienced with life, and certainly more able to stand on their own two feet than I'd been when I'd first arrived in Naples. Yet I will always remember how small and helpless they once were, how they needed my attention, their tiny hands and feet, their eyes, the first time they smiled, their first steps, and their first day in school. After the twins were born, when Paul would peer down at them in their buggy, he would tell me that Arthur and Mela reminded him of two baby birds in a nest. As babies, without hair, tucked in their blankets, they seemed identical. Though one was a boy and the other a girl, he could hardly tell which was which, except that one head looked up and the other looked down, much the same as their personalities would become. When the twins were older, perhaps five or six years, I would tell them, "I love you when you are good, I love you when you are sick, I love you when you are sad, I love you when you are bad...but then not so much." They would get so upset with me and cry. They could never understand how I could love them a little less.

Those first days they were gone, all I could hear was the silence they'd left behind. I remember thinking about their footsteps. Throughout their lives, from the first time they wore shoes, I could always recognize them by the sound of their footsteps, the way they ran up the stairs, through the hallways, or when they first opened the door, each as unique as the sound of their cries. Now there were no more footsteps to be heard.

Their trip took seven days, and I don't think there was a moment that I did not worry. I knew that there was nothing I could do to protect them, but I couldn't help but worry. It was a mother's worry. We recognized that they were crossing international waters. The war had just started. No one knew what to expect or what dangers might be encountered. At night, the ship's lights would be extinguished to avoid the risk of attack, even if it were by accident. All I could picture was a blacked-out ship sitting alone and exposed in the middle of the ocean. I remember our relief when we received word from America that they had arrived and all was well.

I knew Paul and I had ourselves to be concerned about, but as the days and weeks passed, I grew afraid that I would forget the sound of their laughter or Mela's voice when she talked about her dreams. This was her first time on her own and away from home. The hours she and I had spent together with the pensione had brought us so close. I imagine my fear was the kind we all have when a loved one leaves. With the boys, it was different. They had left home before. I knew they would be all right. I always felt that Mela was more vulnerable. It was comforting to know that they were all safe in the United States and that their futures could be filled with opportunity. Paul and I knew it was their turn. Now it was their time. If I was sad, it was because I wanted to be there to share their excitement.

I found it difficult to operate the pensione without Lotte. Celestina, who had been our first housekeeper those months after Paul and I had married, came to my rescue and offered to help. She told me she didn't care about the racial laws. I have always remembered how Celestina taught me my first words of Italian. Then I was helpless, couldn't say a thing, and she asked me what she should prepare for dinner. The only way we could communicate was by playing our own version of charades: she pretending to swim like a fish and me flapping my arms like a chicken. I no longer remember what she served that evening, but I do remember how we laughed that afternoon. Paul, bless his heart, was a big help too. He did whatever he could to lift some of the burden off of me. We still had guests, but not as many. Some rooms stayed vacant, but there was seldom a night that the pensione was completely empty.

Once again, the character of the pensione changed, and this change was one that we had noticed beginning with the invasion of Austria. Most people were afraid to travel and simply stayed home. Everyone was uncertain. Tourists were few and far between. People were in Naples for different reasons, mostly connected with the events of the world and the port in one way or another. Now there were different nationalities. One seldom saw an American. The British had stopped coming. Guests were more careful and guarded with sharing their stories. One could never be entirely certain who was an enemy and who was a friend. I am convinced there were many afternoons when both walked through our doors only to find themselves seated side by side at breakfast the following morning. Behavior was guarded.

The Pensione Alexandra became a way station for many fleeing for their lives. It was apparent that Europe's mass exodus was underway. Once Naples had been the gateway to Southern Italy. Now it was a gateway to various parts of the world. Friends, relatives, acquaintances, and friends of friends joined our other guests and stayed while waiting for their entry visas to the United States or passage for elsewhere. The front door of the pensione always remained open to all, but now the back door became an entrance for those who could find no other place to go.

The word quickly spread that there was always the promise of food and some help at the Pensione Alexandra.

It was such a strange time. Somehow, everything had taken so long, and then suddenly, events happened so quickly. If we were surprised, it was that many of our worst fears had been realized. War is not always about bullets and bombs. It is fear and mourning and dread and suffering and uncertainty. It is that feeling of utter helplessness. For years, there had been more than enough signs, starting with a few small stones rolling down a hill and then becoming so large an avalanche that the terrifying size and speed made it impossible to stop, destroying everything in its path. Sometimes, I think those things directly in front of one's nose are the most difficult to see and certainly to see clearly. The truth is the world paid little attention. It hardly blinked an eye. All the rest of us could do was stand by and watch. There had been more than enough warning, but now this was real. Hitler and Germany were terrorizing the world.

CHAPTER FIFTY

I have heard others say that, before Nazi Germany invaded Poland and provoked Britain and France to declare war, Hitler had informed Mussolini of his plans and expected Italy's support. But Mussolini, despite having signed the Pact of Steel, was not ready. Hitler advanced sooner than expected. Mussolini recognized that the Italian Army was not yet prepared to fight. For that reason, the Italians did not join in the German attack. I don't know if this is true or an accurate depiction of the events as they took place, but at the time, many of us hoped and prayed that Italy would remain neutral and that Mussolini would come to his senses. Now I am sure that this was an uninformed hope, but that was the way we felt. For us, it was not about nationalism and pride; we just wanted to avoid war, another form of patriotism.

As long as the war did not come to Italy, neutrality remained a possibility. Many years later, I read that Britain and France had promised to give up territory in Africa in exchange for Italy's pledge to stay neutral, so I imagine Mussolini was under a great deal of pressure from both sides. Having time to think about this, I am not so certain that he really had a choice. He had made a commitment to Hitler. There would be a price to pay if he chose not to follow through. Mussolini also had his own plans. He expected the German army's support when he was ready to mount his military campaigns in the Balkans. Mussolini had not given up his ambition to recreate the Roman Empire, and he knew he would need Hitler's help.

In Italy, we couldn't help but wonder what the Pact of Steel Mussolini had signed with Hitler really meant. Now that the war was underway and Italy had not stepped in to support Germany, how much was Mussolini gambling? Would Hitler call Mussolini's bluff? Of course, at that time, most of the news continued to be censored. Most of what we learned was months after events occurred and from the stories told by those who traveled through our doors. The civilian population was told very little. As events unfolded, Mussolini would wait for many months to make his decision, and by that time, he was left with only one choice.

From our perspective, the war was taking place on two fronts. There was the external war, and there was the internal war, the war directed against the Jews. Whether Italy was neutral or actively engaged in an external war or not, within Italy, Mussolini's attack on Jews continued, and although it remained that most Italians chose not to embrace anti-Semitism, the propaganda produced by Mussolini and the Fascists didn't stop. Government-controlled newspapers spewed filth and garbage about Jews on a daily basis, so it wasn't surprising that some came to believe what they read. For us, the best approach was to remain cautious while we waited to be called by the American consulate. Paul and I limited our interactions with others beyond the doors of the pensione. That seemed to be the safest approach, and while always angry and disheartened, we remained largely unaffected.

What did become quickly apparent was the shadow of the war. As each day passed, there was less music in the open air, and Naples took on more and more of the look of austerity. You could see it in the faces of those who spent their days on the streets. The quality of life slowly evaporated for all Italians, not just the Jews. One hardly noticed from one day to the next, but it was quite evident when one looked back on the Naples we had always known and that was in our hearts. Lines became longer, tempers were more apt to flare, happiness faded, and more worry appeared. For some, friendships became strained. And for others, friendships were broken. This waiting for war was taking something from everyone. The suffering was felt by all.

From our guests that spring and summer, we learned mostly of heartbreak and anguish, misery and suffering. There was little we could do but listen. Paul's nephew Arthur, from Berlin, with his wife and small infant, stayed at the pensione for a number of nights. Ilse, his wife, told us of her fear and worries for her family. On Kristallnacht, like many others throughout Germany, her childhood home had been destroyed, and her father and brother jailed. They'd been released only after signing everything they owned to the Nazis and agreeing to leave their small town in East Prussia within thirty days. Once wealthy, overnight, her parents had become paupers, relying upon the goodwill of others.

While Ilse had been away at work that night, Paul's nephew Arthur had been taken by the Nazis and jailed too. He'd spent several weeks at Sachsenhausen, the concentration camp outside of Berlin. No one had been able to find him for days. He'd been released weeks later, but only after Ilse had presented camp officials counterfeit documents that showed they would leave for South America immediately. At Sachsenhausen, Arthur had lost more than fifty pounds. He had been starved and beaten.

Thousands of synagogues and Jewish-owned businesses in Germany had been destroyed and looted on Kristallnacht. More than twenty thousand Jews had been arrested. The message was loud and clear. All Jews should leave Germany. They did not belong. Jews were not real Germans.

Arthur explained that they had only left Berlin after months of searching to find a safe place to go once they departed Germany. They had traveled for several days and nights to reach Naples. Traveling by train had been difficult, particularly with their baby, and it had taken time to clear borders. After staying with us, they would travel twelve more hours by train to Brindisi, where there was a ship that was scheduled to take them to an unknown future in Shanghai, China. Ilse's parents had travelled to Trieste and would join them on the ship. Ilse told us she was concerned for their health. She doubted her father would ever recover. Imagine how difficult it was for him to have everything he had spent his life working for suddenly taken. He had always been a proud citizen of Germany. He had fought in World War I. The family had been baptized. They had become Lutherans. Now her young brother had been sent to Scotland. Her two sisters remained in Germany, and she feared for their lives. Nothing made any sense.

I felt so bad for Ilse and Arthur. They were so tired, anxious, and nervous by the time they arrived in Naples. I couldn't begin to imagine their confusion. When they'd left Germany, all they'd been allowed to take was what they could carry and the equivalent of a few dollars. They'd stopped in Naples to retrieve funds that Paul's brother Ludwig, in New York, had wired through a shipping company. Their Uncle Ludwig really was their guardian angel. He had sent enough to pay for their tickets and to help them find food and housing when they arrived in Shanghai.

Another German family who stayed at the pensione before Britain declared war on Germany had passage for only two to Palestine. The mother and father asked us to care for their fourteen-year-old son. They would send for him later, once they were safe and settled. However, when it came time for the son to join them, Britain and Germany were at war, and he could not go. Giovanni stayed with us for a number of months before we could make arrangements for the boy to go to the United States, where he would live in a foster home for the duration of the war. I don't think he ever reunited with his parents.

The situation with Palestine was terribly heartbreaking for so many. Since Palestine was a British mandate, Britain would not allow entry to any enemy foreign national. Once war was declared between Germany and Britain, all Germans, even if they were Jews fleeing persecution, were classified as the enemy and not allowed to emigrate to Palestine. We knew that crushed many dreams. Those who'd left early, before the war had officially begun, had made it. Those who left too late found themselves stranded. In some instances, family members, like Giovanni, had become separated from their families. This was a terrible situation.

There was another time a family of seven arrived, two parents and five young children, all close in age. I am not certain, but I believe they were released from a camp in Libya. It might have been somewhere else. I have no idea how they found their way to our doorstep in Naples, although I had heard that refugees bought transit to Sicily. Everyone was in good shape except for the beautiful young mother, who was crippled by polio and confined to a wheelchair. I remember the day they received a response to their appeal sent to President Roosevelt. One of our happiest moments was learning that their visas had been granted and that the family could all stay together.

Of those who were able and fortunate enough to leave Germany or the occupied areas, nearly all arrived penniless. Some were in poor health. There were those who stayed at the pensione who, later, were sent to Italian camps and not allowed to leave Italy. There was enormous pressure on the Italian authorities to deport them to German concentration camps. I understand that many who were detained in Italian camps managed to survive the war. The same was not true for the countries controlled by the Nazis. We saw several refugees who had been ill-treated in camps before being allowed to leave. Tired and pathetic, some still bore marks on their bodies and faces left from repeated beatings.

There were many difficult stories. People were simply trying to survive the horrors of the war. Some stayed for only a meal or for only the night. Some stayed for several days. Some could pay. Others were dependent upon the generosity of others. Fortunately, our children had gone to school with many children whose parents had various government connections. Some were associated with foreign consulates. We used whatever help we could find, and through the efforts of many good and caring Italians, most of those who stayed with us were successful in leaving. Even in these darkest moments, we saw many instances of humanitarian concern and generosity. There were many people who stepped forward to help their fellow human beings.

Today, I know that those whom we met were the fortunate ones, the ones who had the will and ability to leave. We only saw the tip of a very large iceberg. There were thousands of stories like these, and only a small number passed through our doors. Millions more never had the chance to leave Hitler's and Germany's grasp. Their fates were sealed, and they perished with the world never learning more. Their stories were left untold.

Every day, as long as this exodus continued, we kept asking ourselves: who had the right to destroy the lives of so many? Whose God would allow this to happen? I have lived longer than most. And with this question, I have become no wiser. I will never understand the answer. Even then, watching this unfold before our eyes, I refused to believe that this could happen to us. I always believed Italy was not Germany and Mussolini was not Hitler.

CHAPTER FIFTY-ONE

Nine months after Germany invaded Poland, and Britain and France responded by declaring war, Italy officially entered the fight. It was June 1940. Three-fourths of a year had gone by since the children had left for America. For us, it felt as if the war had gone on forever since Mussolini had declared us to be something less than second-class citizens late in 1938. For others, I am certain the war had gone on much longer. Germany's Jews had suffered through more than seven years of Hitler's rule.

For much of this time, we were bystanders, watching events from a distance, somewhat aware of what was going on but largely unaffected and grateful that we lived in Italy, not Germany. I was so glad that my parents had missed all of this. There was no one left from that entire generation. By this time, only a few of the larger family remained in Germany, cousins and their families. Most had scattered to all parts of the globe. I had tried to stay in touch, but then had come the pensione and now war. Only months earlier, the Nazis had expelled most of the remaining Jews in Koenigsberg. Fifteen hundred had been loaded into cattle cars and deported to camps as the German government moved to clear all Jews out of the German Baltic areas.

My sisters in America knew more about the family. It was such a large family, and our ages were so different. We each kept up with our favorites. Now there was no way to know. I did learn that my brother Martin and sister Jenny were safe in America. Paul and I were the last ones still in Europe. Martin must have had a difficult time in Dusseldorf. He wrote that, on Kristallnacht, their apartment had been vandalized. They were never harmed, but even his prized grand piano had been thrown from their second-floor window. They'd packed up and left as quickly as they could. Given his dire predictions, I am not sure why he stayed as long as he did.

In Italy, the longer it took Mussolini to act, the more we believed that war could be avoided. War is not in the nature of Italians. Italians are a peaceful people and love life too much. At least, that is what I had come to believe. We wanted to believe that we could escape this disruption. What did the war really have to do with Italy? Italy was never Germany. Mussolini's dreams were always different from Hitler's. This was someone else's war. This was about others, not us.

As Jews, we had assimilated. We didn't look like those Jews they drew in cartoons and caricatures, the Jews who were parodied in the newspapers. When I look in the mirror, that is not who I see. I just see a normal human being. And when I cut my hand, I just see red blood that looks the same as any other human. And we all have hearts. I suppose, in some way, I believed that those other Jews were different from us. They dressed and acted differently. We felt that way even in Germany. I know that is not a good thing to say, and I don't believe it now. That was just something we were taught. It is too easy to blame an older generation for our faults. As adults, we must take the responsibility to know better. My generation needed to admit that this was our war, that we never prevented it from taking place. I never believed that the world would allow such inhumane cruelty to exist. Then there came the time when the world could not find a way to make it stop.

That June, the French government declared Paris an open city after German armies invaded France. The French conceded. They made the choice not to defend Paris. In exchange, the Germans promised not to bomb or attack. By declaring Paris an open city, the French government prevented civilians from being killed and injured and historic landmarks from being destroyed. Whether France gave up or not did not matter. In the end, this was a major victory for Germany and a major defeat for France.

Only days before the fall of Paris, convinced that the defeat of his nearest geographic rival, France, was all but certain, and fearing that Germany might get all the spoils, Mussolini took the opportunity and joined Germany in the war against France and Great Britain. The hopes of those of us who prayed for neutrality were dashed. I imagine our hopes were fueled more by desire than by reality. Concluding that Britain would be next, I believe that Mussolini was left with little choice. He would either join Hitler or be occupied by Hitler. Most believed that Mussolini's ego was too big to let Hitler and Germany single-handedly conquer the European continent. Mussolini must have recognized that Germany was too powerful. Italy could never keep Hitler in check.

With his partnership resealed with Nazi Germany, Il Duce was able to renew his dream of rebuilding the Roman Empire. He ordered the Italian army to invade Southern France. And only months later, Italy attacked Greece and invaded Egypt.

There was an immediate response to Italy's decision to enter the war. The bombing of Italian cities began a little more than twenty-four hours after Mussolini's declaration. Because of its strategic location, Southern Italy became an immediate target. Within days, the port of Naples was targeted as the British sought to prevent supplies from being sent to the Italian army for their Africa campaign.

I once read that the British were convinced that Italians did not have the stomach for war, particularly after the ill-fated campaign in Ethiopia. British intelligence officials hoped the bombings would encourage civilians to turn against Mussolini. I am certain that if a vote were ever taken in Naples, many Italians would have voted against the war. The problem was that regime change does not take place easily under a dictatorship. Those who fail are killed. In Italy, Mussolini had all the votes.

The declaration of war brought more changes to Naples, and we felt the effects immediately. Blackouts were imposed for fear of the security of the port, and bomb shelters were encouraged. All unnecessary lights were to be turned off, and those that were essential had to be screened or lowered. No lights were allowed to be visible from homes, shops, offices, restaurants, and other public premises. No cars could be driven with white lights. No more than two people were allowed to walk side by side, and they could only carry blue lights pointing down toward the pavement. We were instructed to never illuminate other people, cyclists or drivers. Cyclists were ordered never to ride side by side but always in a line, and to tone down their lights, which had to be blue.

Naples was Naples, as is its destiny. In its typical way – perhaps it is that way everywhere – not everyone listened, and others found advantage. True or not, it was reported that one of the unanticipated consequences of the blackouts was a rise in crime taking place under the cover of darkness. I am always bewildered by the motives of a few.

We left Naples before the war ended and when most air strikes occurred. By the end of the war, Naples had become the most bombed city in all of Italy. While other Italian cities suffered more casualties, twenty to twenty-five thousand civilians were killed in Naples. I never learned which of our friends were lost, but I am sure there were many. I can't imagine the terror and fear that must have been felt by those living in those areas where there was little protection. While many were evacuated, far too many remained. From the sounds of the bombs, they must have felt death raining upon their heads.

During the months before we managed to leave Naples, nearly everyone we knew was affected in one way or another. That is the tragedy of war. All lives are touched no matter the side, and particularly those of the innocent. Most families had sons or husbands serving in the Italian army. <u>I am so grateful that my sons had fulfilled their military requirements and served in times of peace.</u>

    I will never forget what happened to Mariantonia, the wonderful person who came to our home to mend and clean our clothes for more than thirty years and who was by my side when I needed her help with the laundry at the pensione. She was grandmother to four children who were left motherless when her daughter suddenly died in childbirth. Mariantonia worked so hard to support and raise those children. The daughter's unemployed husband was no help. The eldest grandson grew up under the greatest of difficulties. The family had so little, and he had been asked to sacrifice so much. He could only study at night because he needed to work as a carpenter by day. How proud Mariantonia was when he graduated and became a teacher. Then the war came and he was required to go as an officer. I remember how upset they all were when he came with Mariantonia to the pensione to tell us this news. He was such a tall, nice-looking boy, so good-hearted and responsible. From Africa, he wrote often and sent the family money. Then, one day, Mariantonia began to get nervous. The letters stopped. There was no news from her grandson.

    By that time, I knew that my children were safe in the United States. I received their letters and knew how important it was to hear from my children. Mariantonia continued to come to the pensione every week to take care of our clothes. She always brought us flowers from her garden, and each time she arrived, she would kiss the photographs of our children. She thought of them as her own. She had been part of our family as long as we could remember. When the twins had been born, she'd been the one who'd helped the midwife unwrap the umbilical cord from Arthur's neck when he'd gotten all tangled with Mela.

Mariantonia grew so feeble with worry, and then the air attacks on the facilities at the Port of Naples began. The alarms and sirens would sound, and we would all search for shelter. I became so afraid that Mariantonia might be caught by an attack while she was on the street coming to see us. I told her not to come to the pensione anymore. She needed to stay safe.

Our last week in Naples, as Paul and I were about to leave, I went to see her to say goodbye. How old and tired she looked. She told me she never heard from her grandson again. I am certain there were thousands and thousands of others just like her. I will never understand the enormous sacrifices that ordinary people are forced to make because of the foolish pursuits of their egotistical and selfish leaders. This was an offensive war. Mussolini and the Italian army were not defending our freedom. They were attacking the freedom of others.

CHAPTER FIFTY-TWO

We really never had a choice to make. Leaving Naples for a safer location was out of the question. Despite the periodic air raids, we had to stay in Naples while we waited for our quota numbers to rise to the top. If we had left, I am not sure where we would have gone. We had little money, and we needed to be near the American consulate. But all that changed abruptly in February of 1941, when the Italian government ordered the American consulate in Naples to close its doors and move north to Rome.

That month, British naval ships took the Italians by complete surprise when they shelled the port of Genoa. Bombing raids near the port of Naples had been a continuing threat by air for months, but the port had never been shelled by ships, and suddenly, that became a worry. Although the United States had stayed out of the war,

Italian authorities were fearful that U.S. officials working within the consulate might secretly relay intelligence information about the port to the British. Ordering the United States government to move the consulate away from the seaport to Rome was the most expedient solution to the problem.

When this news was announced, Paul immediately decided that if the consulate was moved to Rome, we needed to do the same. As unsettling as this was, I knew he was right. But I was dismayed. I'd always thought we would stay in Naples until we could leave for America. Suddenly, my plan evaporated.

We had watched the children take their turns sitting at the Naples harbor offices when they'd needed passage to America. Their efforts had paid off. We needed to do the same for our visas. If we had any chance of getting entry visas, we needed to remain near the American consulate. Paul was convinced that our departure to America could happen with little notice. When we became eligible to submit our applications, we would have to be prepared to act quickly. Then the consulate could issue our travel documents, and we could book passage and leave for America. We could not risk losing our place in line. We had waited too long.

Once the decision was made to move to Rome, we were left with little choice but to pack and condense the contents of our entire lifetime in Naples into two suitcases. Whatever we owned was to be sold, given away, or left behind. We could not take more than we could carry. What would the future bring? There would be no extra money to spend for porters to move our belongings. That was a luxury we could ill afford. One thing was absolutely certain: our funds were limited. We had little savings, and once we left Naples, we could not depend on the opportunity to earn additional income. Anything we owned of value, no matter how special or sentimental, had to be converted to cash as rapidly as possible.

At least in Naples, we could rely on the pensione for a little income, even if it was a very small amount. Signor Spinelli always made sure we had a few coins in our pockets, and we knew we had food to eat and a roof over our heads. Rome would be different. We would be totally on our own. We would have to survive using whatever funds we had and would still need to find our way to America.

We always had known this day would come, but in my head, I thought we would be able to take our more cherished possessions. Now where we would leave from and when was far less certain. I suppose, in many ways, I had been making preparations ever since the day we'd waved goodbye to the children. Among their belongings, I'd hid the little jewelry I owned. One never knew what emergency they might encounter in America.

It really did not matter how much we prepared; when the time came, our move seemed abrupt and sudden. We had only a few days to dispose of our remaining possessions. I remember silently wishing we could close the doors, depart immediately, and leave everything behind. It would have been easier. Having two weeks to sift through forty years of belongings only made the process more exhausting, more emotional, and more confusing. One afternoon, I sat on the bed and spent hours turning the pages in the pensione guestbook, reliving the stories and memories of our guests. I had a good laugh thinking about my dear friend the anthropologist from Bombay, who was always so confused when we served him pasta.

How do you pack the contents of a lifetime into a suitcase? Others have asked the same question. I remember gathering far more things than I could possibly take and setting them out in tidy, organized piles on the floor. Then I remember the exact moment when I suddenly understood. This was not a vacation. We would not be returning.

Personal items like pictures and photographs, family heirlooms, my sketches, books, drawings made by the children when they were young, or treasures left by our parents would be secondary. We needed to conserve the few funds we had. There would be no extra money to buy what we could not carry. We needed a few dishes and cooking utensils. We needed my sewing kit. Even the few clothes and extra shoes we could pack would compete with the other essentials.

We only had room for what was necessary: a few clothespins, some string, the address book, a few pens and pencils, important papers and documents that might be required along the way, whatever we might need. We had to be prepared for changes in weather. It could rain. It might become cold. There was no way of knowing how long we might be in transit. Only after the essential items were packed could we consider anything else, and then only those items that didn't weigh too much and take too much space. We couldn't risk the chance of one of the suitcases breaking because it was overpacked. I couldn't imagine having to tie a suitcase together with string. And why should we carry something that might be confiscated along the way?

Life is always filled with little ironies. When the children had departed for America, they'd taken the steamer trunks and most of our other luggage. Now it was our turn to leave, and all that they'd left for us to use were the same two beaten and battered suitcases that Paul and I had carried when we'd first moved to Naples.

Letters were exchanged with the family in America. They needed to know our plans. We knew they were concerned for our safety and doing whatever they could do to assist us in getting out of Italy and to America. They had written of their attempts to appeal to Washington, D.C., for special permits and the efforts to seek assistance from Massachusetts Senator Lodge, who had been helpful but unsuccessful. They had made contact with a cousin in Cuba. Perhaps a visa could be issued for an interim stop. That had been done for others. There was little more that they could do. They wrote and told us not to worry about money for the ship tickets. When the time came for us to depart, they would sell the jewelry and do whatever was necessary to raise the funds. They promised a big family party when we made it to New York. What we had to do was find a way to get there. Remember, America had not yet entered the war. I am not sure what we would have done if Italy had been at war with America at that time.

Within two weeks of learning about the closure of the consulate, we wished farewell to our closest friends and boarded the train to Rome. That morning, I found room for two extra tiny decks of playing cards and my knitting needles. I also managed to find room in my suitcase for the shadow theater I had created for the children when they were young. Made of a little cardboard and paper, it didn't take much space. With its silhouettes of Naples street scenes I had drawn, it would teach the grandchildren about our life in Naples. I couldn't leave it behind. I wanted the next generations to know something of us.

We each carried one suitcase the same way as when we'd both arrived in Naples a lifetime earlier. I remember the morning when Mela left for her trip to America. She told me she wanted to kiss all the walls of the pensione goodbye. Then I laughed and told her that was such a silly thought. It was just like her, always dreaming. On the morning we left, I didn't feel that was so silly. That morning, I understood. My heart broke. I knew what we were leaving. I knew that we would never return to the Naples we had grown to love.

Even today, forty years after we left Naples, I find it difficult to describe what I felt when Paul and I entered the Centrale station. We found a wooden bench and sat by ourselves, quietly waiting for the board to be posted announcing the arrival of our train. When we looked at one another, we both had tears in our eyes. To this day, I still feel the lump in my throat. As I sat, I remembered what I'd felt on the day when I'd first arrived in Naples, when I'd stepped off the train after the long journey from Koenigsberg, when I'd been embarrassed about how I'd looked, that day I'd first met Paul. Back then, I'd had such a rush of emotions. That day at the train station, I had so many similar thoughts. I told Paul I was unprepared, amused, confused, aghast, frightened, and curious all at the same time. Now we were leaving, and Paul told me he felt the same.

Others have asked whether we felt in danger when we departed Naples. I can honestly say no, absolutely not. Neither Paul nor I ever felt we were running for our lives, fleeing, or trying to escape. We didn't feel the way the refugees must have felt when they'd come through our doors at the pensione. No, this was far more normal than that. We were simply leaving. No one was chasing us. We were taking our steps one at a time. We weren't looking over our shoulders. No one was watching us. In fact, no one paid us any attention. We didn't expect anything bad to happen. We were simply moving forward, hoping, and anxious to get on with our lives.

Life always seems to find its balance. When I arrived in Italy, during those first few days, I missed Germany terribly. It was my first time away, and I missed my home. I was so homesick. I remember discovering how different Italy was and how I told myself longingly that Italy was not Germany. Even on my last day in Naples, that day Paul and I sat at the train station, I still knew that Italy was not Germany. Italy could never be like Germany. But on that day, I knew that Italy was much better.

So much of me had changed. By that last day, I knew what I loved most about Italy was that it was so unlike Germany. Italy was passionate and caring. Germany was cold and brusque. I had conquered Naples, and Naples had conquered me. It had become my home. Only, now it had broken my heart, and we no longer belonged. But I was still in love. I couldn't imagine what it must have been like for those still trying to leave Germany.

Those moments were strangely silent – a six-hour train trip with little idea of what would come next. My recollection is that the train was not particularly empty or crowded and the ride was rather ordinary. Everyone was going about their business. Everyone had a place to go. Paul and I? We were simply two more passengers trying to reach the next destination, two more faces on the train. No one on the train that day gave us more than a moment's thought. I am sure that no one understood that Paul and I were leaving Naples forever. What once had been so important now was so unimportant. Our few possessions did not matter. We carried our lifetime full of memories.

We were resigned to our fate. If there were dots to be connected, they did not look like the amber stones Father and I had spotted on the beach in Kahlberg so long ago. That day, there were no dots to be found. There were only empty spaces.

CHAPTER FIFTY-THREE

We knew that life in Rome would be far different than life in Naples. Every place I have ever lived, before or after, has been that way, different, unlike any other, each for its own reasons, each with its own rules. Rome would be no exception. We only planned to be in Rome for a short time, as long as it would take to receive our entry visas from the American Consulate. Although we didn't expect to stay too long, we did need to find a place where we could afford to live, and that was not as easy a decision as it might sound. Perhaps I make things more complicated than they first appear.

It had taken us many years to embrace the Neapolitan way of life. And by the time we left, I think we had. When I'd first arrived in Naples, it had been a big change to leave the Jewish community in Koenigsberg and join the German community in Naples. Ironically, when we left

Naples for Rome, I found myself considering the idea of rejoining the Jewish community. This would be much easier now. We spoke Italian. Oddly, I found myself rebelling and dismissed this thought. Years of living in Italy, in the melting pot of all races and religions, had made me prefer the broader Italian community. That was where I now belonged.

In Naples, since we never joined the synagogue or become part of the Jewish community, we really never gave much thought to who was Jewish and who was not. It certainly was not like the way I had grown up in Koenigsberg. In Naples, this was a distinction few cared about. It was deeply personal, something to be respected, and clearly not something to wear on one's sleeve. Even after Mussolini unveiled the racial laws, I generally found that Italians continued to politely respect one another's differences. This was deeply seated in Italian culture. The few Jews we did know in Naples were much like us, middle class, assimilated, and not particularly religious. Nearly all had been born in Italy. The one thing that made us different was that we had been born in Germany.

Before the racial laws were issued, in all my years in Italy, the only time our Jewishness had been made an issue was by a German at the German club, never with our neighbors or any other acquaintances. In Naples, generations of distinctions and differences had all been thrown together in the same big pot and stirred, like a finely seasoned soup. We were all in the same mess together. And for many, generations of mixed marriages of one sort or another had given most everyone mixed blood. One couldn't tell who had Jewish, Catholic, Muslim, or Protestant blood somewhere in their family tree or who had descended from Teutons, Longobards, Goths, Visigoths, Normans, or Spaniards. What we shared was a common culture, a common tongue, and a common love for Italy. That is how we had become Italians.

I was unsure if Rome would be the same. Our world had changed, and so had Italy. Although Rome was not that far from Naples when measured in miles, distances can be deceiving, and we were totally unfamiliar with the way of life in Rome. The little we knew of Rome was that it was where more than one quarter of Italy's Jews lived, still a very small number compared to the rest of the population but many times the number who lived in Naples.

Someone had told Paul that many of the Jews in Rome were poor, only semiliterate, and deeply religious, and that the old Roman ghetto surrounding Portico d'Ottavia was the only place in Italy where there still was a large Jewish neighborhood with a very strong Jewish tradition. We had no idea whether that was true or not and were unsure where we might fit in. As to whether the Jews in Rome carried out their daily lives as part of Rome's general population or lived within their own segregated world, that remained to be seen.

The one thing I realized was that I did not want us to live in a segregated world. Italy had accepted us and taught us to become part of the greater community. Living apart, mostly within the Jewish community, the way I had lived in Koenigsberg, was not where we belonged. There was no question of our roots or our identity; we would always be Jewish. That was our race. I am always proud of who I am. However, I did not need to live in a community of Jews in order to remain a Jew, much as I did not need to live in a community of Germans to remain a German. All we wanted was for us to be left alone to go about our life until we could figure out how to get to America.

I know that I said we did not feel in danger. That is true. Yet when I am completely honest, I admit to having had concerns about our safety. I was not about to be foolish. We had been told that the Italian government was sending foreign Jews living in Italy into internment camps and removing them from the general populace. In that regard, Paul and I were no longer considered foreign. We had been in Italy long enough, and that restriction did not apply to us. But no one knew what might happen next. Would this order be extended to all Jews living in Italy?

In a selfish, self-centered way, I felt it was better to blend into the general population of Rome and try to remain inconspicuous rather than put ourselves in a neighborhood that was only inhabited by Jews. It wasn't that we were trying to hide. We simply preferred not to be noticed. I am glad that we made that decision. Had we been forced to stay in Rome for much longer than we were, we would have found ourselves in a virtual prison within the four cramped blocks wedged between the Tiber, the Fontana delle Tartarughe, the Teatro di Marcello, and the Palazzo Cenci.

As soon as we arrived at the Rome train station, we went in search of a place to live, and I didn't care about the neighborhood, only that it was safe. Years earlier, I had made an acquaintance with an old woman who maintained a small pensione on Via dei Chiavari, not far from the Piazza di Spagna. She and I had exchanged recommendations from time to time. I knew nothing more of her on that day we suddenly arrived on her doorstep. Every day since, I have thanked my lucky stars and hoped that I have repaid her kindness.

There Paul and I were, appearing out of nowhere to stand at her door, and she could not have been more gracious and understanding. She remembered who I was and listened to our story. She was sympathetic to our plight and genuinely concerned for our welfare. We had no idea how long we might stay or how abruptly we might leave. Yet, she did not hesitate for an instant and rented us the simple one-room attic apartment above the pensione for a price we could afford. This tiny old woman and her husband were more concerned about their fellow human beings than how much rent we might pay. They were truly our Italian angels.

CHAPTER FIFTY-FOUR

As we sat in Rome during the spring and summer of 1941, there was little else that Paul and I could do but wait patiently to be called to the American consulate for our interviews. War activity in Rome was quite different from the way it had been in Naples. There were no air raids, and there was no bombing while we were living in Rome. Although the blackout policy had been imposed throughout Italy and, to some extent, was observed in Rome, it would be another two years before the streets of Rome were under attack. Then the entire working-class district of San Lorenzo was destroyed, and tragically, three hundred thousand Italian civilians were killed by the bombing raids.

Meanwhile, the war raged on elsewhere. Italian forces with German reinforcements fought against the British in North Africa. German and Italian forces invaded

Yugoslavia and Greece. London and industrial cities throughout Britain and Northern Ireland were heavily bombed. RAF squadrons bombed Berlin and Hamburg. And that June, the German army invaded the Soviet Union. In Rome, we were safely out of harm's way, far from any battle. But everyone was on guard. There always was the fear of what might happen next, particularly after the disasters in Greece, which delayed Germany's Russian invasion. There was no question that Italy was at war.

We each took our turn making daily trips to the consulate, hoping that something would happen and our number would be called. In my spare time, I did what I could to help with the cooking and cleaning at the pensione. That helped our finances a little, as our rent was adjusted in return. It made me feel good to contribute. Paul played cards with a few men who lived on the street, and he joined their late-afternoon gatherings on various doorsteps. Some afternoons, I took my pencils and paper and tried to sketch children as they played outside. We spent our evenings in quiet conversation. Sometimes, we played cards with neighbors. Mostly, we minded our own business.

Friends have asked me about the role of the Vatican and the Catholic Church during this period of time. We never sought their help, and I really don't know whether their assistance was available. I do know that many church leaders courageously took it upon themselves to help save the lives of Jews, but I believe most of those actions took place after Paul and I were able to leave Rome.

What I can tell you is based only upon my own personal observations. The Vatican remained neutral throughout the war. While Vatican leaders searched for a diplomatic resolution before war was declared, neutrality, not choosing a side, allowed the church to continue its spiritual mission during the war years. For various reasons, I have always been bothered by how the Church reacted to Mussolini's racial laws when they were issued. To me, it seemed that the Catholic Church was more concerned about who had the authority to set the rules for baptism and marriage than the welfare of Jews. I believe they should have taken more of a stand. During the time we remained in Italy, we rarely saw the Church denounce Mussolini or Hitler for their discriminatory practices or anti-Jewish persecutions. The newspapers reported a congenial relationship between the Pope and Mussolini. I have always wondered about that. I am not a student of history, but I have often reached the conclusion that religions claim little responsibility for man's wars except when it serves their own purpose.

There was no encouraging news from the American consulate. We learned that the U.S. State Department's visa division under the direction of Assistant Secretary Breckinridge Long was putting a higher priority on national security concerns at the expense of humanitarian needs. Long had been America's ambassador to Italy. Even then, we wondered about his relationship with Mussolini. Someone told Paul that Ambassador Long was unsympathetic to the plight of European Jews. Others said he had anti-Semitic leanings.

To our disappointment, weeks turned into months. There were times Paul and I discussed possibly trying to reach a different destination. Paul's nephew and his family had made it safely to Shanghai, and others had found passage to countries in South America, but each time this topic was broached, we ruled it out. America was where we belonged, and we remained hopeful that our wait would not be long. We wanted to be with our children. I wanted to hug my grandson. We wanted to be near family. All I wanted was to be part of their lives.

The world situation seemed to change every day. Mussolini's propaganda machine reported glorious victories. From others, we heard different stories, that these were false reports and that German troops were needed to reinforce the Italian army. <u>Italian soldiers were ill-equipped for war.</u>

Spring became summer. How much longer we would have to stay in Rome became a growing concern. Fewer and fewer alternatives were available. We had met many others trying to find a place to go, and I was told that many countries had closed their doors. We all faced the same issues, and we all had reached the same conclusion. The future seemed inevitable. <u>German troops were entering Italy.</u> Mussolini's role seemed more and more diminished. Most thought Hitler had gained the upper hand and that Mussolini was acting the part of Hitler's puppet. On the streets, this became a very real worry.

Mussolini was a complicated politician. Everyone had their opinions, but not all were expressed. There were some who believed that the bigger danger was not Mussolini as much as those who filled his key appointments. He still had the support of many Italians, but few could understand the motives of those around him. Il

Duce had been surrounded by Nazis ever since he had aligned himself with Hitler. Nearly everyone we spoke with was convinced that, by year's end, Italy would be controlled by Germany in one way or another, perhaps even occupied by German troops. Even in Rome, away from the war, we could sense the growing German presence. Who could predict what might happen next? Would we wake up one morning to learn that Germany had overtaken Italy? The alliance between Hitler and Mussolini might not matter. We heard too many rumors of what was happening to Jews in German-occupied areas. One thing remained certain. There was a clock ticking. We were running out of time to leave Europe and find our way to America.

I do not want to exaggerate the situation as I tell you this story or give you the impression that we were shaking with fear, because we weren't. The entire time we lived in Rome, Paul and I lived a calm and peaceful life. We were largely unaffected by any type of segregation or discrimination. I can't recall any anti-Semitic taunts or threats directed at either of us. Others may have had different experiences. Perhaps living where we did in Rome, fully assimilated with the general population, gave us a certain amount of shelter, a certain amount of confidence. I can't really be sure. For us, the problem was that we were always worried about when the next shoe would drop. It is difficult to remain calm and peaceful with that constant concern. It mattered little what we did. Events were out of our control. Nobody could predict the future.

We certainly were known to be Jewish by the authorities. Anyone who was Jewish was known. When we arrived in Rome, we complied with Italian law and registered our presence. The racial laws had been very clear about that. Two Jewish parents made you Jewish. One Jewish parent, and you could declare your religion. After the racial laws were announced, ten percent of the Jews in Italy chose to convert to Catholicism. This was a choice we never considered. It was out of the question. But that didn't matter. We were both descendants of Jews. We always knew who we were, and I don't believe you can ever change who you were meant to be. If someone wanted to search for us, they could find us. But they never looked, and they never did.

Who was Jewish and who was not had always been known, just like every other ethnic group and nationality, ever since Mussolini had taken power. The government had information about everyone. The census takers collected it. That was the way the system worked in Mussolini's Italy. At the time, we never gave it a moment's thought. Why would we? Until late 1938, leading Jewish figures had always been close to Mussolini. That changed, but for the first sixteen years of his reign, a number of prominent Jews were his supporters and advisers. I can still repeat the words Mussolini said to the chief rabbi of Rome: "Fascism has to contend with too many problems to desire to create more. For us Fascists, there can be no antagonism towards the Jews." When we lived in Rome, it was not my safety that I worried about; it was the uncertainty of our future. That was what kept me up late at night.

I really prefer not to think about our time in Rome. It never was one particular moment or any particularly memory; it was the persistent drumbeat of uncertainty and not knowing what might happen next. My problem was that waiting for our quota numbers to be called dragged on and on. Since the day the children had left on the ship to America, our life had been at a standstill. It was difficult to keep one's balance. We both knew that feeling sorry for ourselves would not change anything, but it was hard not to. We were stuck in mud, and there was not a single thing we could do to get out of it.

Our nights were sleepless and emotional – not every night, but far too many. On those nights, we talked to each other far more than we slept. Too many times, we argued and became angry with one another. There were nights that I threw tantrums. And there were other times when we just cried. Some days, I could not stand to be in the same room with Paul. Other days, I am certain he felt the same way about me. Paul was so concerned that we might need to ask the children for their help with money. We always worried about having enough money, that it would not last. We both wanted the children to concern themselves with their lives and not ours. We promised each other that, whatever they were to spend to help us, we would find a way to repay. It was a difficult time. It didn't matter if the world was filled with millions and millions of people; Paul and I felt very much alone and helpless. Now I know that, every day, there are people who find themselves displaced. No matter the reason, I imagine this feeling repeats throughout the world. It always has. It makes me sad to consider that it always will.

CHAPTER FIFTY-FIVE

We frequently didn't know what to believe. Dictators have their own reasons for choosing their words and generally have the freedom to do and say as they wish. Like many politicians, there are times we thought that Mussolini misstated the facts to support his claims. Vincenzo always encouraged me to let the facts lead me to my own conclusions. Now I wonder how often Mussolini did the reverse, stating his conclusions first and then demanding the facts to justify his actions. In this strictly censored environment, we were only told his reasons, never an opposing view. The reality was that, during the time we lived in Rome, we were given few facts. This made it difficult to be certain about any conclusion.

What we did hear were rumors, always rumors. Each day brought new ones, and frequently, they would be revised and changed. The rumors reminded me of when the children had been small and they'd played the whisper game with their friends. They would sit in a circle. One would repeat the whisper to the next. When it came back to the child who'd started the whisper, the words were all changed. That was how it was with the rumors. Each time they were repeated, the words would change. Sometimes, they would be exaggerated for emphasis. Other times, they would simply be wrong. *We* would be exchanged with *they*. *Possibly* would be exchanged with *certainty*.

Gossip and rumor were part of Italy's culture as long as I lived there. These were national pastimes. In Naples, gossip was a ritual embraced every time one opened a window and joined the neighborhood in conversation. Rome was no different. What distinguished Rome in wartime was the unsettling and persistent question of whether someone who shouldn't hear might be listening.

Throughout Mussolini's reign, we all were aware that one needed to be wary of what was said in public. There were conversations that were acceptable to take place in front of others. There were other conversations, particularly those that criticized Mussolini's government or Il Duce personally, that were only to be shared in private.

That had been our initial concern when Vincenzo had first arrived at the pensione. We had not been sure whether we could trust him when he'd asked questions about Mussolini. There was an invisible line that was not to be crossed. One needed to choose words carefully when talking about Mussolini, whether leaning out windows and sharing the news of the day with neighbors or visiting with friends at the street corner. We always lived under the umbrella of a dictatorship. Individual opinion was not encouraged and, in fact, was discouraged. We were to follow, not lead. What was good for the country always came first no matter who or what was sacrificed. Freedom of speech was a limited freedom. Criticism could easily be misunderstood and mistaken for opposition. It was common knowledge that there were penalties if one crossed over the line. We all heard the stories of Mussolini's Blackshirts tying enemies to chairs and pouring entire bottles of castor oil down their throats to give them chronic diarrhea. Intimidation can be a powerful weapon.

By the time we moved to Rome, the Nazis had already begun to share Mussolini's stage. We had even seen evidence of this in Naples, when we'd thought there were Nazis amongst our German guests, infiltrators posing as businessmen. We never could be one hundred percent certain. In Rome, people always claimed this was true, that there were German agents living among us, Nazi spies. We never knew who might be listening. Not all Germans were Nazis, but not all Nazis were German.

With our carefully censored news, most of us were suspicious of war reports broadcast on the radio and appearing in the newspapers. Yet even if we didn't always believe what was reported, we knew it was important to pay attention. There were subtleties. Sometimes, we had to read the tea leaves. At times, the smallest announcement was a hint of what might come next. One could never forget that the news in Italy was controlled by the propaganda authorities. Editors were sent detailed guidelines about what to stress and what to omit in order to conform with Mussolini's agenda. One thing we all knew was that whatever was reported, whether true or untrue, was what Mussolini wanted us to believe.

Throughout our stay in Rome, Paul was always troubled by the news. We were both frustrated by our inability to separate rumor from fact. What we learned from the news weighed heavily on Paul. Our lack of confidence in the facts only made the weight heavier. I suppose that Paul was the eternal pessimist and I was the eternal optimist, just like our twins. I hope that by our merger, the result was a couple of realists. I believe that was how we assessed most situations.

From those fleeing Germany and the growing list of places occupied by Hitler and the Nazis, we heard reports that Jewish travel was becoming more and more restricted. If memory serves me right, during that summer of 1941, Germany continued to issue exit papers and permitted Jews to leave after anything owned was confiscated by the Nazis. But we also learned that the policy was changing, and we began to hear something different. We were told that, rather than be encouraged to leave, some Jews were being denied exit papers. They were forced to stay and sent to work camps. Reportedly, others were deported to concentration camps in Poland and elsewhere, especially those unable to work. Again, the rumors were flying. The speculation was chilling, horrible, and unbelievable – a barbaric behavior with atrocities that hardly seemed possible in our day and age.

War made all sides suspicious. We learned that Great Britain had confined many Germans and Italians to internment camps and classified them as enemy aliens.

There was a concern that some might be enemy foreign agents. I suppose that many thought segregating the possible enemy from the general population made sense. I can understand how German bombing raids on Britain's industrial centers could produce not only a sense of anxiety on the streets of London, but also a reactionary kneejerk response by politicians and government. What didn't make sense was why the British would do this to those who had fled in search of safe havens and to seek asylum. They were clearly not Nazi spies. I remember when Paul's nephew told us about his wife's fifteen-year-old brother, who had been sent to Scotland only months before war was declared. British officials had sent him to an internment camp on the Isle of Man. They thought he might be a foreign enemy.

We heard so many things, most true, some exaggerated. An acquaintance of Paul's told him that the new Vichy government in France had issued racial laws patterned after those in Germany and Italy. There was a rumor that Mussolini was actually saving the lives of Jews by sending them to camps in Italy so they could be protected. Someone else told us that Jews in France were no longer permitted to leave, that they were being rounded up and sent to camps. We heard that Jews in occupied countries like Poland and Austria were confined to ghettos until they could be deported to concentration camps. One person told Paul that it was as if these people had disappeared from the face of the earth, never to be heard from again. All communication had ceased.

CHAPTER FIFTY-SIX

What I remember most are the contradictions. What made our wait in Rome so tiresome and confusing was that we were always receiving mixed signals. The Italian racial laws were quite clear in their restrictions, but Italian authorities, even Mussolini's militia, were not always aggressive in enforcing the regulations. We weren't sure what to make of that. It was as if we were walking on eggshells all the time, waiting for the next shoe to drop. One official might be kind and understanding, another abrupt and demanding.

I believe much of this lackadaisical attitude when it came to enforcing the racial restrictions was common because ordinary Italians had larger concerns. Despite Mussolini's rules, Italians recognized that Jews were not the problem. For ordinary Italians, the war had changed so much in their daily personal lives. With each passing day, everyone found themselves more affected. Families were concerned about their loved ones serving in the armed forces. Many food items were in short supply or were no longer available. Jobs and incomes were disrupted. Mothers and fathers were concerned about the welfare of their children. On the streets, people would talk about the war, not the Jews. It was a stressful and difficult time for everyone.

One could tell that Italians were growing weary of war. Mussolini had been pursuing his dream of a new Roman empire for as long as most Italians could remember, and now they were becoming tired. While Mussolini continued to silence his opposition, cracks were starting to appear among his supporters. They were no longer as vocal.

It hadn't helped that the Italian army had sustained disastrous and humiliating defeats. Many lives had been lost in the north African campaigns. Success had only come with the reinforcement of German troops. There was little enthusiasm when Italian troops were sent to the Eastern Front to support the German invasion of the Soviet Union.

The problem for Mussolini was that he had been backed into Hitler's corner. And for many, the bigger issue was clear: Mussolini's debts to Hitler continued to grow, and it made the situation more difficult to predict. The apprentice was now clearly the master. Would Mussolini be strong enough to listen to what the Italian people were saying, or would he have no choice but to follow Hitler's demands and demonic actions?

As the Nazi presence continued to grow in Italy, we heard rumors that Hitler and Germany were pressuring

Italy to deport Jews to concentration camps, an action similar to what was taking place in the countries Germany occupied. If that became true, Paul and I might be in significant danger. But again, there were the contradictions. We were told that Italian military authorities had resisted and refused to comply with Germany's demand. Mussolini was either unable or unwilling to force the issue. Some went so far as to claim that Italian authorities were protecting Jews in Italian-occupied territories by evacuating them to the Italian mainland so they would not be deported to concentration camps, a signal of a more tolerant view by Italy's leadership.

The one thing we knew for certain was that the lines at the American consulate were growing longer every day. It was obvious that there were more refugees in Italy and that more people were running for their lives.

Our biggest fear was that, as confidence in Mussolini faded in Italy, he would be forced to turn more and more to Germany for support and inspiration. And no one knew what that could mean. If the frightening rumors of what was happening to Jews elsewhere were true, then we needed to leave Italy as quickly as possible. We had little choice but to act on rumor.

CHAPTER FIFTY-SEVEN

Needing to leave and wanting to leave were not the same as being able to leave. That remained our dilemma. With all the rumors and contradictions, it was impossible to assess how much longer we could stay in Italy without putting our lives at risk. No one could answer that question with any certainty. And even if we knew the answer, our choices of where to go next remained limited. America remained unquestionably our first choice, but there continued to be many others anxiously standing in line ahead of us. There was no guarantee. Unless something were to change dramatically, we were stuck waiting in Rome no matter the risk.

I need to give you a better explanation. That summer of 1941, for those still allowed to leave, finding a way to the United States was at the top of everyone's list. America was quickly becoming the last and only choice. The list of other places one could go had become dangerously short. And the stark reality was that, for far too many, it had become too late. The Nazis had closed their borders. They had missed their chance. They had no way out.

Leaving was a complicated process. There with many pitfalls. In order to leave, one had to move through a series of tightly locked doors with little assurance of what was waiting on the other side. Much like trying to find one's way through a maze, locating the keys was only the first of many issues. Little was obvious. The only way to reach the end required passing each door in the proper order. There were many obstacles. Some were known. Others might suddenly appear and make one start over.

For us, the most critical issue remained obtaining entry visas from the American consulate. Although Paul and I had been Italian citizens for nearly forty years, we had been sent to Germany's long line. By that summer, we had been on the waiting list for more than eighteen months. All we were told was that it might be six more months before our applications could be considered. Then we would be called for interviews. While waiting, there were other issues to consider.

Being allowed to enter and granted an entry visa was only one thing. Everyone also was required to have permission to leave. This had nothing to do with the American consulate. In our case, permission had to be granted by the Italian authorities. Government officials had to stamp passports with no objections. Sometimes, they had to issue exit papers. Each country had its own set of rules. Some countries severely limited the possessions one could take. For example, Germany limited silverware to one everyday place setting per person. Everything else that one owned, including money and property, had to be left behind except for the equivalent of four dollars, which one was permitted to carry. Italy restricted the amount of Italian currency we could take. As I recall, this was little more than one hundred dollars per person. Another rule limited personal clothing to four of each item. Lists needed to be filled out and approvals granted for everything to be taken. No gold or jewelry was allowed. Any taxes owed had to be paid, any legal issues resolved, any police matters dealt with. Many visits with the authorities might be required. There were stages to this process. Some items could be taken care of days in advance. Other activities, like searching suitcases and departure taxes, were handled by officials at the border on the day of departure. Rich or poor, most of us found ourselves destitute by the time we left.

Fortunately, Paul and I had little trouble complying with these regulations. We no longer owned property and had little money. All of our possessions had been left behind in Naples. Everything we owned was packed in our two old suitcases. We had been friends with the police officials in Naples, so getting their approval had not been an issue. The chief of police was supportive and understood our situation. Perhaps others found this step more difficult.

Another major concern was finding our way to a European seaport where ships were sailing. The seaport issue had changed because of the war, and many ports had closed or had important restrictions. By the summer of 1941, finding an open seaport posed a significant problem. When Italy entered the war in June of 1940, nearly all transatlantic passenger ships ceased departing from Italy. After Germany's occupation of France and the fall of Paris, nearly all the other exit routes from Europe evaporated. Lisbon, in neutral Portugal, and an occasional port in Spain remained as the last remaining escape routes for anyone fleeing Europe and the war. We had little choice. At the appropriate time, we would need to find our way to Lisbon.

Reaching Lisbon could be difficult. Portugal had been overrun by refugees trying to escape Europe. To control the situation, Portuguese officials had limited entry to only those who had proof that their passage was booked on a scheduled ship. Many refugees without bookings chose to enter Portugal by foot from Spain in order to avoid having to deal with the border entry issues. We rejected that notion. Portuguese officials in Lisbon checked papers carefully, and they quickly expelled those who had entered illegally. We didn't need that problem hanging over our heads. Neither of us felt that we could endure the adventure of walking over mountains into Portugal or the thought that, if caught, we would find ourselves in a camp somewhere in Spain.

Finding a ship and purchasing tickets presented another significant hurdle. There was no reason to purchase tickets on a ship until we knew which country would accept us. Most companies reviewed entry documents before releasing tickets for their ships. Berths were in great demand and expensive. Prices often increased daily, and bookings had to be paid in American dollars, yet another obstacle. Crossing the Atlantic while a war was raging might be perilous, but traveling by ship was the only affordable alternative. As was our experience when the children left, often, spaces would become available at the last possible moment, an element of surprise that could change how all the other issues were handled.

For Paul and me, the only choice we really had was picking the safest place to live while we waited for the American consulate to act. We had some idea of the situation in France, no idea of the situation in Spain, and were not comfortable with the idea of waiting in Morocco. Those choices really didn't matter, because we needed to be in Rome, near the American consulate. Only after we received entry visas to the United States would we be in a position to proceed to Lisbon. Then we could worry about the border crossings, transit visas, ship tickets, and funds. Whatever route we were to take would have its own set of obstacles.

CHAPTER FIFTY-EIGHT

Suddenly, all of our plans were thrown into the air. We had no forewarning. The U.S. State Department issued a new directive to its consulates. Paul and I always knew that submitting an application would not automatically result in being granted an entry visa, but we never considered that our approval could become an issue. Applications were carefully reviewed by State Department officials and could be denied for an assortment of reasons. There were strict rules to the approval process, and we were prepared to follow every single one. We had spent the better part of two years waiting in line and never contemplated the remotest possibility that our applications would not be accepted. But now there were new rules that called our departure into question.

Only many years later did I learn of the bitter debate that took place among State Department officials that summer. My old friend Vincenzo was right. Too many people had never met a Jew. They only knew what others had told them. Generations of false impressions and misleading images had nurtured an unconscious form of anti-Semitism. Why else would America think we might be the enemy? There was no other explanation.

Consuls general were instructed not to admit anyone to the United States if there was any doubt about their political reliability. While we could not imagine how that could become a problem for us, that July, a second regulation was issued. It forbade the granting of a visa to anyone who had close relatives in an Axis-occupied territory. That second regulation changed everything, and it was issued with the intent to do so. No one could give us a clear definition of who might be considered a close relative. All visa applications would be reviewed in Washington, D.C., by a committee made up of State and Justice Department officials, military officials, and the FBI.

For most German Jewish refugees, the process became longer, and it became virtually impossible to get a visa. Nearly everyone had left a close relative behind. My cousins remained in Germany. There was no way to prove or disprove how close or distant our relationships might be. Unless our quota number came up and our applications could be reviewed, we had no idea whether we would be granted visas. We both agreed. Given the political climate, there was the very real likelihood that the American consulate would not approve our immigration application no matter how long we waited. Then what would we do?

Throughout our time in Rome, the troubling question we avoided and hoped we would never be forced to address was: if we were unable to go to the United States, what would we do, and where would we go? This was the unthinkable problem, and I always refused to entertain the notion that we would go elsewhere. We longed to see our children again. Having each other to lean upon was not enough for me. We were comforted knowing that our immediate family was safe in the United States, but as a mother, I wanted to put my arms around my children. I needed more. I needed to hug their necks. I needed to look into their eyes and know that they were happy with their lives.

Now my longing did not matter. We were forced to consider the alternatives. The risk of staying in Rome any longer was too great. It was time to leave Italy. We would have to worry about America later. We turned our attention to Cuba. I had a family connection in Havana. We had considered going to Cuba once before, even before we left Naples, but had ruled it out. Then we were told there was no possibility. But now Cuba had a new president, Fulgencio Batista, and it was time to consider Cuba again.

CHAPTER FIFTY-NINE

At one time, Cuba was considered a safe waiting area for refugees trying to reach the United States. By purchasing Cuban landing certificates, European refugees could disembark in Havana, where they would wait temporarily for their U.S. entry visas to be processed. Others would often frequently proceed from Cuba to countries in Central and South America. My sister Jenny was able to reach the United States by going through Cuba.

When Paul and I first explored this option, we were advised against pursuing it. There were many issues. Cuban policy had been chaotic and inconsistent. At varying times, its borders had been closed and then reopened, only to be closed again. Ships had been turned around and sent back to Europe. Passengers had been denied entry. At one point, U.S. officials advised Cuba that European refugees stopping in Cuba might not be eligible for American entry visas. Then Cuban officials became worried that refugees on temporary visas would be forced to stay in Cuba. Once again, they revised their policies and closed their borders. What made matters even worse was the fact that Cuban immigration officials had a long history of corruption.

Most of us considering Cuba were familiar with the story of the M.S. *St. Louis* and shared the concern that it could be repeated. In May of 1939, the luxury ocean liner M.S. *St. Louis* set sail from Hamburg for the two-week voyage to Havana. Nine hundred and thirty passengers were aboard. They were carrying landing certificates purchased from Cuban officials for their temporary stay in Cuba. When the ship arrived in Havana and the passengers waited for permission to disembark, no one had any idea that the landing certificates purchased from the Cuban immigration office were fictitious. These tourist visas had been declared null and void by the Cuban government because they had been issued illegally. Apparently, the certificates had been sold as part of an elaborate moneymaking scheme by the then director-general of Cuban immigration.

Only twenty-eight of the passengers were allowed off the ship in Havana that day. The others remained aboard, waiting for the matter to be resolved. Prolonged and frantic negotiations took place. The Cuban government refused to negotiate as long as the ship remained in Cuban waters. The U.S. government refused to intervene. Intervention would contravene the United States' Good Neighbor Policy with Latin America. Urgent appeals were made to President Roosevelt and others. Even officials in Canada were asked if the refugees could be accepted there. Some speculated that there were Nazi spies on the ship. Cuban officials made demands for financial guarantees that kept changing.

I once read that, before the ship left Hamburg, Germany's Nazi government had been made aware of the fake landing documents. Knowing this, they chose to allow the M.S. *St. Louis* to depart anyway. They wanted to use this incident as propaganda. The Nazis wanted the entire world to see that no country would allow the Jews to enter their borders. And indeed, that is what the world learned. This story made the front pages of newspapers across the globe.

Three weeks after setting sail for Cuba, the M.S. *St. Louis* turned around and returned to Europe with more than nine hundred passengers still aboard. On the return, the desperate passengers travelled close enough to the United States that they were able to see the lights off the Florida coast. They were never given permission to disembark. The M.S. *St. Louis* was not the only ship that met this fate. Two smaller ships carrying Jewish refugees sailed to Cuba that same year. Both the French ship the *Flandre* and the British vessel the *Orduna* were refused permission to dock in Cuba. There were similar reports of others.

Despite these and other incidents, the regime in Cuba had changed, and we had reason to believe that the country might now offer us a possibility. My first cousin's daughter lived in Cuba. She had married a Cuban man and moved from Berlin to Havana a number of years earlier, well before the war. They'd raised their family there. We had reason to believe that the daughter had some connections within the Cuban government. Her parents, my first cousins, had been passengers on the ill-fated M.S. *St. Louis*. She'd wanted her parents to join her family in Cuba. Their journey had been successful. They'd been two of the fortunate twenty-eight passengers allowed to disembark the ship that day and remain in Cuba.

Time was running out, and so were our options. We asked our family in America to make another appeal to the cousins in Havana. We desperately needed their help. Communication was limited, and mail from America took days to arrive. Letters were sent via airmail using the Pan Am Clipper, but the mail from America arrived in Marseille and had to find its way to Rome. In early September, we received an official letter and documents forwarded from immigration officials in Havana. If we were able to find passage to Cuba, the Cuban government would grant us permission to live there until such time as we could immigrate to the United States. A second envelope contained two tickets. Somehow, our children had been able to find and book passage for us on a ship that would leave Lisbon that November.

Many years later, I learned how they paid for the tickets. My old jewelry had been sold, but the money received had not been nearly enough. Paul's brother Ludwig, who'd died only a few months before, left them just enough for the balance. It was their gift from heaven, and all the money they had in the world. Ludwig had helped Paul's nephew's family. Now Ludwig's funds were used to help us. Our children never complained about their own struggles. They used their inheritance to pay for our tickets and never asked that it be repaid. Sometimes, it takes a family of angels to carry those in need from one dot to the next. Indeed, this was one of those times.

CHAPTER SIXTY

After all those months of waiting in Rome, the next chapter of our journey to America was about to begin. Armed with the documents allowing us to leave for Cuba, Paul and I were anxious to find our way to Lisbon, where we could finally board the ship.

The war had not come to Portugal. Antonio de Oliveira Salazar, Portugal's heavy-handed prime minister, had managed to maintain a position of neutrality and to stay on the sidelines despite extraordinary pressures exerted by both the Allied and Axis powers. Everyone wanted Portugal's tungsten ore, a major material needed to manufacture weapons for the war.

In Lisbon, we would finally leave behind many of our worries. It promised to be a welcome relief. We were tired of the uncertainty and couldn't get there soon enough. Our stay in Lisbon would be short, perhaps a few weeks.

That would depend upon the length of the journey to get there. As for how long we might stay in Cuba, we had no idea, but we were resigned to that fate. At least we could look forward to Lisbon, where the lights would brighten and there would be no more blackouts. For all of us trying to escape Europe's horrors, Lisbon was the city of hope. It promised to be the start of a new future. For that, we were grateful. I was weary. I needed some hope.

We quickly learned of the challenges involved with getting to Lisbon. And once again, we found ourselves confronted with rumors and an absence of facts. How many times would we ask the same questions? How often would we find ourselves in situations where there were no answers? We knew which borders would have to be crossed but had little idea how long the trip might take, what obstacles might await, or what costs might have to be paid. Ordinarily, the journey by train would require two to three days, but these were not ordinary times. With the war underway, everything was impossible to predict. Even with our angels watching over us, connecting the two dots between Rome and Lisbon would require closing our eyes and taking a long leap.

I had hoped we could begin the journey immediately, within days of receiving the official travel documents. But that wish was quickly extinguished and replaced by more anxiety and confusion. Obtaining transit visas to travel through Spain, Portugal, and war-divided France was more complicated and time consuming than we had been led to believe. We were hesitant to leave without these required papers in hand. It was better to remain in Rome and wait for the transit visas to be issued. We knew how to survive in Rome. Neither of us wanted to risk being detained or delayed at an unfamiliar border crossing as we made our way to Lisbon.

Others have asked me why we hadn't already applied for these transit visas sooner. There were months of waiting in Rome when our applications could have been reviewed by the proper authorities. The answer was simple. We could not apply. It was not possible. And there were a number of reasons why this was so.

No European country we travelled through would consider a request or issue a transit visa unless a transatlantic ship was booked and bona fide immigration papers granted for a destination somewhere. No country wanted to risk the possibility that Jewish refugees would become stranded within their borders. No country had the willingness to provide protection, nor did they possess the financial resources to care for and feed the thousands like us trying to reach Lisbon. Certainly, neither occupied nor Vichy France had any desire to do so. They each wanted the refugees to enter and exit as quickly as possible and not to stay within their borders longer than necessary. Each country wanted the assurance that refugees would be permitted to enter the next country along the route to Lisbon.

Portugal, in particular, was deeply concerned about the growing number of refugees in Lisbon. Transit papers for Lisbon were in great demand, and Portugal limited the time one could stay to less than thirty days. Documents were carefully scrutinized. Many that were carried were forged or fictitious. Those more desperate took their chances and hid in the darkness of the shadows. This was an exodus. Everyone could breathe a sigh of relief when the refugees left the shores of Europe.

Portugal was the key. We needed approval from Lisbon. That was the very first step. With Portugal, luck was on our side. The Cuban immigration visa enabled the Portuguese consul in Rome to transmit our request for a Portuguese transit visa to Lisbon for approval. This was significant. Portuguese consuls could no longer provide visas. All transit visas had to be issued by the authorities in Lisbon. Portugal had changed its rules and tightened its restrictions. Lisbon had been overwhelmed by refugees when the Portuguese consul in Bordeaux, Aristides de Sousa Mendes, had issued some thirty thousand transit visas within a few-day period following Germany's occupation of France. Although he was credited with saving the lives of thousands trying to escape the horrors of the Nazi regime, he had been recalled and punished by the Portuguese government. As a result, the new rules required requests for Portuguese transit visas to be closely screened by Lisbon officials to prevent this from happening again. Though delayed for several weeks, our application was eventually approved.

Spanish officials refused to even consider any request to travel through Spain until approval was received from Portugal. While Spain was also officially neutral, it was cooperating with Germany. It had been two years since Franco had won the civil war, and Spain was a dangerous place for Jewish refugees. It was besieged by the local secret police, and members of Germany's Gestapo remained there. Refugees with the right papers could transit through Spain, but it was not safe to linger because of the strict enforcement of the rules. After France had surrendered to Germany in June 1940, tens of thousands of refugees had flocked to the Spanish border, hoping to reach Spanish or Portuguese seaports. Thousands without visas to their final destinations crossed the border by foot and became stranded in Spain. Franco wanted nothing to do with them. They were either detained in camps or immediately sent back to France.

The French transit visa was easier to obtain, particularly for Italian citizens. That request was submitted to the Armistice Commission in Turin. Finally, we had to find our way through the bewildering bureaucracy of the Vichy regime in Southern France. They had their own set of requirements, some of which we were not able to resolve until we passed through Marseille.

By the second week of October, our papers were in order. Within a matter of days, we arrived by train in Lisbon. The trip was uneventful, and I remember few details of the journey. I was very nervous. Sleep became my best remedy. It was as if I fell asleep in Rome and awoke in Lisbon. Paul sat up awake and dealt with matters for the entire trip. Later, he told me that the trip had been surprisingly simple, almost ordinary, and without delays. Having the transit visas in hand helped. At the border crossings, the officials were all abundantly clear. Nobody had invited us to stay. Everyone wanted to see us leave. They were pleased to see us go.

There is one additional topic that I must discuss, and I want to be certain to describe it correctly. There should be no misunderstanding. When Paul and I left Rome, it was beginning to become difficult and close to impossible to depart. Yet there was still time. Conditions favored our departure, and we were being encouraged to leave. This was not true for many others.

In Italy, the number of refugees trying to leave was small compared to elsewhere in Europe: thousands, not hundreds of thousands. There were many Italian Jews and Jewish refugees in Italy who were stranded because they had no other place to go and no way to get there. But the situation under Mussolini and the way Jews were treated in Italy pales in comparison to the horrors faced by those in areas controlled by Hitler and the Nazis.

Despite the complicated process to obtain transit visas, we generally felt safe as we made our journey from Rome to Lisbon. We never experienced danger, only the onward wishes by officials at the borders. Within weeks, the situation would change for those in Germany and German-occupied countries. And by the time Paul and I made our way, for far too many, it was already too late. Some had waited too long to leave and had lost their chance. Others were denied the opportunity. Now they had no way to leave and, sadly, for most, their fates had been decided.

By the summer of 1941, when we left Mussolini's Italy, the German government was preparing plans for the mass extermination of all Jews remaining in the German empire. My brother Martin had been right four years earlier when he'd warned that there would come a time when

Germany would not know what to do with the Jews who remained in their empire. Now Germany had made its decision.

By November of 1941, most borders would close, and few Jews would be allowed to leave. In December of 1941, Chelmno, located in a part of Poland annexed by Germany, began operations as the first killing facility. Already by that time, more than half a million Jews had been executed when the Germans invaded the Soviet Union. By early 1942, Hitler's Germany would fully embrace the *Final Solution*. Jews would be deported to concentration camps and to death camps, where they were murdered. Germany had decided what to do with the Jews who remained in their empire. Germany would solve this problem once and for all. The Jews would be gassed and burned and exterminated from the human race.

How could the Nazis believe that the world would be grateful? As long as I live, I will never understand.

CHAPTER SIXTY-ONE

Frequently, I am perplexed by the little moments that I remember, those long-forgotten incidents that always seem so unremarkable when they occur but so unusual when they return as ancient memories. The moment Paul and I stepped off the train at the Lisbon station, we both stared at one another and laughed. Like Dorothy in *The Wizard of Oz*, we were both blinking and rubbing our eyes, I from too much sleep and Paul from too little. It was as if we had taken two different journeys, ridden on different trains, and were completely surprised to see each other standing there.

And once again, I felt the wave of emotions I always sensed when I arrived at a new place. I found myself unprepared, amused, confused, aghast, frightened, and curious all in the same instant. I was so grateful to have Paul by my side. With him, I knew we would make our way to

America. I didn't know how long it might take, but I knew we would make it. Fate had given me such a good-hearted man. I needed his comfort and his calm resourcefulness. He was my patience. I was his anxiety.

Some days, I still think of my childhood, when I considered my reflection in the mirror, the way I pictured how my life would unfold. Today, I find it difficult to be absolutely certain whether these memories are real or not. Am I dreaming, or have I actually lived this life? Does the difference really matter? My emotions are the same.

Here in Portland, at the assisted living center, they schedule movie night one evening each month. Personally, I think they should really change the name because it is misleading. Instead, they should call it "movie afternoon without popcorn" because we are all returned to our rooms by 5 pm. There was a time when they served popcorn, but that was stopped after the disappearing dentures incident. There is no need to elaborate on those details. They are not relevant to the story I am trying to tell you.

Late last year, we watched the old movie *Casablanca*. My grandchildren have seen it and have asked me what I thought since we lived through those times. Actually, I found it very entertaining. The movie gave the viewer many impressions of the time: trying to get to Lisbon, escaping Nazi persecution, the highly prized letters of transit. I suppose, in some ways, it made me reconsider how I remember those years. As compelling as the movie was, it was made for the cinema, and Humphrey Bogart and Ingrid Bergman romanticized it for the screen. Paul and I and thousands of others survived the events that actually occurred. I am sure that there were those who dressed and acted the way they did in the movie, who had the money to spend their evenings in smoked-filled fancy cafes with piano players, but we never saw any of that take place. Of course, our journey was different. We never passed through Casablanca, so perhaps I missed these things. I do not know what I might have missed. Most of us just took each day one step at a time. We did the very best we could.

Happy would not be the word to use to describe our time in Lisbon. All we hoped was to keep moving forward, that each step would get us one step closer to our final destination. Clearly, we all shared a sense of relief, but coping might be the best word to describe how we spent our hours as we waited to go onward. It was not so much a journey of survival as it was a journey of surviving. We were buried in our emotions. We prayed to see our loved ones again. I cannot speak for others. For me, I would rather forget that time. When there is so much to life, why waste precious time on those memories. <u>I mourn for the past, but I live for the future.</u>

Lisbon remains Portugal's capital and largest city. I imagine, like most great cities of the world, it has grown considerably. Then, when we arrived in late 1941, it was a lively seaport of about a half-million people living in an underdeveloped country of six million. With its port, lovely harbor, and surrounding hills, Lisbon reminded me of Naples. It had that same gritty, hustling, and bustling feel. I had the sense that there were many people going about their business busily engaged with their work. Like Naples, it felt like a city of survivors. At least, that was my impression.

Finding a place to stay was difficult. Accommodations were scarce, and there was still a little more than two weeks before our ship would depart for Cuba. We had been very careful with our money. In Rome, I had been fortunate to reduce our living costs by helping out at the pensione. Still, we needed to continue to conserve our resources. Every penny counted. We knew we would probably have to rely upon the support of others once we reached Havana, but in Lisbon, there were so many others whose travels had been far more difficult and were far more in need. The resources of the volunteer organizations were severely stretched. We chose to pay our own way. We wanted to be responsible for ourselves for as long as we could.

Many Lisbon hotels had put in extra beds and opened up their basements to provide lodging. A number of the Portuguese residents made rooms available in their homes. With the assistance of one of the many refugee services in Lisbon, we were able to find a small room with a shared bath in a private home in a neighborhood on one of the lower-level streets. The owners seemed pleased to have us as guests. We had heard stories about the outlandish rates that were being charged for rooms, but we didn't have that experience. We were asked to pay only what we could afford. They knew our stay would be short and our funds were limited. Once again, we were met with kindness. Paul told me I must have an angel on my shoulder. That was a nice thought. It made me sleep well that night.

I don't know if the wealthier gambled in the Estoril casino standing next to officers of the German Reich or whether they stayed at the posh Aviz Hotel. We never saw them. Most of us had little money, and we found ourselves living in the Baixa district, the historical heart of Lisbon, bound together by a series of squares.

We spent our nights confined to tiny cubicles or small bare rooms with no way to prepare food. For most of us, days were spent dealing with visits to consulates, aid organizations, and shipping offices. Many had medical issues to attend to. Our spare time was spent walking the narrow cobblestoned streets of the Baixa, resting on park benches, or sitting in one of its modest, small outdoor cafes and restaurants, sharing a small meal or coffee, usually under the watchful eyes of the secret police.

These outdoor venues became our daytime homes and living quarters. We benefitted from the sunshine. Often, a coffee could last for hours. We were all suffering from the sense of isolation. Finding familiar faces at a cafe became part of the daily ritual. We recognized one another, and our differences disappeared. Spending time in the company of others gave us the warmth of camaraderie, the sense that we were not alone. There were days I felt as if we still lived in Naples, when the gossip was exchanged each morning, when the windows were opened and the clothes hung out to dry in the open air.

Whether rich or desperate, together, we shared a certain common anxiety. In Lisbon, there was always a noticeable undercurrent of activity: silent, secretive, and worrisome. Activities were taking place that we were not to know about. Suspicions were constantly aroused. Documents were repeatedly examined. We all had the fear that one of our papers might not pass scrutiny. We didn't see many, but we did see a few who were whisked away on the streets and became invisible.

Lisbon might have been our oasis, but we were not in a desert. There was no forgetting that a war was going on. Everyone we spoke with during the brief time we were there was aware that Portugal's neutral position could easily be upset by either the Axis or Allies with little forewarning. Rumors constantly circulated just as they had ever since we'd left Naples.

I have never learned how many of us there were who escaped through Portugal. My only observation was that the numbers might have been greater during the year before we arrived. That was when Lisbon had suddenly faced the massive influx of refugees without documents or transportation enabling them to reach their final destinations. Somehow, an army of courageous volunteers and relief agencies had found the way for most. However many, I am sure the numbers were overwhelming. By the time Paul and I arrived, in October of 1941, I think most of those who could had already left. With borders closing, many others would never reach Lisbon.

The biggest surprise took place when our stay in Lisbon was nearly over. We had been there two weeks, and our ship was to leave the next morning, when Paul and I stumbled on a sight that left us both speechless, a moment I will never forget. Late in the afternoon, we were sitting on a park bench in the Praca da Figueira, near the covered market, right by the statue where everyone feeds the pigeons. That was when I noticed an older, rather distinguished-looking, gray-haired man wearing a beret. He clearly was deep in thought and oblivious to anything around him as he patiently painted on a stretched canvas sitting on an easel. What caught my eye was the rather noticeable and unusual large paint smudge near the breast pocket of his jacket. I knew I had seen that smudge before. Seated next to him, silently observing, was an elegantly dressed, quite refined-looking young woman with a very long and graceful neck. I had to watch them for several moments to be absolutely certain. I could not believe what I was seeing. Mein Gott! Josef and Kaethe were in Lisbon too.

CHAPTER SIXTY-TWO

Josef and Kaethe will always remain locked in my heart as a much-loved mystery. I couldn't help but recall the first time I'd met them, that day I'd mistaken them for father and daughter, when they'd arrived at the Pensione Alexandra in need of a room. At the time, we'd thought their story was strange: Germans living in Paris; he so much older than she; he always talking, she always listening; their honeymoon of sorts. Even after we got to know them well, there were always questions that were left unanswered.

I remember when Lotte, Mela, and I stayed up late that first night speculating. We wondered who they really might be. We couldn't believe that they were who they said they were. And they always seemed to appear at the strangest of times: that day when Josef left Kaethe sitting on a park bench and old Consolato suggested that a room might be available at the Pension Alexandra; or the time they arrived when there were no tourists in Naples and Europe appeared to be on the brink of war; and now, suddenly here in Lisbon. I remember how Mela tried to convince us that they were secret agents on some type of undercover mission. Mela and Lotte could not understand how Kaethe, a girl so close to their age, could become involved with a man nearly as old as Paul.

Paul and I were curious too. We remained unclear about their unexplained circumstances: the years that were not accounted for when Josef told us about his life; why Josef left Berlin so quickly only days after Hitler took power and the Reichstag was burned; how Kaethe could suddenly move to Paris and sever all contact with her family in Berlin.

For me, Kaethe was always the strange one. I loved her as if she were my own daughter, and she always embraced me as if I were her mother, but there were things about her I could never quite understand. It was easy to compare her to Mela. They were so close to one another in age, but their differences could not have been greater. I could not imagine the two as sisters. One liked to talk and rarely knew when to stop and listen; the other preferred to listen and seldom knew when to begin speaking. One always appeared busy; the other always appeared idle. One ventured opinions; the other remained silent. One was inquisitive; the other rarely asked a question. One laughed and cried with frequency. For the other, emotions were an infrequent occurrence. One tended to be a little clumsy; the other appeared to be graceful. One showed signs of immaturity and uncertainty; the other never did. Their differences were profound. I always understood Mela's feelings. With Kaethe, I seldom had a clue. I often wondered who she really was and how she'd become this way.

I agreed with Mela and Lotte. How could two people thirty-two years apart in age possibly meet and fall in love? Paul smiled wryly when he told me it was possible. I told him to quit smirking and to stop imagining. These were questions far too personal to ask, so we never did, but I always wondered why Kaethe had chosen to devote her life to a man so much older. Now little of that mattered. They had become close and dear friends. Their last visit to Naples had meant so much to us. They'd brightened up some very dark days. I will always be touched by their generosity. They were the guests who departed but who always returned.

The war had intervened. Our friendship had become interrupted. All contact had stopped. We had no idea where they might be. Who knew what they thought might have happened to us? Why would I ever expect to see them again? They must have felt the same. And now here they were before us – Josef painting, Kaethe watching, just as they had in Naples. It was if nothing had changed. I am not certain who was more surprised. It was Kaethe who spoke first. I had never seen her so animated. She rose from where she was sitting, shouted "Mamarella!" as she ran to us, and gave us both hugs.

Sometimes, the only explanation for these inexplicable moments is fate, when that invisible hand gently positions the dots so they intersect. Why else would totally random paths cross? I am convinced that our chance meeting in Lisbon was one of those times. I have no other way to explain this particular moment.

CHAPTER SIXTY-THREE

We would have little time to spend together, not nearly enough, just the one evening. What time we did have was spent huddled in conversation. The story of how they'd found their way to Lisbon took most of the remaining hours. Since the last time we'd seen them, Josef and Kaethe had experienced a remarkable journey.

There was no mistaking the irony that their France and our Italy were now declared enemies of one another and engaged in a war that made little sense. Here we were in Lisbon, each having been born and raised in Germany, and each trying to escape the world's madness. How could the people of our homeland, those we had grown up with, be the ones responsible for all this horror? How could our parallel journeys be so entirely different?

To me, it didn't seem possible that nearly three years had passed since we had last seen Josef and Kaethe, when they'd surprised us with their visit to Naples and when everyone had been worried about war. So much had happened since then: the children leaving for America, the start of the war, leaving the Pensione Alexandra, living in Rome, finding our way to Lisbon. And the worry, confusion, and uncertainty? They had experienced so much of the same, but always from a different side. I kept thinking of two trains on adjoining tracks, racing in opposing directions, and the flickering moments when passengers can stare across through the windows to the opposite car and watch the startled looks on the faces staring back as they quickly race by.

They had been in Lisbon for a day or two before we'd unexpectedly spotted Josef quietly painting and Kaethe patiently watching near the covered market. We learned that their final arrangements for departure had been resolved only within the previous week. Transit visas and other necessary documents had been signed in Marseille, where, somehow, U.S. officials had approved their immigration application. They would leave for the United States after the first of the year. Until then, they would remain in Lisbon. Their ship, the *Nyassa*, was booked to leave in February. Even the contents of their Paris apartment had been packed into crates and would accompany them: Josef's piano, his library, the furniture, his paintings, and his other possessions. America would become their new home. It had all been arranged.

There was a part of me that couldn't help but say to myself, how could this be? I never asked them, but how had they passed by us in the line waiting to go to America? How had their application been approved when so many had been denied? Wasn't Kaethe considered a threat? She'd once told us her brother was a soldier in the German Army. Who had given them transit visas to stay in Lisbon for two months when Portuguese officials had limited stays to thirty days? Who had approved their documents? How could they travel with their cherished possessions when we had left so much behind and could carry so little? What really was their secret? I admit to having been more than a little jealous.

Josef told us of their discomforting return to Paris following their last stay at the Pensione Alexandra. Unexpectedly, they had been detained for several days at the French border after they'd passed through Switzerland. Their documents were confiscated and examined by French border officials. Evidently, war with Germany already seemed inevitable to French authorities. France was on guard. Security officials had been instructed to take heightened precautions at border areas. Although Josef and Kaethe were traveling on French passports and were no longer German citizens, the French authorities were concerned about their German nationality. They questioned the couple's reasons for travelling to Mussolini's Italy. Needless to say, suspicions were raised. French officials were wary of any Germans entering France, whatever the reason.

Because he was Jewish, years after he'd left Berlin, Germany had stripped Josef of his German citizenship. If the documents he carried were fraudulent and he actually was not a French citizen, he would be stateless, a possibly different issue. This had to be verified. His citizenship records in Paris needed to be located. For Kaethe, the situation was also worrisome. Although she had become a French citizen, there had been a question of whether she had renounced her German citizenship. While Kaethe assumed that this was a minor distinction, Josef thought that she might have aroused more concern, particularly when it was learned that she continued to have another strong German connection. Her brother, sister-in-law, and nieces still lived in Germany. When she tearfully told border officials that she had severed all contact, they chose not to believe her. This wasn't right. What kind of person was she? Why would she leave her family? It did not make sense. They could not understand this behavior.

They were interrogated and interviewed for several hours, together and apart. One border guard argued that Josef and Kaethe could not be married. He had his own anti-Semitic beliefs. Why would a Gentile marry a Jew? It was not possible. Did they have proof? When and where did their marriage take place? At one point, he insisted on seeing their marriage documents. One young man even rudely accused Josef of immoral behaviour. How could an attractive young woman like Kaethe possibly be interested in an old man like him? Their German accents even became an issue. What were they hiding? What was the real reason she was travelling with him? Were they secretly working for Mussolini? Perhaps they worked for the British? It took days to resolve these matters, and extensive consultation with French authorities in Paris were necessary. The entire situation left Kaethe quite shaken.

Days later, as they arrived in Paris and finally made their way to their apartment in the eleventh arrondissement, they were surprised to see so many war preparations underway. Much had changed during the twenty days they had been away. Throughout Paris, city workers were digging trenches to be used for bomb shelters in city squares and parks. The following month, gas masks were distributed to many civilians, and Parisian civil defense officials began posting signs with directions to shelters.

Despite these measures, Josef hung onto his slim hope that diplomatic negotiations would still prevent war from actually occurring. Perhaps the non-aggression pact with the Soviet Union would make a difference. Many of the newspapers had been censored, particularly those with Communist leanings. Josef and Kaethe found it difficult to have a clear sense of the events. It appeared that British officials were still pursuing a policy of appeasement. Josef couldn't understand. Hadn't they already learned their lesson? Even the Vatican had become involved. But then more ominous signs appeared. And more preparations for war were apparent.

They heard rumors that workmen were removing the stained-glass windows from Sainte-Chapelle, the royal chapel within the medieval Palais de la Cité. Others said that curators at the Louvre had returned from their vacations to pack and catalog major works of art. With the assistance of nearby department store employees, valuable pieces were stored in crates labeled with codes disguising their contents. The Winged Victory of Samothrace statue, the celebrated Hellenistic marble sculpture prominently displayed at the Louvre, was removed, carefully loaded onto a truck, and taken to the Château of Valençay in the Loire Valley. There were reports that a continuous convoy of vehicles, without headlights and under the cover of darkness, were carrying very important collections of paintings and other priceless works of art to be hidden in safe destinations.

Late in August, the French government began evacuating children out of the city to safe areas surrounding Paris. Street lights were turned off as a measure against German air raids. Normally busy, the streets suddenly became quiet at night. Those who were able began leaving Paris.

Finally, news reports said that negotiations had stalled. Germany had flexed its muscles and invaded Poland. The Germans claimed that their action was defensive, that they were defending themselves from attacks Poland had made along the border. Without fear of Soviet intervention or reprisal, Hitler did what he'd promised to do. He would rebuild the German empire and defend the German people. He would conquer territory for his fellow Germans. Germany would never be defeated by a lack of resources. And so it happened. France and Britain responded and kept their word. They stood with the people of Poland. They struck back, and two days later, they declared war on Germany. The fuse had been ignited. Europe's fear of an all-out fight for dominance had been realized. World War II had started.

CHAPTER SIXTY-FOUR

On September 3, 1939, the day France and Britain declared war on Germany, Josef said the streets of Paris remained quiet, almost too quiet, in a way he had never seen. Parisians did not know what to expect. There was a sense of foreboding, the feeling that something bad was about to occur. Despite expectations of impending darkness, though, little happened. Whatever fighting that might have taken place that day took place elsewhere, far from the streets of Paris and away from the countryside of France. The sea battle, the Battle of the Atlantic, would start immediately, but it would be eight months before Germany would begin its major offensive ground operations.

The quiet did not last for long. Parisians were accustomed to living their lives on the streets and boulevards of Paris, in cafes, in shops, at the market, in the small squares and parks, in the Tuileries, along the Champs-Élysées. As days turned into weeks and weeks turned into months, most Parisians regained a sense of normalcy, and much of pre-war Paris returned. Children who had been evacuated were reunited with their families. Others who'd fled from the city returned. Restaurants found themselves once again filled with patrons. Shops and cafes reopened. Fisherman, booksellers, and street performers returned to their favored places along the banks of the Seine. Even many of the streetlights brightened, at least for the early evening, when people had errands to run. Theatres and cinemas scheduled their matinees and early evening performances just as they had before. For much of Paris, it was business as usual.

Many of the expected wartime inconveniences became minor. Yes, newsboys and newsstands did run out of newspapers, and there was a clamoring for the news, but a simple solution solved that problem. Once read, newspapers were left on café tables for others to share. Ration cards were issued for food, meat, and gasoline. Yet if milk, butter, eggs, and other daily necessities were in short supply in Paris, it was hardly noticed. Supply and demand remained at equilibrium. The people of Paris needed less. Josef said it was because so many men had been sent away to war.

Whether France was fully braced for war always remained a question, particularly in Paris, where so much of daily life was back to normal. Still, Josef told us that, in Paris, they could always see the preparations. Sandbags were stationed near public buildings. Posters with directions to bomb shelters were still hung on most street corners. He had read that some school classrooms had become overcrowded as students doubled up. Apparently, schools suffered from a shortage of teachers. Many had joined the army. Automobiles could only be driven at very slow speeds. Strips of paper could be seen covering the glass windows of many shops to prevent glass from shattering should an aerial attack occur. Josef thought that there were more men in uniform on the streets, although, in Paris, seeing men in uniform was not an unusual sight.

Many agreed that France was haunted by memories of World War I. This time, the army would take the time necessary to build up its forces. The politicians said that they would be prepared, but their plan would be passive and defensive. The French did launch a brief attack on Germany in an attempt to divert attention from Poland, but this failed to significantly reduce the pressure on the already collapsing Polish front. Rather than risk the consequences of any further offensive action, the French army positioned itself to be ready for the German attack. The men would wait in the fortifications of the Maginot Line. Later, journalists and politicians would refer to this period as the *Phoney War*, or the *Sitzkrieg*, the months at the start of World War II when there were no major military land operations on the Western Front

Mostly, it appeared that old habits refused to die. Paris had always been a city where the Parisians enjoyed their outdoor time. As time passed, life for most returned to the way it had always been. Most is not all, and Josef and Kaethe were not like most Parisians. They found that the *Phoney War* had a major impact upon their lives. For Josef and Kaethe, a sequence of events began that would eventually lead them to Lisbon.

Of the two, Josef was the first to feel the impact, but listening to their story, I am not sure if Kaethe didn't feel it more. Josef fit a certain profile. He was a German male residing in France. His past political activities had become known and were suspicious. There were many questions about his leftist leanings and the reasons for his sudden departure from Berlin. Within days of the declaration of war, he was summoned from his work at the hospital and ordered to appear before French authorities. France required all German males living in France under the age of sixty-five to report. Until such time as his situation could be sorted out, Josef was considered an *enemy alien* and would remain in the custody of French authorities. For Kaethe, this was a frightening time. She was left to stay by herself. She would be on her own. Although she had lived in Paris for a number of years, she still could barely speak the French language and only with a distinct German accent. She had no other friends. Her entire life was devoted to Josef. She had no interests or hobbies to occupy her time. There was little she could do but wait for Josef to return.

CHAPTER SIXTY-FIVE

Detaining *enemy aliens* was not a new concept. Taking this action was not unique to France and certainly was not unjustified. In times of war, every nation is concerned about the security within its borders, as is their right and responsibility. I am not about to criticize this. Then or now, I want my government to protect me. And in the rush to judgement, I suppose it is normal to take a broad brush and identify anyone who arouses suspicions or may have a past connected in some way to one's enemy. But I wouldn't want anyone punished until more is known. That is an entirely different matter. I just want to feel safe. Better to be safe than sorry.

Having seen it firsthand, I know that even the threat of war creates an atmosphere of caution, an absence of patience and common sense, a certain mass hysteria, an indiscreet desire to act, and a widespread sense of fear.

Often important values and civil rights are overlooked while answers are being found. I imagine that the generals would tell us that war is a complicated business, much more complicated than the world would ever know. The words may be simple, but the actions seldom are. Sometimes, the first reactions are blindly emotional and require time and order to sort things out.

During World War II, Britain detained Germans and Italians living within their borders, the United States did this to the Japanese, and France interned Germans. I am sure other countries did the same in their own way. What makes this topic so messy is that most of those rounded up and detained may be the most convenient targets, but they are often the most innocent. Most have sought political asylum, have fled from persecution, or have arrived to find a better life. They probably aren't the enemy, but it is the remaining uncertainty that we are most afraid of.

Josef was swept up in this large and complicated net. He told us he was immediately sent to Les Milles, to a former brick factory converted into an internment camp in the commune of Aix-en-Provence. He and a number of other men were loaded onto a train and taken there. He wasn't certain but thought that it housed several thousand prisoners. He met many others, people from all walks of life. He understood that there were several of these camps and, supposedly, this was one of the more bearable. Josef told us that the living conditions and food were adequate. He slept on the floor, but he saw no evidence of disease, although he said that it seemed that there were rats everywhere, so disease was certainly possible. The guards were respectful but a bit unsavory and could not be trusted. There was little to do. Everyone suffered from boredom.

He had been surprised to encounter an old friend, a Russian artist he had met years earlier in Berlin. At the time, the artist had been in Berlin displaying his works in a one-man show at the Der Sturm gallery. That was when they'd become friends. The last time they had seen one another was over dinner in the early 1920s, when Moishe had returned to Berlin on a failed mission to retrieve his paintings that had been left at the gallery. The paintings had disappeared, and he was very distraught. Since that time, Moishe had gained much international notoriety. He had changed his name and now was known as one of the world's leading artists and living in Paris. Like Josef, Moishe had been swept up in the large net and sent to this camp.

Moishe had helped Josef find his way around the camp, and Josef had been fortunate to be housed with a group of about two dozen artists. The guards had allowed them to work on their projects and even supplied them with paints, brushes, and canvases. Josef told us that some of the artwork had been confiscated and there was a rumor that paintings by certain well-regarded artists, including one by his friend, had been taken to Paris, where they had been sold in galleries to unsuspecting buyers. Kaethe and he had been able to write to one another. He had been permitted to receive mail and to post letters to her three times each week.

Josef said he had been resigned to his circumstance. He hadn't liked it, but it was what it was. He'd never felt in danger, just uncomfortable, and recognized that this was one of the unavoidable things that could happen in war. Most of the men had felt the same way. There was little that they could do. It could have been better, but it could have been worse. His biggest concern had been Kaethe. How had she managed? She was not prepared to live by herself.

It was not long before he was released, just short of five weeks. Several of his colleagues at the hospital had interceded. They'd vouched for him and agreed to sponsor his release. A few days later, he had been returned to Paris and been able to resume his work at the hospital. There was little more to say except that he had missed Kaethe terribly. While Josef spoke, Kaethe never interrupted. She just carefully watched him and held his hand. Paul and I could see the tears in her eyes. I am sure it was a very difficult and frightening time for both of them.

As I listened to Josef, I kept thinking of Paul and how anxious and worried I would have been if something like this had happened to him, how I would have needed to be in the company of others, how difficult it would have been to be alone. I would have thought it unfair and reacted with anger, but neither Josef nor Kaethe had reacted that way. Josef seemed to choose his words carefully as he described his experience. Perhaps he was shielding Kaethe from the worst, but I'm not really sure. I don't believe Kaethe knew any more than what we were told. That was all we learned about Les Milles. The last thing he said about Les Milles was that it had occurred almost two years earlier. He was glad that he had renewed his friendship with Moishe and was so pleased with his success. He only wished that he had kept one of his friend's paintings. Perhaps, someday, that would have made him a wealthy man. Then he laughed and said that he would never learn to call Moishe by his new name. No one else knew him as Moishe. Now they called him Marc. As for Les Milles? It was clearly a memory to be forgotten, something he had already put in the past.

CHAPTER SIXTY-SIX

We learned that there had been a second incident, one that occurred several months later. The *Phoney War* ended in May of 1940, when Germany invaded Belgium, the Netherlands, and Luxembourg. France's fears were realized, and the invasion of the Low Countries marked the beginning of the Nazi incursion into French soil. Within days of the German onslaught, large red posters appeared on the streets of Paris announcing that all *ressortissants allemands*, all those from Germany, were to report to the Vel' d'Hiv in Paris for interviews and investigation. This time, the net was expanded, and both Josef and Kaethe were detained. Along with thousands of other *enemy aliens*, they soon found themselves separated before being sent to the southwest of France. Kaethe had been confined in the Gurs camp.

Gurs was one of the first and largest camps established in prewar France. Previously, it had been used as a detention camp for political refugees and others fleeing Spain after the Spanish Civil War. When the Germans invaded France, Gurs was converted as a camp to detain Germans living in France and other political prisoners. Just to the south of the village of Gurs, the camp was located in the foothills of the Pyrenees, about fifty miles from the Spanish border.

Kaethe told us that, at first, she was sent south to a small village near Marseille. She wasn't certain, but she thought this had to do with her enemy classification. They had handled her differently from Josef. French authorities were concerned about the military status of Kaethe's brother in Germany. They claimed that he was known to hold rank in the German army. For several days, she was kept under armed guard at an old, dilapidated, and overcrowded hotel. Much like Josef, she said very little about the details of her situation. Suddenly, one day, without explanation, she was transported by bus to the Gurs camp. She had no idea why they moved her to Gurs. The ride must have been difficult. It was a very long trip that took nearly an entire day, and the bus windows were covered so French citizens could not see in. She could not understand why they were taunted and spat upon, but then she was told that the villagers assumed that French guards were transporting the German enemy.

During this same time, Josef was sent to the camp at Saint-Cyprien. Thanks to a friendly official, he learned that Kaethe was confined to Gurs, and they were able to get word to one another. Like Gurs, Saint-Cyprien was first created to house refugees and immigrants fleeing the Spanish civil war. Josef never spoke about the conditions there.

Within weeks of their internment, France fell to the Germans. When the Armistice was signed, toward the end of that June, many of the detainees at Gurs were released or escaped. The French guards were either indifferent or wanted to keep the prisoners out of Nazi hands. Gurs was virtually abandoned. Thousands walked out. Kaethe chose to remain. She had no place to go and was afraid she would lose contact with Josef.

A little more than a month later, in August, Josef was released from Saint-Cyprien when the majority of its detainees were released. Somehow, he was able to find his way back to Gurs, where he arranged for Kaethe's release. Once again, they were reunited.

CHAPTER SIXTY-SEVEN

Listening to their stories, it was difficult to imagine all that they had been through. Paul and I found it hard to believe that Josef and Kaethe were sitting with us in Lisbon so far away from the daily worries of the war. We chose not to interrupt or ask any questions. We kept our silence. This was too personal, too private, and we understood how Josef and Kaethe valued their privacy. I have no doubt that there many words left unsaid. I would not be surprised if there were moments they had chosen to keep from one another. I know now that the conditions they'd found themselves in had been far more hazardous, debilitating, and demoralizing than either ever said, and I feel certain that they softened their descriptions. They knew our emotions. It was obvious that little had been said to one another about these times. I am convinced that they had never shared these stories with others. Even today, I can't imagine that they would have ever repeated their stories again to anyone but themselves. Like I said before, sometimes, it takes willing ears to sit patiently, listen, and not judge.

Since those hours spent with Josef and Kaethe, I have seen, heard, and read far too many stories created by war. Josef and Kaethe had survived, and to my knowledge, neither had been harmed, at least not physically in any serious way. By nearly every standard, their journey pales in comparison to the losses so many others suffered during that time. Far too many lives were lost. Far too many questions were never answered, and far too many stories never were given the opportunity to be heard. I can't help but think of my childhood mirror. Who would ever look to the future and dream of this?

That evening was our last in Lisbon. With Paul and me, Josef and Kaethe had found familiar faces to tell their story. Even the most private sometimes need listeners. They knew we would leave in the morning. There was little chance that our paths would ever cross again. Life would lead us on our separate journeys. Sometimes, I believe they told me their story because they knew that I would be left with the key to unlock the stories that will soon be long forgotten. Isn't that a strange thought?

For Josef and Kaethe, there was more to tell. All of what had been told thus far occurred well more than a year before they were to arrive in Lisbon. Together once again, and free from their imprisonment in internment camps, they chose not to return to Paris, at least, not until such time as they felt safe. With the Germans in control, they faced an entirely different issue. Kaethe was no longer the enemy. Josef was. This time, it was not because of his German past. It was because Josef was Jewish. Already, the Jews in France were being rounded up and deported to many of these very same camps. And this time, it was with far less compassion.

When Paris fell that June and Germany conquered France, more than half of France was occupied by the Germans and administered by German military officials. One month later, in close collaboration with the Nazis, the newly formed Vichy government was installed and took control of the unoccupied areas. French citizens were to suffer on both sides of the divided nation. Within months, Jews living in France began to be imprisoned in concentration camps. By late 1941, as the four of us sat together in Lisbon, many were already being deported to Germany's killing centers and murdered.

When they were reunited after leaving the camps, Josef and Kaethe wanted to be as far from this madness as they could possibly be. Much as we found ourselves stranded in Italy until we could find a place to go and a way to get there, they were confined to France with few options for their future. After Josef found Kaethe at the Gurs camp, he brought her to Soumoulou, a tiny village in the southwest of France. Fewer than five hundred people lived there. Nobody would know them there. In Soumoulou, they could remain invisible. They could hide. The Nazis wouldn't come looking for Jews in Soumoulou.

⇌ ⇌

Over the years, as I have thought about their story, I have always remained curious why Josef chose Soumoulou. How had he known about this very small village in the southwest of France, and how had he become reunited with Kaethe after he was released from the Saint Cyprien camp? How had these dots connected?

Perhaps my memory fails with the details, but these questions only add to the mystery of Josef and Kaethe. There must have been someone else who helped them along the way. Neither Josef nor Kaethe ever said, but you will learn that I do have reason to believe that his old friend Moishe, the famous artist, played a bigger role in their story than they ever said. I have always found it odd that Josef and Moishe had not seen one another for twenty years, ever since Moishe's paintings had gone missing, when they encountered one another at the Le Milles camp. I remain convinced that there was more to this story and that they had a stronger friendship than Josef chose to share. But I have never been able to learn any more details. Some mysteries are never solved. Some questions are never answered. I am sure that Josef had his reasons.

CHAPTER SIXTY-EIGHT

It was Kaethe's turn to tell the story. She loved Soumoulou. She had never lived in such a wonderful place. Josef and she could be together all the time. They were free to do as they pleased. A farmer rented them a small house on his property. If he or his wife cared about who they were or whether Josef was Jewish, it was never mentioned. They were able to live the perfect life. Kaethe had always been a city girl. She had always lived in either Berlin or Paris. In Soumoulou, she could tend to a garden. She could grow flowers, something she had never considered before. Josef could paint every day. There were so many scenes to be painted. The landscapes were breathtaking, the old farm buildings so interesting.

Kaethe laughed as she told us of the time they'd borrowed bicycles from the farmer. They had packed a picnic and ridden to a nearby village for needed supplies. They had even brought two bottles of wine. Before the day was over, they both had drunk so much that they could hardly ride. Everything had fallen from their bikes, even the eggs, though not a single one had broken. They'd laughed so hard that they'd cried. In Soumoulou, she could have Josef entirely to herself. She had never been happier.

After the first month, once they were settled in, they decided it was safe to travel to Paris. Of course, now their circumstances were different, but traveling together, they thought they would be safe. And they were. Everything worked out, and they made it to Paris without any issue. No questions were asked.

In Paris, they were able to close up their apartment and arrange for everything to be crated and stored. They would only carry a few of their possessions back to Soumoulou. Little was needed. Life in Soumoulou was so much simpler than it had been in Paris. Josef explained that when he'd checked his mail in Paris, he had been surprised by some very important news from the strangest of places. An attorney in the United States, from San Francisco, had sent him a letter. Apparently, the mother of his first wife had died, and Josef had been named as a beneficiary in her will. He had been left seven thousand dollars. His only contact since his first wife's death twenty-five years earlier had been to send birthday wishes to his former mother-in-law each year. From these cards, she had known of his plight and had left these funds in her will specifically to help them flee Europe. Josef had never received an inheritance before, and the news could not have arrived at a better time. He understood that the estate was being settled and that a bank in New York would hold the money. Upon learning the news, Kaethe and he immediately decided to move to America. They agreed to go to the American consulate in Paris the next morning to register and apply for entry visas.

But then they encountered an unexpected problem. They discovered that the U.S. embassy in Paris had closed its doors and followed the new government to Vichy. In order to apply for entry visas, they would have to find a safe way to travel to Marseille in the South of France instead. It was no longer possible to apply for an American entry visa in Paris. This would have to wait for another day.

Before leaving Paris, Josef and Kaethe made one last stop. Josef wanted to find his old friend Moishe once more. Perhaps Moishe could help. He thought Moishe might have some connections. He knew Moishe was planning to move to America. When they went to see Moishe, he gave them the name and address of a man in Marseille and a note to present to him. Then, with nothing more to do in Paris, Josef and Kaethe found their way back to Soumoulou. They would have no reason to ever return to Paris again.

CHAPTER SIXTY-NINE

Josef told us that, together, they had left Soumoulou only on one other occasion before beginning their journey to Lisbon: when they'd gone to see the man in Marseille. Josef had been afraid to take any other chances. He'd known the new government in Vichy was aggressively searching for Jews and sending them to camps for deportation. Even in Soumoulou, there had been a frightening moment.

One day, a group of German soldiers happened to pass by the farm. Josef and Kaethe ran to the fields and hid. Josef didn't believe this patrol was actually looking for him that day, but he remained concerned that someone could report his presence or that there could be a chance encounter. Neither he nor Kaethe could bear the thought of being separated again. They had made a solemn promise to one another, and each carried the pills Josef had retrieved from his medical supplies in Paris should that ever occur.

Moishe had given Josef the name and address of Varian Fry, a young American from New York who was working in Marseille as an agent for the Emergency Rescue Committee, a group assisting Jews trying to flee the Nazis. Fry had set up an elaborate network to circumvent French officials, who were refusing to issue exit visas to Jews. With the support of a small group of volunteers, Jewish refugees were hidden at the Villa Air-Bel, a château outside Marseille, until they could avoid detection and be smuggled out. Then they were taken across the border to Spain, where they then traveled to the safety of neutral Portugal.

Apparently, Fry worked closely with a senior U.S. State Department official based in Marseille, a man sympathetic to the situation and who was able to issue entry visas to those in need. From Marseille, the Emergency Rescue Committee also worked closely with the Unitarian Service Committee in Lisbon. They were able to help these refugees find berths on ships. Josef mentioned that someone else was able to secure the necessary transit visas needed for Spain and Portugal. He had never learned who that person was.

When Josef and Kaethe travelled to Marseille to see Mr. Fry, they carried the personal note that Moishe had written. The note requested Fry's help. Money was not an issue. Josef had money at the bank in New York. Weeks later, after they returned to Soumoulou, Josef and Kaethe received word that the necessary documents had all been prepared. They were told to depart at once. They would be hidden at the Villa Air-Bel outside of Marseille for several days, until it was safe for their journey to America to begin.

Suddenly, just as they were about to leave Soumoulou, they received another message. This time it was frantic. Their plans had been cancelled. They should remain in Soumoulou. That had taken place two months ago. Josef learned that Vichy authorities had been watching Fry for quite some time. Under constant surveillance, he had been detained and questioned by the authorities on a number of occasions. Only days before Josef and Kaethe were to leave Soumoulou, the Vichy regime had acted. Varian Fry had been ordered to leave France and sent back to America. That was when Josef and Kaethe had received the frantic message to cancel their departure.

What the Vichy authorities did not know was that another group based in Marseille was also secretly assisting Jews who were trying to leave France. Josef and Kaethe had received a message from them. This time, because she had German papers and it was safer for her to travel, Kaethe had travelled to Marseille by herself to meet with the organizers. Additional funds had been necessary, and more time required to make this second set of arrangements; however, this time, their plans had not been thwarted, and they'd been told to begin their journey. They had left Soumoulou ten days before our surprise encounter in Lisbon. That was how they'd made it to Lisbon. That was how they would be able to go to America.

CHAPTER SEVENTY

Late that night, we said farewell to Josef and Kaethe. I doubted that our paths would ever cross again. It didn't seem likely. Their journey would take them to New York, where they would begin their new life. Our journey was far less certain. Much remained to be seen. Before hugging and walking away in opposite directions, Josef told us that he had an invitation from an old friend, a physician he had once been associated with in Berlin, who was now practicing in New York. There might be an opportunity at his hospital. He hoped he would be allowed to practice medicine again. His medical career had been rewarding, first Berlin, then Paris, and now perhaps New York. They would experience life in another big city. That was their plan.

As for Paul and me, we did not know what the future would bring. We hoped our stay in Cuba would be short and temporary, but we would still have to wait for entry visas to be issued before we could find our way to America. We had no idea how long that might take. If we were allowed to live in the United States, our home would probably be outside of Chicago. My sister Marie had written when her husband had passed away. Jenny, our other sister, the frustrated spinster who had stayed in Koenigsberg to care for our parents, had moved in with her when she'd come to America. There was one more vacant room in the house. Paul and I could live with them for free if we wished. Given our financial situation, we knew this was a pretty good offer, and I knew that Mela lived nearby.

It was very late when we went to bed. We had to be up early the next morning to board the ship, but I had a difficult time sleeping that night. There was so much to think about, and my mind refused to slow down. I was excited. We would turn the page and begin a new chapter. We were ready to leave. I felt as if, over the last years, I had used all the tears that God had given me to last my lifetime.

Spending the final hours with Josef and Kaethe had been emotional. In bed that night, I found myself thinking about their story. They had become such close friends, a magical friendship, and being with them had been a perfect way to spend our last night in Lisbon. First, they'd vanished, and then, suddenly, they'd reappeared. I had grown to love Kaethe like a daughter. She was always so patient as she listened to my stories. I was happy that I had been able to do the same for her. And she had been so good to Josef. He was lucky to have her in his life. Without her return to Marseille to make the arrangements, I am not sure they would have ever found their way to Lisbon or whether we would have ever seen them again.

Josef was a good man, but I never could understand why Kaethe would choose to devote herself to a man well more than twice her age. I wouldn't make that wish for Mela. What kind of life would that be? He would become old while she would remain young. But I suppose Kaethe never had a mother to give her advice. I have always wondered how they met. How is it possible for an eighteen-year-old girl to meet and fall in love with a fifty-year-old man?

I suppose this was one of the secrets they chose to keep and never share. I can only imagine that they had their reasons. I never pried; it would have been inappropriate to ask, and they never saw fit to offer. Now it will be forever left unsolved. That night, as I struggled to go to sleep, this was the unsolved mystery that kept me awake. As Paul put his arms around me and fell off to sleep, he whispered that he loved me and said I was still *crazy in the head*.

At first, I thought that Josef must have been a friend of Kaethe's father. It seemed a likely explanation, but I ruled it out because I knew that her father had met Josef for the first time in 1932, four years after Josef and Kaethe had become lovers. Another possibility was that Kaethe had been a patient of Josef's, that he had treated her for some type of medical condition or ailment. But I remembered

Josef once saying that he could never understand why Kaethe refused to see him for any medical issue, so I eliminated that possibility. A chance encounter had merit, but I quickly dismissed it. What were the odds that would occur? Their social and economic circles were worlds apart. I considered whether Kaethe could have been a clerk in a department store, but then recalled a conversation when Kaethe had said that she had never worked in a store. I was nearly asleep when I dreamed of an accidental meeting on a trolley, probably the result of some book that I'd once read. I eliminated this when I realized that if she had given up her seat to an old man, she probably would not have been attracted romantically. And if the roles were reversed, if an older man had given up his seat for someone so much younger, that could have been odd and perhaps offensive. Another explanation was that, somehow, they'd been introduced. In the absence of being able to find someone who might confirm or deny this possibility, particularly at that time of the night in Lisbon, this explanation remained and was never rejected. My final explanation seemed most likely. Was it possible that she had worked for him? If she had been a clerical assistant in his office, a relationship might have been explored. She did seem familiar with his medical practice. One can see how an eighteen-year-old girl might be infatuated with a much older man in that kind of setting. That is all I remember before Paul woke me up to tell me it was time to leave for the ship. Until that last night in Lisbon, solving this problem never kept me up late at night. I only share it with you now because I have run out of possibilities and you may wish to consider it as you fall asleep one evening.

CHAPTER SEVENTY-ONE

The next morning, we arrived at the harbor with our two suitcases in hand and our thoughts on Cuba. It had seemed so distant. Now Cuba appeared so real. Havana could become our home. And there was little news. It was difficult to find any information about what might happen there. The last report we heard was troubling. Cuba, once again, had suspended any new visa and citizenship applications. President Batista had announced that Cuba had admitted all the refugees that it was able to absorb. Their borders would be closed, and new arrivals would be turned away. This latest order was to be applied to any person born in any of the Axis countries or in territories occupied by the Axis powers. We didn't know what to think. This would certainly apply to us. Would we travel to Cuba only to be sent back to Europe?

We were told that visas issued by Cuban consulates in Europe to emigrants in this category would be automatically invalidated. Our remaining hope was that my cousin's daughter in Havana had continued her good connections with the Cuban government. The fact that our papers had been approved and issued in Havana, not Europe, was reassuring and seemed to point in our favor. We hoped that this would make the difference. Yet we remembered what had happened to the passengers on the *St. Louis*, and that was a worry.

We boarded the ship early that day. Once again, our documents were examined carefully, and we were relieved when we were allowed to board. That was another good sign. Ship officials refused to board passengers whose papers were suspect or when they expected someone to be denied permission to depart the ship.

The facilities on the ship were a surprise. Paul and I had no idea what to expect. She had only arrived hours earlier. This was the first time we'd set eyes on our ship. We learned that the ship's journey had begun in Balboa, the seaport in Northern Spain. We had understood all ports in Spain had been closed for months, but we now learned that a few ports had been reopened to assist with the current situation.

In Lisbon, we had heard numerous stories about various sailings across the Atlantic during wartime. It was common knowledge that there had been several ill-fated crossings, a concern we all shared. We also learned that there had been other issues. Over coffee one afternoon, someone told us the story of the *Navemar*, a refugee steamer that had sailed to Cuba and New York two months earlier. She had begun her journey in Seville and stopped in Lisbon to pick up additional passengers. There had been quite an uproar. Portuguese officials and others had refused to let the *Navemar* leave the Lisbon harbor without making a number of health and safety improvements. Apparently, conditions had been miserable. There were reports of a limited and questionable water supply, overcrowding, poor sanitation, and inadequate sleeping areas. Deck space had been severely restricted because four huge oxen had been penned on the afterdeck to furnish meat for the passengers. Fresh meat had to be butchered because the *Navemar* had no refrigeration facilities. Before arriving in Lisbon, many passengers had suffered from the poor quality of food and unhealthy water. There were many reports of illness. A number of passengers had been removed from the ship and sent to Lisbon hospitals.

Fortunately, our ship was affected by none of these problems. It was well maintained. The captain and crew were professional and courteous. We traveled in comfort. The journey to Cuba took nearly two weeks, and the seas remained calm with the exception of a three-day period of choppy weather. The weather didn't turn until we had been aboard for several days. That really helped. By then, we had become accustomed to the roll and pitch of the ship. Neither Paul nor I felt any twinge of seasickness, which was a big relief. I had suffered from that malady the only other time I had traveled by ship and did not wish to repeat the experience. This time, I knew to avoid our cabin, remain in the fresh air, and to resist the temptation to try every food that might be available.

The ship might have been a bit smaller than many of the more modern transatlantic liners, at least, that is what others said, but I don't believe it lacked for comfort. It held slightly more than five hundred passengers. While the sleeping quarters and berths were confining, as they are on most ships, the abundant space on the open decks was a blessing. None of us felt crowded. There was room to walk. Of course, as with any ocean crossing during the war, safety protections were taken to lessen the risk of detection, particularly at night. Passenger ships had suffered casualties, and the possibility of danger did exist. At first, I was a little unnerved when we were drilled in the procedures to be followed in the event of an enemy attack. But we were never inconvenienced, and there were no encounters with enemy ships or U-boats. All in all, the trip was quite pleasant and peaceful.

The public areas were more extravagant than we had imagined. There was a movie theater, a large hall, a music room, and the dining room. We even watched a few movies, but I found it too embarrassing when Paul fell asleep. The ship was Spanish owned, and the dining area was decorated in the style of the manor houses of Northern Spain. It had the appearance of a courtyard with Moorish arches. Even the food was quite good. I can't say that we suffered at all.

We met and visited with many of our fellow passengers. We were all nervous and excited. In general, it seemed that there was an atmosphere of jubilation throughout the crossing, but I don't want to overstate this. I think all of us on board wanted to believe that we had left the dangers of the European wars behind. I know we shared a common desire to look to the future, but I suspect everyone on the ship had many cracks in their armor. One could see it in the eyes. Sometimes, you could hear it in the voices. Try as one might, relief cannot entirely mask sorrow. We all had lingering memories that could never be forgotten. War carries a hefty price, and we all had paid.

Somehow, no matter the circumstance, children have a way of injecting joy and hope into the air. I believe we all were infected. There were a number of young children on the ship, and their antics kept us all entertained. They were always staging parades or playing one game or another, even putting on puppet and magic shows. That helped everyone. The brisk breezes, gentle seas, and salt air added to the calm of the crossing. Most of us spent our afternoons wrapped in blankets, comfortably napping in our deck chairs. I seldom felt bored. Paul found others to talk to and played cards with a group of men. As for me, there is always room in my bag for a deck of cards, a sketchbook and pencil, and a little yarn and a few knitting needles. Some habits don't change. My hands were not idle. I had more than enough to keep me entertained.

CHAPTER SEVENTY-TWO

We all bristled with anticipation. The day could not have been more perfect as we approached Cuba and Havana's harbor. The temperature was marvelous, the sky was clear, and the sunshine abundant. Yet suddenly, I experienced a very strange sensation. I wasn't alone. I think everyone aboard felt it. The sun still shone brightly, but it seemed as if a cloud had darkened the sky. Paul and I felt the mood shift the moment it occurred. Everyone became anxious and uncertain, more serious and somber. We all felt a chill in the air.

Paul told me that one third of the ship's passengers, one hundred and seventy, were bound for Havana and expecting to depart the ship that day. Those of us departing all carried papers of one sort or another. We all hoped and prayed that our documents remained valid and that

Cuban authorities would allow us to enter. The others would remain on the ship. Their visas allowed them to continue to the United States. Cuba would not be the final destination for most of us planning to get off the ship in Havana. We hoped that our stay would be short. We were all tired. Our journeys had taken years. We were ready to reach the end. Now we were all concerned. Nobody knew if we would be allowed to stay. What if Cuban officials blocked our entry?

Our first sight was the tall, rounded stone tower, the lighthouse of the Castillo de los Tres Reyes Magos del Morro. Someone shouted when they spotted it from a distance at least two hours before we sailed into Havana's harbor. It was so tall that it could be seen from more than thirty miles away. We all watched it as the ship drew closer. Finally, we could see the fort that surrounded the lighthouse. Perched high on a rocky bluff for more than three hundred years, the fort had protected the entrance to the harbor from pirates and foreign invaders. Now we hoped it would not keep us out.

I have read many stories about when the *St. Louis* first arrived, how small boats went out to greet the passengers, how there were cheers and celebrations, how there were relatives there to meet the ship. None of this occurred when we arrived. There was no one there to greet us that day. We had the sense that we would be on our own.

I have also read about how difficult it was for the passengers on the *St. Louis* to understand their situation when they first learned that they would be unable to leave the ship. They had followed the rules. They had purchased their tourist cards. I can't imagine their confusion and disappointment. Knowing their history is what made us so worried and concerned. We weren't about to celebrate. No one wanted to face the disappointment. All we wanted was to learn our fate, to connect two more dots on our long journey.

It happened quickly. The process was organized and arranged. There were no delays. Upon our arrival in Cuba, most of us were taken to Tiscornia, a temporary holding camp for all refugees and immigrants located on the other side of the Bay of Havana, on the Isla de Pinos. We joined others who were housed in army-style barracks surrounded by barbed wire. It was so odd. Throughout our journey, ever since we'd left Naples, Paul and I had never spent one night apart. Now we would, he with the men and I with the women. I never imagined that would be how I would spend my first night in Cuba. Oh, how I missed being held in his arms that night.

Cuban officials were polite and encouraging. There was no problem, only a bureaucracy. We were told that we would stay in the camp temporarily, perhaps for a few days, no more, while our status was investigated. Once cleared, we would be officially allowed into the country. Then we would be free to do as we pleased. I looked forward to seeing my cousins.

Paul and I were thrilled to learn that we would probably remain in Cuba for only a few weeks, at most one month or two, while we awaited our American visas. If all went well, our U.S. entry visas would be expedited. It was possible that we would ring in the New Year surrounded by our family. I could not have been happier when we learned this news.

And then an event occurred that entirely changed the world. On December 7, 1941, within days of our arrival in Cuba and while we were detained and waiting for our release from Camp Tiscornia, Japan launched the devastating attack on the United States naval base at Pearl Harbor. The war had come to America, and everything stopped, frozen in place.

CHAPTER SEVENTY-THREE

I can't tell you the exact day or time we heard the news. All I remember was that it was sudden. Confined to the camp, it was difficult to keep track of the days. They all ran together. We all, even the guards, were in a state of confusion.

What I can tell you is that, the day after the attack, the United States declared war on Japan. Days later, Germany and Italy declared war on the United States, and the U.S. reciprocated with its own declarations of war. The global war was underway. There was no question whose side Cuba was on. The Cuban government stood firmly with the United States. <u>Cuba immediately declared war on Japan, Germany, and Italy.</u>

That was all we knew. We received no other news. And that was all we would know for quite some time. We had no radios or newspapers. We were not allowed to communicate with the outside. We could not have visitors or send or receive letters or use the telephone or telegraph. There were no messages to or from family. The Cuban government had more pressing priorities. It would be many weeks before they could get to the question of what to do with us.

There was another problem, and it was significant, a serious issue that distinguished Paul and me from the others: now it no longer mattered if we were Jewish. Our papers were clear. Paul and I were not like the German refugees who had been declared stateless when Germany had rescinded their citizenship. Paul and I were different. Our citizenship was known. Cuban officials did not care where we were born. There was a war going on, and they wanted to understand who we really were. We were their mystery, and the only evidence was our documents. We carried Italian passports. Our citizenship papers said we were Italian. As far as Cuban officials were concerned, Paul and I were their enemy. We were suspected enemy agents. Pending further investigation, we would be detained as *enemy aliens*. One could never be too careful. This was a time of war, and Italy was Cuba's enemy.

CHAPTER SEVENTY-FOUR

When I rose from my bed this morning, I found a note passed under my door. This was not unusual. That's how they often communicate with me. Since my hearing and eyesight are both so poor, it is a system that works. I am sure that they do this so I do not get frightened when someone suddenly opens the door and enters my room. I suppose they are afraid that I might have a heart attack or that, perhaps, I will faint. Neither strike me as good adventures.

Today's note reminded me of a few things: first, that my visitor will be returning but would not arrive until the afternoon, and second, that my room will be cleaned this morning, which means that I will be spending some time in the hallway with my playmates, a normal Friday morning occurrence. The note also reminded me to put on my hearing aids. They remind me of that all the time.

I hate those things. I keep telling them that they don't make a difference. This disagreement has been going on for years. By now, I am through with arguing. I just wear them to make everyone happy. Since I don't put the batteries in, I know they will never work. But they don't know that. It is just one of my little secrets, one they forget to ask about. There are other secrets. Those I will keep to myself.

Actually reading the note is just as much a problem. Every time they hire a new employee, I have to teach them to write in very large block letters. Even with my magnifying glass, that is the only way I can make out what they say. Somedays, it is all I can do to find and pick up the piece of paper that they write on.

I don't want to be too critical of their system of passing me notes. The people here, my caretakers, take good care of me. They tell me I am becoming a bit more forgetful at times. I can't be certain that is true, but they do remind me of things, and I know that I must believe them. I imagine that is another reason why they slip notes under my door. I know what I remember, but they know what I forget.

There is one minor thing, hardly worth mentioning, that irks me, and I am not sure when it started. Today's note was addressed to Mama O. Now, I ask you, who addresses a ninety-eight-year-old woman that way? When I was a child, my name was Elsa. As a young married woman in Naples, the help would refer to me as La Signora. Then, when the children teased, they would call me Mamarella. I adore that name. It was Alex's idea, and that's the name that stuck. They have called me that for a very long time.

Now even their friends call me Mamarella. The grandchildren and great-grandchildren have all invented their own names for me. There are too many to remember, but I find them all endearing. I suppose none of this matters too much, particularly since I can't hear when they call my name anyway.

I laugh sometimes when the great-grandchildren visit. I am sure their parents have told them to speak loudly and clearly when they talk to me. Often, the young ones will yell each syllable of each word one at a time at the top of their lungs. I can see this by how they move their mouths. Everyone in the building must hear them. I know it annoys their parents, but I always enjoy telling the children that my hearing is bad and ask them to speak a little louder.

But now the people here want to call me Mama O? I'm not sure what I think about that. I am not sure that it feels right. I ask you, who calls an old woman Mama O? Today, though, I have a more important issue to consider. The note said that my visitor will be returning. I find that more concerning. I am pretty sure I had a visitor here every day this week. Given the state of my eyes and ears, sometimes, it is pretty hard to be absolutely certain. Here is my dilemma: today, I cannot be certain that I know who this person really is.

Don't be alarmed. This has happened before. This is not the first time I have been faced with this problem. Here is what usually happens. When my visitor first arrives we hug each other. It rarely matters who the visitor is. Everyone hugs an old lady. Then we kiss one another's cheeks, first the left and then the right. That's when I ask myself whether I know the answer. Sometimes, my sense of smell helps. Truthfully, whether I know or not changes very little, because I do what I always do. I do what life has taught me. I smile, and I nod politely. Then I start talking. I go on with the rest of my story.

When you really think about it, isn't that what we all have to do sometimes? Just put one step forward, smile, nod, take a giant leap, and see how the dots are connected.

CHAPTER SEVENTY-FIVE

That Afternoon

I told Mamarella I would be back in the early afternoon to finish hearing her story. We had been together every day that week. I had enjoyed every moment, but that morning, I wanted to spend a few hours with the others before returning home. Our generation was not getting any younger. We all cherished our time together, and there was never enough. Although we lived far apart, East Coast, Midwest, and West Coast, ever since we'd arrived in America, we'd made it a point to try to see each other at least once a year. We always celebrated the important occasions, cheered one another's successes, and commiserated whenever there were heartbreaks. This time, we had celebrated Mamarella's ninety-eighth birthday. It was such a wonderful event. She seemed so happy. She really was more than amazing.

We had always been close, and for all these years, Mamarella had been the center of our attentions. Her family was the most important part of her life. At first, every month we each sent typed letters with carbon copies for all. Later, by the time we could afford long distance telephone calls, we all dismissed the idea. The cost of long distance was a luxury, and old habits were hard to break. The letters remained our way to stay in touch, a reminder of our past. Perhaps the struggle and journey we shared made us always remember all that we had in common.

I will always remember that last afternoon when I arrived at the center. Mamarella had promised me to finish the story. The chaplain was there to meet me at the door. He had been expecting me and took me aside to explain. It had happened only a short time earlier. Mamarella had died.

She had not been alone. She had been sitting in the hallway with others. It had been peaceful. Mamarella had closed her eyes, fallen asleep, and never woken up. There was no disturbance. She had not suffered. Yes, it had been sudden. Death always is. But it had been gentle. She'd had no warning. She was happy. She knew she was loved.

I was the first to learn this news. There had been no time to call the others. I needed a few moments to collect my thoughts. Then I would let them know. As I sat and considered the moment, I couldn't help but smile through my tears. I thought of her playground without swings or slides, the haunted house she'd wanted to organize with her playmates, and the protest over the "lights out" rule she'd wanted to stage. Mamarella had been through so much, but she'd kept her sense of humor and sense of justice until the very end. No, cherish is not love; Mamarella knew she was loved.

I really can't say that any of us were surprised by her passing, perhaps a few of the grandchildren and great-grandchildren, the ones who had never experienced the death of someone close before, the ones who hadn't found the time to stop by for a visit. What a remarkable life. How many people can say that every one of her descendants is still alive? Few people who live to be ninety-eight are able to make that claim. All she'd ever really wanted was to see each of them grow. That was what kept her hopes alive throughout her journey. That was what she wanted most and that was what she did. She had been to the marriages, celebrated the anniversaries, witnessed the births, and played with the children. She knew us well. She looked into our eyes and knew we were happy. That was the first question she always asked.

I remember when Mamarella told me how she'd reacted to the deaths of her parents and Papa's mother. It was the advice she'd given us when Papa had died, the advice she had once been given. She said that their deaths happened in the natural order; never expected but not unanticipated, not unimagined, sudden, and sad, but not surprising. I suppose that is how I felt that afternoon. I imagine the others felt much the same way. When she'd talked about the Pensione Alexandra, how many times had we heard her say, "Guests arrive, guests depart, life goes on?" Perhaps that is true about our lives as well. She always reminded us how, no matter what, she had to go to the train station and look for the next guest. She had to do what she had to do.

Ninety-eight years and a full and complete life. It wasn't without hardship, but she'd made it. Her remaining wish had been to see the moon one more time. I wish she had. I wish I had arranged it. She loved to tell us that she would be remembered because her ears didn't work and her hands were never idle. I can assure you she will be remembered for much more. I know she felt that her life made a difference, and for all of us, it did. That strikes me as a good way to be remembered.

I had heard Mamarella's story many times. We all had in one way or another, mostly in bits and pieces, sometimes more, sometimes less, often with minor revisions. This week was the first time I'd heard it from beginning to end, well, almost the end. A lifetime ago, she had told me that, one day, it would be my turn to tell the story. I would inherit her role and should add my pages. I would become the keeper of the stories, left with the key to unlock the stories that will soon be forgotten, a responsibility passed from one generation to the next. I don't know why she selected me: perhaps fate, just because I was there for that particular moment, a gentle hand connecting our dots. The others were far more qualified and certainly more deserving. I know the key is passed from one innkeeper to the next. It is that I just never thought I would be given this key so suddenly or so soon.

Papa and Mamarella were able to finally find their way to America, but it took much longer than they had hoped. They were detained at Camp Tiscornia for several months before they were released by Cuban officials and allowed to live a normal life in Havana. Like she said many times, "War is a complicated business." She told me that after the first few months, camp officials became sympathetic and understood their situation. Their guards came to realize that they posed no threat, that they were not the enemy. They were never mistreated in any way, but Camp Tiscornia had not been the most pleasant of places. Without any contact, they always worried about us. It simply took time to sort things out. She grinned when she told me that Papa finally convinced the guards to allow them conjugal visits.

As for their time in Cuba following their release from Camp Tiscornia, little was ever said. I am not entirely certain why Mamarella chose not to say too much about that time. She did tell me that their German accents had been a problem. Cuba was at war with Germany, and Germans were avoided. We were able to correspond with them and learned that money was a big issue. Although theirs was a desperate situation, they found it difficult to ask any of us for support. Alex organized things, and we all pooled our resources. We each contributed five dollars and, through one of the Cuban relief organizations, were able to send them twenty-five dollars each month for food, housing, and other essentials.

My impression is that they lived a very quiet life and kept to themselves. I don't think they had many interactions with the cousins in Cuba and don't know why.

One More Moon

Mamarella was always interested and curious about everything, so in some respects, Cuba must have been an adventure. But I can only assume that, by this time, she and Papa were so tired of their journey that they no longer had the energy to do much of anything.

In early 1943, three years after they'd left Naples, Mamarella and Papa finally received word that their entry visas had been approved by the U.S. State Department and that they could come to the United States. It must have been sudden, because we didn't learn of this until after they'd arrived and passed through immigration in Key West, Florida. The following weekend, we were all there to greet them when they stepped off the train at Grand Central Station in New York. I have never seen a happier occasion.

As we all returned to our normal lives, they did move in with Mamarella's sister outside of Chicago. Mamarella loved to talk about those times. They were so happy those first years in America. That was when they got to know the grandchildren and spend time with all of us. At first, Papa pretended to be ten years younger so he could find a job as a stockboy in a grocery. He turned his age back ten years because he needed to be sixty-five. His dignity required a paycheck. The war was still going on, and in Chicago, there were no jobs for a man seventy-five years of age who barely spoke English. Mamarella tried to help their financial situation by making puppets and stuffed animals to sell to department stores in downtown Chicago. She rode the bus and walked the streets with great, big, purposeful strides. She was so excited when one of the stores agreed to put her creations on their shelves. But

Papa was reluctant about this. I am sure he had his reasons. He still insisted that he was the breadwinner. Self-esteem – that always meant so much to Papa. That was his battle. Life was always trying to take it away.

By 1960, Mamarella was the last remaining member of that household and of her generation. Everyone else had passed away: Papa, Jenny, Marie, all the brothers and sisters. She sold the house and began commuting. Each year was divided into four quarters: three months with each of her children. I cherished the moments we were to spend together. She was never idle. She spent her days with the things she always loved: playing solitaire, knitting, reading, her drawings, making birthday gifts for her grandchildren. She never purchased a birthday or holiday card. She made each with her own hands, always with one of her sketches.

By 1973, she became too old to commute. After her ninetieth birthday, Mamarella moved into the home in Portland, where her life ended. Mamarella made a lasting mark on her family. She was just as she was in this story.

CHAPTER SEVENTY-SIX

Twenty-Five Years Later

It was a spectacular fall day on the Outer Banks of North Carolina, the kind of day one waited for and wished would never end. The surf was gentle, and the saltwater warm and comforting. By early evening, four of Carova's wild horses were quietly grazing the dune, undisturbed. Now the beach was empty. The tourists were gone. The season was over. The locals and the horses were reclaiming their land.

Most would argue there is no better way to capture the picturesque beauty of the Outer Banks than to drive down the beach in the four-wheel drive area just north of Corolla to Carova. At the ramp, NC 12 continues on the sand on this narrow strip of beach for thirteen miles before ending at the fence that separates North Carolina from Virginia.

It is not unusual to see dolphins playing in the surf, brown pelicans skimming the waves, the fins of sharks, and even an occasional right whale off in the distance. One has to drive slowly, with caution, particularly when the tide is low, to avoid the exposed timbers of old shipwrecks and the petrified cypress tree stumps that remain on the shore.

I imagine if you'd been sitting near Swan Beach, enjoying the peaceful early evening breeze, you might have noticed the slightly battered and rusty Jeep Wrangler pass by. The top was down, and there were three people riding, two passengers and the driver. The rather old woman riding in the back might have been easily mistaken for someone much younger. She was wearing a baseball cap and appeared to be elegantly dressed in a navy-blue pantsuit. If you had looked closely, certainly, you would have noticed her long, graceful neck, a distinguishing reminder of her former beauty.

Kaethe was having the time of her life. The grateful smile on her face masked her ninety-five years. She was still able to make her twice annual trek to the Outer Banks, a place that, for most of her life, she'd never known existed and could not have imagined. Now it was a little more difficult to visit than it once had been. They'd sent her the plane ticket and arranged for a car and driver to shuttle her back and forth from the airport in New Jersey to her apartment in the city. They wanted her to move in with them, even kept a room in their house where she kept all her things. She had her own closet, where she kept the clothes she would only wear at the beach, like the pantsuit that she would never consider wearing anywhere else and certainly not the city.

One More Moon

Their offer had been genuine and caring, but she had refused. The time was no longer right, and she felt too old. She had always been a city girl, ever since she'd grown up in Berlin and when she'd lived in Paris. By now, she was set in her ways and chose to remain in her New York City apartment off Broadway on Riverside Drive for the days that were left. It was true that the neighborhood had changed. No one she knew lived there anymore, but she had been in the same unit for sixty-three years, ever since they'd arrived in America in 1942. Now she was not prepared to move.

Josef had loved living there. He had loved their long walks along the Hudson, and she felt comforted being surrounded by all the familiar things that reminded her of his presence, all their possessions that had followed them on their long journey from Berlin to Paris and to Lisbon so many years ago. She kept every item exactly as it was meant to be. Now the sixteen-piece china set was missing a few teacups, and a plate or two were chipped, functions of age, wear, and an occasional mishap. But the paintings on the walls were just as Josef had placed them, reminders of their travels to Naples, his hikes in the Alps, and the months in Soumoulou when she'd had Josef all to herself.

Everything remained the same: the piano, the books, the silver service that she polished every week, the hairbrush on the dresser in the bedroom, even the clock on his desk, which she wound each morning. She even kept the letters he had written during the months they'd been apart. They were hidden in a special compartment in the desk. After Josef had died, when she'd first been alone, the others had been concerned for her safety and that she would become lonely. But she preferred her privacy. She did not need the company of others. She was never alone as long as she kept Josef in her heart and she had his letters as reminders of his love.

She could no longer remember who'd inherited who, but that no longer mattered. Now she was doing what she most wanted to do. Kaethe was spending the week with her closest friends in the world: Mamarella's grandson and his lovely wife, Ginger.

It hadn't always been this way, but now all the others were gone. For so many years, she had always been the youngest. Now, suddenly, it seemed that she was the eldest. One by one, they had faded away until she was the last one remaining, the last one left who knew this story, the story she had told Ginger and Mamarella's grandson for the first time this week.

Life is funny, the things that are never expected. How could she have imagined finding someone like Ginger? She was the daughter Kaethe had never chosen to have, yet the daughter she'd always wanted. Josef would have loved her too. He would have been enchanted. They had never wanted to have children. There had been a time when they could have. But the world had been broken, and neither had been particularly interested in raising babies. Those moments were so far in the past.

But then Ginger? She was Kaethe's gift from heaven and a reminder of herself. She was such a wonderful listener. Kaethe had never spoken so much. Ginger was respectful and caring, and she always knew how to make Kaethe laugh. The only other ones who had done that for Kaethe were Josef and her father and, perhaps,

One More Moon

Mamarella's son Alex and his wife, Lotte, who had become such close friends for so many years. When Mamarella had come to live with Alex and Lotte each year, Kaethe had spent many hours by Mamarella's side, listening to her stories as if she were her daughter.

First Mamarella, then Kaethe, now Ginger. It was just like Mamarella had always said. Who could have connected those dots? Three people so entirely different and so closely connected, not by family or birth, but by fate, by some invisible hand gently encouraging each to share in one another's lives.

The events that connected them had been odd and unlikely, instances that could never be repeated, moments that could never be planned, but that somehow managed to start at the beginning and conclude by the end. Who could have arranged for Mamarella to become the mother Kaethe had always yearned for? How could it be that Kaethe would be the last one to hear Mamarella tell her story? Indeed, it was a curious path that linked Kaethe to Mamarella and finally to Ginger. How else can one explain fate?

⇌ ⇌

Their passage on the Nyassa from Lisbon to New York had been largely uneventful. Sitting on the foredeck one sunny afternoon, Josef, as was his nature, had engaged another couple in conversation. Much younger than Josef and closer in age to me, George and Nina were delightful companions during our eight-day journey. And once again, I found myself cast in the role of the listener. They too had experienced a harrowing journey and had suffered much personal loss. Like us, they hoped to find their peace and a much-needed fresh start in New York City.

In the course of conversation, Josef spoke of our surprise Lisbon encounter with old friends from Naples. George remarked that, a few years earlier, they had attended the wedding of an old childhood friend in Naples, Lotte, who had grown up in Koenigsberg and been sent to Naples to avoid the events in Germany. They had stayed at a delightful pensione overlooking the Bay of Naples, the Pensione Alexandra.

As we began our new life in New York, our friendship with George and Nina continued. Together, we enjoyed celebrating one another's birthdays, anniversaries, and moments of success. And there were many. Josef was able to continue his medical career at a nearby hospital just as he'd hoped for. Nina's acclaim as one of the leading sculptors of her generation continued to grow as her works found homes in some of the finest museums of the world, including the New York Metropolitan Museum of Art and Whitney Museum of American Art.

Weeks after our arrival in America, we were joined by a third couple one evening. What a surprise it was to be reunited with our mutual friend, Lotte, whom we had first met in Naples, and her husband, Alex. Despite our many stays at the Pensione Alexandra, we had never met

One More Moon

Mamarella's son Alex. We both fell in love with Alex as soon as we met him.

That night, we learned that Mamarella and Papa had been detained in Cuba because of the war and had never been able to move to America. I remember how shocked we were. Josef insisted that we contribute to the funds they sent to Cuba each month. Alex was grateful and assured us that there would be a family celebration when Papa and Mamarella arrived and that we would definitely be included.

It was one year later, in the spring of 1943, when Lotte telephoned with the wonderful news. Mamarella and Papa had arrived in America. Could we join their family the next day? Their train was scheduled to arrive at New York's Grand Central Station.

I will never forget the moment. We were all there to greet them. If you happened to be at Grand Central Station on that particular day, you would have noticed the celebration. It was as if everyone in the station cheered their arrival. Nina even had created a bronze sculpture for Mamarella, two children on a seesaw. Mamarella had suggested this idea to her years ago, when they'd been in Naples. I think Josef and I were the biggest surprise. We were the guests that always departed but always returned.

We cried so much that night. For me, there couldn't have been a better ending to their journey.

※ ※

Tonight, when Kaethe, Ginger, and Mamarella's grandson returned to the house, they would have their own celebration. It was not a birthday, not an anniversary or anything like that. No, this was better. Kaethe had finished what she had set out to do. Many years ago, that night when she and Josef had sat with Mamarella and Papa in Lisbon, she had promised to become the keeper of the stories. Everyone had been through so much, and they all agreed that, since Kaethe was the youngest, it would be her task to someday tell this story. Mamarella had told her there would always be secrets. One of her most important responsibilities would be to keep the secrets and only share the stories.

And that was what Kaethe had done this week. She had spent each afternoon telling them this story, and she had kept the secrets. Now it was time to pass the key forward. She had always known that Ginger would be the one. Kaethe could think of no one better. Ginger knew how to keep the secrets and tell the stories. That evening, she told Ginger it was her turn to keep the key to unlock the stories that would soon be long forgotten. It had been a long week, five days to tell this story, but she had told it just the way Mamarella would have wanted, and using Mamarella's words. Tonight, they would drink a glass of wine and stay up to watch one more moon. Kaethe had fulfilled Mamarella's wish. Now she was finished. She had only one last thing to say.

※

Fate has a way of connecting the dots, an invisible hand that guides from one to the next, sometimes gently, sometimes forcibly, but always watching, always there. I have always prayed for that invisible hand. Fate is what connected me to you.

POSTSCRIPT

I first met Kaethe (Katie, to me) in 1978 In Englewood Cliffs, New Jersey, at a family reunion to celebrate Uncle Alex's birthday. As Ralph and I had only been dating a few months, this was my first exposure to most of his family. They were amazed that I shared the same birthday with Mamarella.

On the periphery of this somewhat boisterous affair sat a reserved, well-dressed lady with a slender, long neck. Being somewhat timid amongst all these laughing, joking Italians, I naturally gravitated toward this quiet but smiling lady. The rest is history.

For the next twenty-five years, Katie was my "surrogate" mom, mentor, and friend, filling a tremendous void in my life. My birth mom died when I was thirteen, and my relationship with my later stepmom can only be described as complicated.

Katie and Josef had emigrated to New York City in 1942, where they lived and worked (he practiced medicine) in a large apartment near the George Washington Bridge. They were close friends with Alex and Lotte, whom they had become reacquainted with through mutual friends. Many of these friendships grew from a common heritage during a tragic period of world history.

I never met Josef; he died in 1961 at the age of eighty-three. But I felt like I knew him, as he was clearly the love of Katie's life and she talked of him and their adventures often. His photo was on her nightstand, and she carried it with her whenever she traveled – to keep him near.

Ralph and I spent many weekends with Katie in her apartment, dining out, going to the orchestra and Broadway shows, and taking long walks. She had refused to change or modernize anything in the apartment...I suppose to keep Josef's memory alive. One entire room was filled with his medical textbooks. Much of the furnishings, china, and silver had come with them from Berlin. Josef's watercolors adorned the walls.

As our relationship grew, she became less reserved. We laughed a lot. We had smiles and tears holding my infant granddaughter. She was quite opinionated about world events. She could also be quite critical about manners and dress. She was proud to be a "city girl" and proud of her independence. But there was always a hint of the mysterious about Katie, particularly concerning Josef.

Some of my fondest memories are of her visits to see us on the Outer Banks of NC. I convinced her to wear pants for the first time in her life, but she refused to take them home to the city. She became more carefree in our casual environment, even using our outdoor shower!

When Katie died, at age ninety-six, she made sure that Josef's and her legacy continued. Having no children of her own, she left something for Mamarella's descendants, her adopted family.

She was so special to me, and I've thought long and hard about how best to keep her memory alive. I am forever grateful to Ralph for telling some of her story. She lived through an incredible, turbulent period and had an amazing journey. She loved and was truly loved.

And now, as my tribute to her, I will keep the secrets and continue to share the stories.

Ginger

ACKNOWLEDGMENTS

When I finished writing my first book, I was convinced there would never be another. I didn't have a story. I didn't have the patience. I didn't want to have to think that much. But something about creating a book can get into your blood and convince you to do it again.

There are many expressions used to describe the knowledge and wisdom that comes with age. I cannot claim much on that score other than to say that the years have taught me that I have some awfully good and interesting roots. I wouldn't dare to compare with others. Every family is unique, and in one way or another, I hope they are all dearly special. I am convinced that they all are interesting and they all have stories.

Over the years, I have learned that my mother's mother, my grandmother, had an artful ability to write things down: descriptions of family members, descriptions of family moments, literally scraps of paper to give future generations some clues to the past. If these were diaries, then, by the time I saw them, they were missing most of the years and most of the pages. The few pages I did have, fewer than ten, allowed me to look through her window to gain a glimpse of her world as she saw it, to learn more of her personality, to find her humor, joy, sadness, and to understand her strength – the things that, as a ten-year-old child, I paid little attention to. I can't imagine what she would think now were she to read this story. But I would be remiss not to acknowledge her contributions to my life.

A book like this cannot be written without real-life characters. Now all deceased, they have given me literary freedom. I am fortunate that they, too, were part of my life, and each must be acknowledged as well – Kaethe and Josef; my mother, Mela; my uncles Arthur, Alex, and Theo; my aunt, Lotte; my grandfather, Paul; and all the others who took part in this story, even Renato with his rooster, a story I heard as a child. Each, in their own way, made writing this story a love affair for me.

There are so many others; not characters in the story, but real people in my life today who helped make this book come to fruition. First and foremost is my wife, Ginger, my collaborator, best friend, and lifelong partner. Perhaps written in invisible ink, her fingerprints are on every page. Without her encouragement and critical review, I am sure that I would still be writing about the rise and fall of Mussolini and the book would become so lengthy that it would never see the light of day. Some topics are better left for historians and history books. I know with certainty that she is happy to have our conversations move on. While she was unrelenting with her support, I can be unrelenting with my chatter.

Many thanks to those who reviewed the final draft and offered their opinion and reactions: my son, Michael "Zak" Patterson, who has impeccable judgement on any and all matters and the amazing ability to simplify things that I often complicate; my talented friend of forty-five years and old work colleague from a lifetime ago, Barbara Ifshin; my sister, Joan Webster-Vore; my cousin Ruth Mendelson; and my friend and neighbor Dr. Scott Starsman, who, in addition to being a World War II history buff, has an amazing ability to find all the details that don't quite comport and can be improved; the team at Eichner-Fukui Design, who created the cover; the folks at CreateSpace, who organized the pages. My editor, Jefferson at FirstEditing, deserves special recognition. This is the second project we have worked on together, and this book is improved by his tireless effort to find and fix all the things that I have missed. The final thanks goes to you, the readers. You allow me to share the story, and that makes it all worthwhile. I will be forever grateful.

Ralph Webster, 2017

ABOUT THE AUTHOR

Award-winning author Ralph Webster received worldwide acclaim for his first book, *A Smile in One Eye: A Tear in the Other*, which tells the story of his father's flight from the Holocaust. Voted by readers as a Goodreads 2016 Choice Awards Nominee for Best Memoir/Autobiography, *A Smile in One Eye: A Tear in the Other* and this second book, *One More Moon*, are proven book club selections for thought-provoking and engaging discussions. Whether in person or online, Ralph welcomes and values his exchanges with readers and makes every effort to participate in conversations about his books. Now retired, he lives with his wife, Ginger, on the Outer Banks of North Carolina. In addition to writing, he enjoys spending his time with family, playing tennis, hiking, and traveling the world. Ralph can be reached through his website www.onemoremoon.com.

Made in the USA
Middletown, DE
28 February 2018